KV-482-554

WITHDRAWN
FROM
UNIVERSITY OF PLYMOUTH
LIBRARY SERVICES

The Economic Regulation of International Air Transport

Ramon de Murias

The Economic Regulation of International Air Transport

McFarland & Company, Inc., Publishers
Jefferson, North Carolina, and London

Acknowledgments I take this opportunity to express my thanks to the following individuals for their assistance to me in the research for this work: Professor Joseph Sweeney of the Fordham University Law School; John J. Casey, vice chairman, and Li Wah, librarian, of Pan American World Airways, Inc.; Thomas McGrew of the DC Bar; and the following officials of the Air Transport Association of America: James E. Landry, general counsel, Nathaniel Wilson, International Division, and Marian Mestrick, librarian.

British Library Cataloguing-in-Publication data available

Library of Congress Cataloguing-in-Publication Data

de Murias, Ramon, 1916–
The economic regulation of international air transport.

Bibliography: p. 249.
Includes references.
Includes index.
1. Aeronautics, Commercial—Government policy.
2. Aeronautics, Commercial—Deregulation. I. Title.
HE9777.7.D4 1989 387.7′1 88-42534

ISBN 0-89950-343-8 (lib. bdg.; 50# acid-free natural paper) ∞

Manufactured in the United States of America.

McFarland Box 611 Jefferson NC 28640

TABLE OF CONTENTS

1. INTRODUCTION

The economic regulation of international air transport may be said to have two aspects: the regulation of national companies engaged in international air carriage and the regulation of foreign companies engaged in international air carriage. The regulation of the technical aspects of international air transport is dealt with herein only incidentally.

The extent to which the economic activities of international airlines should be regulated is a topic that is at present widely disputed throughout the world. Historically, international air transport has been closely regulated everywhere, with few exceptions. Before discussing the history and the validity of particular forms of regulation (or deregulation), it appears desirable to review the elements that are dealt with in the economic regulation of international air transport. These are treated in this introduction under the following perhaps arbitrary headings: (1) What Is Regulated, (2) The Right to Regulate, (3) The Modes of Regulation, (4) The Motives for Regulation, (5) The Instruments of Regulations, and (6) Tangential Matters.

What Is Regulated

Routes, including the matter of entry, are the most fundamental elements of regulation. Each country must first decide whether to allow foreign aircraft to operate in its air space, and between what points it will allow operations.

Capacity is also subject to regulation. Capacity is generally reckoned as the frequency of operation of the flights (or, the number of times a flight is operated over a given period, for example twice a week), times the number of seats installed or the cargo carrying capability of the aircraft used. Sometimes only the frequency is regulated and in rare cases only the carrying capability of the aircraft is regulated, but in most cases, if one element is regulated, both are.

Fares and rates are subject to regulation. Fares are generally considered to be the amounts charged for the carriage of passengers and rates are generally considered to be the amounts charged for the carriage of cargo and mail. Collectively, they are sometimes referred to as "tariffs," and sometimes as "rates." There are also ancillary charges which are subject to regulation, such as excess baggage charges; valuation and insurance charges for baggage and cargo; delivery charges, C.O.D. charges and the like.

Traffic is subject to regulation. This concerns how much and what type of passengers or cargo an airline is to be allowed to carry. For example it may be allowed to carry cargo and mail, and be forbidden to carry passengers, or vice versa. Restrictions may be placed upon the number of passengers that may be carried, or upon the class of passengers that may be carried. The airline may be forbidden to carry passengers who do not have their origin or destination in its home country ("Fifth Freedom") or its carriage of such passengers may be limited. Similar restrictions may be placed upon the carriage of cargo. Mail is also subject to restrictions, but they tend to take a somewhat different direction, because the carriage of mail is commonly regulated by the postal authorities, rather than by the aeronautical authorities. Typically, permission to carry cargo or passengers is automatically accompanied by permission to carry mail. Beyond the initial permission to carry it, the carriage of mail is governed by the provisions of the Universal Postal Union Convention and the Provisions Concerning Airmail.[1]

Scheduled Service vs. Non-scheduled. In considering "what is regulated," it is desirable also to focus on the type of service that is regulated. In the earliest days of air transport, scheduled services were the only services that it was possible to offer on a scale that justified serious commercial promotion by the carrier or economic regulation by governments.[2] Therefore scheduled services were regulated from the beginning whereas other services which were generally offered at high rates on small capacity aircraft were considered too sporadic and insignificant to require extensive regulation. This attitude appears to have persisted until 1944 when the Chicago Convention was negotiated.[3]

Since 1944, there has appeared a class of charter flights which, although they are not offered as part of a traditional regularly scheduled service, differ radically from the type of non-scheduled flights that were considered too insignificant to call for regulation. Nevertheless, because of the historical background and its reflection in the Chicago Convention, scheduled and non-scheduled services have been dealt with separately in the economic regulation of air transport and scheduled service has continued to be the dominant mode, although charter flights have become increasingly important and the subject of regulation in recent years. In the main, when reference is made herein to the economic regulation of air transport, scheduled service is meant. When the subject is charters or non-scheduled service, it will be specifically identified.

The Right to Regulate

The law with respect to the right of states to regulate the economic activities of foreign aircraft operating in their air space is clear. States are sovereign in the air space above their territory and they may exclude or regulate the activities of foreign aircraft operating there. In the absence of some limiting agreement this right may be exercised unilaterally.

It should be noted that the reference here is to sovereignty over the "air space" above the territory of a state. The claim is not that sovereignty extends into "outer space." A problem remains with respect to where air space leaves off, and outer space begins, but this is a scientific (and political) question which does not need to be resolved for present-day aircraft, which require the air to navigate. The problems of rockets and satellites are real, but they are outside the scope of this work.[4]

In 1911, just eight years after the flight of the Wright Brothers at Kitty Hawk, Harold Hazeltine, LL.D., an American lawyer who was at the time a reader in English law at Cambridge University, published a paper in which he summarized as follows the then state of the law with respect to the right of nations to regulate the entry of foreign aircraft into their air space:

> There are two great groups of theories as to the rights of states in the air-space above their territories and territorial waters. There are first the freedom of the air theories. Of these there are two: The theory that the air is completely free, and the theory that the air is partly free. Some of those who maintain that the air is partly free give the state certain rights, without restricting the exercise of those rights as far as the height of the air-space is concerned; while others restrict the exercise of rights by the state to a limited zone in the air-space, the upper regions of the air being completely free. The second group of theories may be designated the sovereignty-of-the-air theories; theories which accord the state rights of legal and political supremacy—rights of sovereignty—in the air space. The first of these theories concedes to the state full sovereign rights, without any restriction, up to an indefinite height above the state's territory and territorial waters. But some of the sovereignty views do not go this far, for they concede to the state only a limited sovereignty; either a sovereignty which extends only up to a certain limited height (and this view may be compared to the zone theories of adherents of freedom), or else a sovereignty which although unlimited in height is yet restricted by the reservation of a servitude of innocent passage—that is a right of innocent passage for all balloons and other air vehicles.[5]

Hazeltine concluded that the proper view was that states are sovereign in their own air space, and he pointed out that every time a state had been called upon to act concerning this subject, it had acted consistently with this view.[6]

Hazeltine's description of the assorted views is definitive and his analysis has stood the test of time. Although there have been many theoretical arguments for a "freedom of the air" analogous to the "freedom of the seas," there has never been a time when the prevailing practice favored "freedom of the air."[7]

Prior to the first World War, as Hazeltine says, there were theoretical arguments advanced in favor of a "freedom of the skies" analogous to the freedom of the seas, the best known proponent of such theories being Paul Fauchille of France.[8] As the destructive capability of airborne vehicles became more apparent with the arrival of heavier-than-air aircraft, it was considered necessary to modify this theory to give the subjacent state the right of self-preservation, and finally, in 1911 the Institute of International Law allowed the subjacent state to forbid foreign aircraft to pass through its airspace.[9]

Bin Cheng, Wagner, Matte, and Johnson review the debates on this subject at length.[10] The debates included numerous and ingenious qualifications of the doctrine of "freedom of the skies," such as that it was limited by a territorial belt, like the territorial sea, or that it was limited to the right of innocent passage by aircraft of foreign states. Nevertheless, since the earliest days, where sovereignty over the airspace has been an issue states have acted as though they had it, and in view of the damage that can be done by hostile aircraft, it is hard to see how they could have acted otherwise.[11] This attitude was confirmed for good at the close of the first World War in the Paris Convention on the Regulation of Aereal Navigation of 1919[12] which included as Article 1 the provision that

> Every power has complete and exclusive sovereignty over the airspace above its territory.[13]

The United States participated in the drafting of this treaty, and was one of the original signatories. The United States did not, however, ratify the convention because it formed part of the group of treaties arising out of the Paris Peace Conference after the first World War, which the United States refused to ratify.[14] Nevertheless, the United States has consistently taken the position that it has sovereignty over the airspace above its territory.[15] In 1926, with the passage of the Air Commerce Act,[16] the United States officially declared that

> The Government of the United States has, to the exclusion of all foreign nations, complete sovereignty of the air space over the lands and waters of the United States, including the Canal Zone.[17]

The Pan American Convention on Commercial Aviation signed in Havana in 1928, to which the United States was a party, followed the Paris Convention in declaring that each nation had complete sovereignty over the air space above its territory.

The Paris Convention of 1919, and the Havana Convention have both been superseded by the Chicago Convention (negotiated and signed in 1944 effective in the U.S., 1947). The Chicago Convention continues to provide for national sovereignty over national airspace in the following terms:

> Article 1, *Sovereignty*. The contracting states recognize that every state has complete and exclusive sovereignty over the air space above its territory.[18]

The concept of state sovereignty over the air space is now so firmly established that Cooper, Bin Cheng, Matte and Wagner all indicate that the quoted provision of the Chicago Convention is merely declaratory of the existing customary law.[19]

Although it is now settled law that states have exclusive sovereignty over the air space above their territory, it is useful to be aware of the history behind the development of this concept, because it is still possible to argue that ideally state sovereignty over the air space should be limited.[20]

Modes of Regulation

Having seen that routes, capacity, traffic, and fares and rates form the principal subject matter for the economic regulation of commercial air transport, we can now turn to a review of the ways in which this regulation is accomplished.

The regulation of *routes* is relatively straightforward. Either directly, or by means of intergovernmental agreements, the government of a state tells each foreign airline what points it may serve en route to, within and beyond its territory. The description of routes can be either more or less restrictive. At the most restrictive end of the spectrum would be a route description that names specifically each point that may be served for the entire length of the permitted flights. (Obviously, in such case, the fewer points named, the more restrictive the route description would be.)

At the least restrictive extreme would be a provision that any airline could serve any point in the country on flights to or from any point abroad. This formulation appears never to have been adopted, even as a concession to the airlines of a single country. About the most liberal route description in current use applies to the airlines of a single country and reads more or less as follows: "from points in the home country to named points in the granting country and beyond." The requirement that the flights originate in the home country of the airline, or at least that they go through the home country, is very nearly universal. This requirement is evidently a result of the concept that each aircraft (and each airline) has a "flag," and that each country sponsors its own airlines. This concept goes back to the provision of the Paris Convention of 1919 that registration of aircraft should endow them with national character.[21] Airlines have traditionally been considered an essential part of a nation's "air power."

Since each airline is regarded as having a nationality, and each country has traditionally been jealous of granting access to its market except as part of a trade whereby it obtains foreign market access for its own airlines, it is not surprising that nearly all international route descriptions require the airline to originate and terminate its services in its home country.[22]

Given the nationalistic bias in the regulation of air transport from the very beginning, it is probably inevitable that virtually all schemes for the regulation of air transport have started out from the premise that the primary legitimate function of an airline is to carry the traffic to and from the state whose nationality it possesses. This is the underlying premise of the requirement just mentioned that airline routes have their origin in the country whose nationality the airline possesses. Similarly, most schemes for regulating capacity are based primarily upon the requirements for the carriage of traffic to and from the homeland of the carrier.

Because of their relevance to routes, capacity and traffic, it will be helpful to describe at this point the so-called "Freedoms of the Air." The concept had its origin in the International Air Transport Agreement, which was signed at Chicago in 1944, but never became effective. In that agreement, the "five freedoms" are listed as follows:

> Each contracting state grants to the other contracting states the following freedoms of the air in respect of scheduled international services:
>
> 1. The privilege to fly across its territory without landing [the "first freedom"].
> 2. The privilege to land for non traffic purposes [the "second freedom"].
> 3. The privilege to put down passengers, mail and cargo taken on in the territory of the state whose nationality the aircraft possesses [the "third freedom"].
> 4. The privilege to take on passengers, mail and cargo destined for the territory of the state whose nationality the aircraft possesses [the "fourth freedom"].
> 5. The privilege to take on passengers, mail and cargo destined for the territory of any other contracting state and the privilege to put down passengers, mail and cargo coming from any such territory [the "fifth freedom"].[23]

So far as this writer is aware, no current air transport agreements, other than the International Air Transport Agreement, whether they be bilateral or multilateral, express themselves in terms of these "five freedoms." The agreements between nations by means of which airline routes are granted typically describe the routes in terms of points that may be served or in terms of such general expressions as "via intermediate points," or "and beyond," rather than in terms of "freedoms" that may be exercised. Nevertheless, the "five freedoms" and their definitions continue to have great currency in discussions about commercial air transport rights, to describe the type of traffic concerned.

In the jargon of air transport regulation there has arisen also the concept of "sixth freedom" traffic, which refers to traffic carried between two states, neither of which is the state whose nationality the aircraft possesses, via a point in the territory of the state whose nationality the aircraft possesses.[24]

So-called "sixth freedom" is sometimes considered a special case of fifth freedom traffic, and it is at other times analyzed as a combination of third and fourth freedom traffic, where the passenger is carried from the country of origin to the home country of the carrier as a fourth freedom passenger and is then carried from the home country to the country of destination as a third freedom passenger.

The concepts underlying these classifications have particular relevance for the Bermuda Agreement.

Bin Cheng also mentions a "seventh freedom," which he says relates to traffic carried on a service which does not touch the homeland of the carrier and an "eighth freedom" which he applies to traffic carried between two points in a single country (generally referred to as "cabotage").[25] Neither of these two latter "freedoms" has much currency in the special vocabulary of air transport regulation.

The regulation of *capacity* can be carried out through direct limitations on the number of flights that a particular airline will be allowed to perform. Such limitation usually applies to flights performed on a given sector over a particular period of time, usually one week (for instance, "three flights per week between A and B"). This can be accompanied by a further limitation on the carrying capacity of the aircraft employed. This latter limitation can be accomplished through a requirement that a particular aircraft configuration must be used, or it can be accomplished by a limitation on the number of seats and amount of cargo lift that may be offered, without any requirement that a particular aircraft configuration must be used. (In regulatory jargon the latter device is often referred to as "roping off" capacity.) Sometimes regulatory requirements insist that a particular type of aircraft be employed with a particular seating configuration.

The regulation of *traffic* follows the same general pattern as the regulation of routes and capacity and can produce the same general results. It is not the same thing, however. The limitation of traffic rights can take the form of a prohibition on the carriage of traffic between a given pair of points, in which case it is similar to the regulation of route rights, but it differs in that if only local traffic rights are withheld, the airline may nevertheless operate between the points concerned, carrying traffic other than that between the two points to which the limitation applies. This can be a valuable commercial right, and is referred to in regulatory jargon as a "blind sector right." (The commercial value of such a right consists in the ability to combine on a single flight service between the two points in question and other points on the carrier's route. For example, it would have been a valuable right for a United States airline to be able to operate a single flight from Dallas/Fort Worth to both Paris and Frankfurt, even though U.S. airlines did not at the time have the authority from the French to carry traffic between Paris and Frankfurt. The right would enable the U.S. airline to serve both Paris and Frankfurt with a single trans-Atlantic flight from Dallas/Fort Worth, in circumstances where the capacity of one aircraft was sufficient for the traffic between Dallas/Fort Worth and those two cities.)

The limitation of traffic rights can also take the form of a restriction on the amount of traffic that may be carried, in which case it resembles a limitation of capacity. Such traffic limitations may take the form of restriction of the number of passengers that may be carried on a particular service (such as a daily flight from A to B), or they may take the form of restriction of the number of passengers that may be carried over a given period. Traffic restrictions differ from capacity limitations in both cases, however, because, being *traffic* restrictions, they limit only the traffic to and from the country imposing them, leaving the balance of the capacity of the aircraft free for the carriage of traffic other than that to which the particular restriction applies. It is also worth noting that a restriction on the number of passengers that may be carried on individual flights is far more onerous than a similar restriction on the number of passengers that may be carried over a given period. (For example, a restriction to 100 passengers per flight on a daily service would be more onerous than a restriction to 700 passengers per week on the same service, because with the weekly restriction the carrier could make up for days when it carried less than 100 passengers by carring more than 100 passengers on other days, whereas with the per-flight restriction, the carrier could never carry more than 100 passengers per day, and thus could never make up for days when it carried fewer than 100.)

The regulation of *fare and rates* poses a special problem, because it is almost impossible to regulate them unilaterally with any degree of effectiveness, and it is extremely difficult to regulate them effectively even on a bilateral basis. In fact, fares and rates can be regulated with relatively complete effectiveness only by agreement or acquiescence of the governments over a very wide area. There are two basic problems; the first is that for a country to regulate unilaterally what it charged for travel in-bound to its territory, requires it to regulate the sale of transportation which is made in another country. This is very difficult to police. The affected country cannot intervene directly in the sale; all it can do is to refuse to allow the service to operate while it charges the offending fares. Moreover, the attempt to regulate charges for transportation that is sold in another country is likely to cause that country to feel that its sovereignty has been infringed.

A further, and more fundamental problem affects both unilateral and bilateral attempts to regulate fares and rates. This is that fares and rates throughout the world are interrelated because of the worldwide network of connecting services. This means that a passenger between any pair of points usually has many routings available to him, so that he can shop around for the routing that gives him the best price. Where the routing selected is via a point in a third country, the two countries between which the passenger is travelling are often unable to control the price. For example, suppose the following fares A–B = $150; A–C = $50; C–B = $50. A passenger seeking a cheap routing between A and B will purchase tickets and travel A–C and C–B and will pay a fare of $100 ($50 + $50), thus defeating the A–B fare of $150. If it is appreciably cheaper to travel via the circuitous routing, that is the way the traffic will go, and the cheaper fare will be the effective fare for the journey despite the efforts of the two governments directly concerned to control it. Because of this interrelation of airline fares, and the need to produce an integrated tariff structure, it has been generally recognized that if airline fares are to be established uniformly by agreement, the agreement must include all major traffic points in all major routings and hence must be multinational in scope.[26]

To be successful, agreement on airline tariffs probably must take the form of pure haggling among airline personnel. Once matters of prestige or principle become involved (which they are likely to do in governmental discussions), agreement becomes extremely difficult. In addition, establishment of worldwide tariff structures requires an intimate knowledge of traffic flows and commercial conditions that could only be obtained first hand by airline personnel. In recognition of these considerations, as well as for other reasons, it was agreed at the time of the Bermuda Agreement in 1946 to allow the airlines to act as surrogates for the governments in reaching agreements on fares and rates through the International Air Transport Association (IATA). The fare regulating portion of IATA consists of a conference system similar to steamship rate conferences where the airlines agree to fares and rates on a global basis and then submit the resultant agreed fares and rates to governments for approval. Without the approval of all governments concerned, the fares and rates do not become effective.

In recent years, the United States has objected to the IATA system on doctrinaire grounds and almost forced an "open rate" situation, where no IATA-agreed fares and rates were in effect on the routes to and from the United States. In this situation, pricing is established individually by each carrier, subject to whatever limitations may be imposed unilaterally or pursuant to intergovernmental agreement by the governments of the countries affected by the pricing. In the absence of agreement, each government can prevent the service from operating at prices of which it disapproves. (This follows from the sovereignty exercised by each state over the air space above its territory.)

Governmental agreements have taken the following main forms:

1. The fares shall be subject to the approval of both governments concerned. Sometimes this is accomplished by a provision that the fares shall be agreed by the carriers of the two nations concerned, either bilaterally or through IATA, usually accompanied by a further provision that in the absence of carrier agreement, the governments will agree on or consult concerning the fares between their respective territories.

2. The fares shall be subject to the approval only of the country where the transportation to which they apply originates.

3. The fares proposed by a carrier shall become effective unless both governments concerned agree that they shall not become effective.

4. The fares proposed by a carrier shall become effective irrespective of government approvals or disapprovals.

The commercial and competitive importance of fare and rate regulation is obvious.

In recent years, there has been considerable controversy concerning whether there should be government supervision of fares and rates, either directly or through the medium of IATA. The United States has taken the view that airline pricing should be set exclusively by market forces, with governmental intervention limited to cases where market forces are inhibited from acting. Most of the rest of the world has taken the view that governments should continue to regulate airline pricing, preferably through IATA, although some of the Europeans are approaching the U.S. view.

Motives for Regulation

From the very earliest days, the operation of international air services has been closely regulated. The original thought was to regulate the operation of aircraft as a means of avoiding threats to national security.[27] Early on, however, the element of protecting the national airline from competition by foreign airlines became a central element in the regulation of international aviation.[28] Sometimes this solicitude for the national airline has taken the form of obtaining adequate traffic rights to enable the national airline to compete. This has been a primary thrust of United States air policy. Often, however, it has taken the form of a frank intention to suppress the competition.

One reason given for restricting foreign airlines for the benefit of the national airline is to protect the country's sovereign interest in the national resource which air traffic constitutes. In a number of countries in South America, there is a deep-rooted feeling that oil and mineral resources in particular form part of the "national patrimony" and must be reserved for exploitation by nationals of the country. It has been argued that the airline traffic generated in the country is such a national resource and forms part of the "national patrimony" which the government has the obligation to protect. This appears to be less of a real reason in itself than an attempt to invoke the emotional climate surrounding the exploitation of natural resources in the extractive industries to induce the government to impose restrictions on foreign airlines for the benefit of the national airline.

In fairness, however, it must be noted that although protection of the national airlines seems to have been an important objective in the regulation of foreign airlines throughout the world, there is a perfectly respectable and widely held body of opinion that all forms of transportation for hire require close government supervision.[29]

Thus, in virtually all countries where there is a developed air transport industry, entry by national airlines is tightly controlled and the activities of the airlines are closely supervised by government regulators. This is as true of domestic transportation, where there is no question of protection against foreign competition, as it is of international transportation. The United States is unique with its recent program of "deregulating" its air transport industry and until recently it followed the worldwide pattern of governmental regulation for national airlines engaged in both domestic and international air transportation.

The rationale behind this type of regulation is in part that behind the regulation of other public utilities: the operator is using a form of monopoly granted by the sovereign and in return must accept regulation by the sovereign to see that he does not abuse it; and it is in part a consideration applicable especially to transportation enterprises: that in the absence of regulation they would engage in cut-throat competition to a point where either all the competitors would collapse or one would emerge in a position to engage in an abusive monopoly.[30] Remaining through these theoretical considerations, however, is the fact that the practical effect of most of the regulations imposed on international airlines has been to protect the national airlines from competition (in some cases to protect them from unfair competition).

One would think that ensuring safe and cheap transportation for the public would most often be assigned as the major reason for the economic regulation of international air transport. Curiously, however, the only instance where it appears to have been cited as the primary reason for governmental action in this field has been in the recent attempt by the United States to convert the rest of the world to "deregulation," where a regime of little or no regulations of international air transport would be established.

It is probably true, however, that policies directed toward protecting the national carrier have as an objective preserving the access of the national public to air transport under terms acceptable to the government as well as promoting the prosperity of the national airline.[31]

Still another reason for the economic regulation of international air transport is to achieve national goals in some other sector of the economy which would be affected by air transport. For example, in an informal conversation among American and German airline and government representatives in Bonn in 1979, in which the writer participated, the United States group observed that the fares for intra-European air travel were higher than one would believe could be justified on the basis of costs. The German representatives replied that if the air fares were reduced this would result in a diversion of traffic from the railroads to the air. Such a diversion would necessitate a reduction in rail service, as had already happened in the United States, which in turn would result in unemployment among rail workers. Since high employment was one of the primary goals of the German government, it made no sense to them to reduce air fares where the result would be unemployment in the railroads. Similarly, the point has been made that Brazil suffers from a shortage of capital which would be aggravated by a need to obtain added aircraft to carry increased traffic that might result from unregulated rate competition.[32]

Environmental considerations are another motive for the economic regulation of international air transport. Excessive capacity can result in unacceptable noise and pollution levels and this could be a reason for objection to promotional fares that might lead to increased capacity.[33]

A consideration of the motives for regulating air transport must also encompass the motives of governments in wishing to foster their own national airlines. From the earliest days, military considerations seem to have weighed heavily in the governments' interest in national airlines. Oliver Lissitzyn writing in 1942 says, "In any event, however, the world may be organized, or disorganized, after the war (World War II), commercial air transport will remain the auxiliary of military air power just as the Merchant Marine remains the indispensable auxiliary of the Navy."[34] Lissitzyn lists and describes the following aspects of air transport and national interest: Economic (How air transport helps exporters)[35]; Air Mail Speeds

Up Business Correspondence; Business Men Fly; The Airplane as a Freight Carrier; Air Lines Help to Develop Isolated Areas; Air Express Traffic; Psychological and Administrative Considerations (Air Transport and National Propaganda); Cultural Influences and Air Transport; Air Lines an Asset in Diplomatic Competition; Air Transport and Imperial Unity; Military (Matériel); Planes Carry Troops and Supplies; Personnel; Air Line Pilots at Peak Training; Air Routes and Ground Organization; Wartime Communication; and Wartime Administration of Transport Systems. Whether or not Lissitzyn's list is still valid in all respects as a description of world conditions, it certainly is a useful explanation of why governments originally became interested in fostering their own airlines and it gives a good indication of why that interest continues, although in recent years the military value of commercial air transport has been discounted.[36]

A national airline operating abroad is often regarded as a contributor to the national prestige, particularly in "developing" countries.[37]

The operation of a national airine can serve to enhance the national balance of payments, or at least give a government the illusion that it will do so.[38] A national airline can serve as a means for the state to project its power abroad, and this is a subject that is bound to be of interest to the state. A national airline is an important link in maintaining the cohesiveness of an overseas empire.

A national airline can help promote tourism to the country. It can also be useful in developing a national aircraft manufacturing industry.

A further reason for governmental support of national airlines in certain countries is that commissions on aircraft and other major items of equipment form a coveted source of income for certain high military officers and other government functionaries. This doesn't exist in every country, or at all times in particular countries, but it has been a reason in certain countries for support of an international government airline.

National airlines are also sometimes fostered as a means of providing extended careers for air force officers. In countries with relatively small air forces, it is often customary to retire the officers at an early age in order to open up promotions for those below. If they can be assigned as airline pilots, the retired officers can continue to be paid more or less as though they were on active duty.

The Instruments of Regulation

Having established that each state may exercise its sovereignty to exclude or to regulate the entry of foreign aircraft into its territory, the question remains to what extent and by what means does a state allow commercial operations by foreign aircraft, and how are they regulated?

At the most fundamental level, entry is allowed by means of a permit issued directly to the airline, and regulation is accomplished by means of national laws and regulations, on a completely unilateral basis.

International agreement on a multilateral basis has not prospered as a means of granting and regulating commercial air transport rights. The Paris Agreement of 1919 roundly rejected a multilateral approach to the granting of air transport rights when it was amended in 1933 to provide that

> Every contracting state may make conditional on its prior authorization the establishment of international airways and the creation and operation of regular air navigation lines, with or without landing on its territory.[39]

The 1933 amendment was the result of a controversy over the meaning of the 1919 Convention, but its effect was to foreclose a multilateral approach to the grant of commercial air traffic rights.[40] The Pan American Convention of 1928 to which the United States was a party appears to allow a measure of "freedom of the air," but it was never interpreted in that sense.[41] Other attempts to establish a multilateral agreement on a general waiving of sovereignty over the national air space in favor of scheduled commercial operations have been unsuccessful up to the present time.

The International Civil Aviation Organization has not until relatively recently concerned itself in a major way with the economic regulation of international air transport. After the initial failure to reach agreement on a multilateral agreement for the exchange of commercial rights, there seems to have been a consensus that ICAO was to be used primarily for technical matters.[42] Recently, however, largely in response to pressure from so-called "Third World" states, ICAO is being pushed into the arena of economic regulation.

The primary means for exchanging international traffic rights and for agreeing on the rules for the economic regulation of international air transport has been and continues to be through bilateral international agreements.

The so-called "Bermuda Agreement" of 1946 between the United States and the United Kingdom formed the cornerstone of the United States' International Air Transport Policy until it was revised in 1977. The Bermuda Agreement exerted a considerable influence on the air transport agreements of all countries throughout the world. The chief areas of influence of this agreement were its undertaking to recognize the International Air Transport Association as a rate-making body and the provisions governing the regulation of the capacity of the two nations' airlines. The Bermuda Agreement was superseded by a revised agreement in 1977.[43]

As has been observed earlier most of the existing bilateral air transport agreements relate to scheduled airline service. Non-scheduled service (and "charter" service, which is difficult to define as distinct from "scheduled" service) has been mainly regulated unilaterally. As "charter" flights have become more commercially important, those countries interested in fomenting them, notably the United States, have entered into bilateral agreements for charter service. Most of these agreements, however, cover only ancillary matters, and leave the decision whether or not to allow the operation of a particular charter flight to the unilateral judgment of each party. The United States has entered a number of bilateral charter agreements pursuant to which each country agrees to admit charters that originate in the territory of the other party, provided they qualify for operation as charters pursuant to the laws of that party ("Country of Origin Agreements"). Charter bilateral agreements relate primarily to traffic between the two countries concerned. The assumption evidently is that "fifth freedom" charters will be prohibited.

Inter-carrier agreements which are promoted by government pressure and are sanctioned by government approval, either formal or informal, are also vehicles for the economic regulation of air transport. Foremost under this heading is the establishment and operation of the International Air Transport Association (IATA). This body was the result of a governmental proposal, but was established by private agreement among the carriers and its existence was sanctioned by government approval. The fares and rates agreed by the airlines in IATA are subject to governmental approval and they do not become effective without that approval. Thus IATA is essentially a way for governments to delegate to the carriers the establishment of fares and rates.

The same device could be used to achieve carrier agreement on capacity, but it has never been attempted.[44]

Although there have not been multinational carrier agreements on international capacity through the medium of an IATA-type organization, there have been numerous bilateral carrier agreements limiting capacity and also a number of multilateral carrier agreements among the airlines of various states on capacity, all with governmental blessing, so that they can be considered governmental capacity regulation by surrogate in much the same way as IATA agreements on rates can be considered surrogates for governmental rate regulation. A number of bilateral air transport agreements specifically provide that the capacity offered on the routes between the two countries shall be agreed between their two national carriers, with the governments intervening only in the event of their inability to agree.[45]

Airline pooling agreements[46] can and often do introduce an element of capacity regulation which is little different from open agreement among the carriers on capacity (or from governmental agreement, where they are subject to government approval). Bin Cheng[47] gives an excellent description of pooling. He points out that the ideal justification for a pool is to avoid concentration of service at peak times and to provide adequate service for the public and a fair distribution of traffic for the airlines at all times. A less benign use of pools is as a means of blackmailing foreign airlines anxious to participate in the local market, where the price of an operating permit is a pool in which the local airline obtains advantages.

Pooling may involve the sharing of equipment or the splitting of costs and revenues. In a revenue pool where the airlines operate the same type of equipment over the same route, the formula for dividing costs and revenues can be fairly simple. Where there are different equipment types or different routes, the formulas become very complex.

Pools necessarily involve carrier agreement on capacity and this adds to the suspicion and antipathy with which they are regarded by the United States government.

Stephen Wheatcroft, writing in 1956,[48] delivers a strong case against the practice of pooling. He demonstrates that the pools in the European area were not producing the benefits that were claimed for them: They did not improve airline load factors; they did not permit reduced operating costs and if they produced a better spread of services throughout the day, this same result could be achieved without pooling. Moreover, Wheatcroft found that pooling has an adverse effect by eliminating the benefits of competition which might otherwise result in lower fares and improved service.

Tangential Matters

In addition to the more direct types of economic regulation, there are a number of devices for the economic regulation of air transport, which are analogous to "non-tariff barriers" in the import and export of goods. These devices are similar to direct regulation, in that they appear to have as their ultimate objective to obstruct the ability of foreign airlines to compete with the national airline; where they differ is that they are ostensibly intended for another purpose. For example, the Japanese have in recent years advanced a number of technical reasons (absence of fuel facilities; lack of ground transportation; noise problems) for their refusal to allow foreign airlines to increase their services at Tokyo. The suspicion has been raised, however, that the real reason for the refusal is to protect Japan Airlines and that the Japanese have seized upon this pretext because they have signed bilateral agreements that would prevent them from acting directly.

Another oblique way of exercising economic control over foreign airlines under the guise of technical regulation is through the assignment of "slot times." Modern international airports have a genuine problem in allocating landing times ("slot times") among the airlines that serve them. It is sometimes evident that where governmental authorities are in charge of this function, they carry it out so as to give the favorable landing times to the national carrier, to the detriment of foreign airlines, or even to deny such times entirely to certain foreign airlines.

An analogous but more direct regulation of landing times is to be found in the Argentine Air Policy Law, which provides that foreign airline schedules must avoid "super positions of schedules which are prejudicial for the national carriers in either an operational way or in an economic way."[49] Similar provisions are found in Bolivia, but such frankness is unusual, and landing slots are generally dealt with on an at least ostensibly technical basis.

The allocation of airport space can also be used as a device to discriminate against foreign airlines in favor of the national airline. Similarly, a number of countries announced that their landing fields were not suitable for jet operations until the national carrier was in a position to order jet equipment or that their airport terminals could not handle the increased traffic resulting from the use of wide-bodied equipment, until their own airlines were in a position to obtain wide-bodied aircraft.

Despite its extremely liberal attitude in recent years toward the regulation of airline routes and capacity, the United States was accused of engaging in technical regulation that had an undue economic effect on foreign airlines in connection with its implementation of Part 36 of the U.S. Federal Air Regulations, which established increasingly strict noise standards for application to aircraft landing at American airports. Although these regulations were viewed by the United States as being environmentally necessary, they had the effect of precluding the use for service to the United States of a number of very popular aircraft (including the Boeing 707 and the Douglas DC-8) unless a very expensive program of modifications was performed on them. Countries without the ready funds to perform the modifications or to obtain alternative equipment tended to accuse the United States of trying to put their airlines out of business.[50]

Other practices that are similar to "non-tariff barriers"[51] are regulations on doing business that affect the ability of foreign airlines to compete with the national airline. An example of such a regulation is a provision that only the national airline may sell computerized reservation services to other airlines in the country. In most countries, this will have the effect of facing foreign airlines with the choice of buying the services from the national airline or of doing without them entirely, because the markets for foreign airlines in most countries are too small to justify the expense of operating a computerized reservation system for a single foreign airline, and the prohibition prevents them from establishing a jointly operated system among several foreign airlines. When the foreign airlines are compelled to buy reservations services from the national airline, they are likely to find that the reservations system is skewed so as to give an advantage to the national airline and its pool partners in the way their schedules are presented to travel agents. The national airline also obtains access to the reservations lists of the airlines that participate in its reservations system, and this can be valuable competitive information. If the foreign airlines opt for refusing the service of the national carrier, they are left in the competitively disadvantageous position of not having access to a computerized reservation system, which is likely to be very serious where the system is used by travel agents. Another example is restriction on the opening of local offices by foreign airlines. Sometimes this is accompanied by a requirement that the national airline be retained as general sales agent. Still another example is restrictions on the convertibility or remittance out of the country of local currency obtained as the proceeds of sales of air transportation in the country.

Sometimes restrictions are imposed directly on the prospective passenger. For example, in a country where there are currency restrictions, passengers may be allowed to obtain a foreign currency allowance for their trip only if they use the national airline. In other cases, foreign visitors may be unable to obtain hotel accommodations unless they use the national airline.

This type of restriction can be encountered sporadically in any part of the world. In countries with non-market economies, such as China, the Soviet Union and the eastern European countries, restrictions on market access are the inevitable consequence of the way of doing business. Where the government controls the entire economy, including the national airline, it is logical from its point of view to forbid free market access by foreign airlines.

The United States has in recent years sought to alleviate the problems created for its carriers by foreign restrictions on doing business, which it lumps under the generic heading of "discriminatory practices," but it has been an uphill fight.

2. EUROPEAN AIR TRANSPORT POLICY, 1919–1944

An historical review of the United States National policy with respect to the econonic regulation of international air transport is necessarily closely related to the history of the operation of international air service. As a natural consequence of geography and the characteristics of aircraft (their speed and the fact that they operate in the air which has few natural boundaries between nations), commercial international flights were operated in Europe before they were operated in the United States.

In Europe, the nations are relatively small in area, so that to achieve the distances that took full advantage of the speed of the new means of transport, it was desirable and practical to extend air routes over two or more countries. In the United States, the internal distances are so great that full use could be made of the advantages of the new medium without going abroad, and in any case the range of early aircraft was too limited to be practical for long distances, many of them over water, between the United States and major traffic centers abroad, even those in Canada and Mexico. Thus, as one would expect, international air transport had its earliest development in Europe and the related regulatory policies were first developed in Europe.

These European laws and policies naturally had a profound influence on the development of laws and policies in the United States. Geographical, economic and technical conditions in Asia, Africa, Australia and South America were such that these areas did not figure in the international commercial airline picture until relatively late. In the United States, the early technical and regulatory development related to air routes exclusively within the national borders.

Prior to World War I (1914–1918), there were no organized commercial air operations anywhere. There was, however, a lively intellectual ferment in Europe concerning how the new medium could best be regulated. Originally, with considerable optimism and idealism the idea of "freedom of the skies," analogous to the "freedom of the seas," was propounded, but by 1911, it could be said "that states already view themselves as sovereign within their own aereal space."[1]

The sober and prophetic outlook that led to this insistence upon control of national air space is well expressed by William E. Von Hessen, writing in the British publication *The Aero* in 1911:

> In conclusion may I point out that the aeroplane is going to upset our present standards of warfare very very much indeed; so much so that I cannot do better than quote the opinion of a famous Continental Officer, 'Heaven help the nation without aerial craft next war, for god alone knows what an aeroplane could do, he alone knows.' And my experience leads me to believe this officer is sound in his mature judgment.[2]

These concerns were fully justified by the damage done by aircraft in World War I, which although small by modern standards, was extremely impressive to those who experienced it, and the concept that each country has full sovereignty over the air space above its territory was firmly established in the Paris Convention (Convention on the Regulation of Aerial Navigation of 1919)[3] which formed part of the series of treaties arising out of the Peace Conference in Paris after the war (which were not ratified by the United States).

By the end of World War I, the technical development of aircraft was sufficient to permit their use for the carriage for hire of mail and passengers. According to an early British writer, Semphill, May 1, 1918, the date of a British Air Ministry order first permitting air services, may be called "the date on which civil aviation commenced" and on August 25, 1919, "the first machine on the first regular commercial air route in the world left Hounslow, then the official London Aerfield, for Paris."[4]

This flight was made by the British Company Air Transport and Travel Ltd. According to the World Airline Record, the world's first "international commercial flight" was made over the same sector by Farman Airlines, a French Company on February 8, 1919.[5] The Farman Airlines flight was evidently not part of a regularly scheduled service.[6]

It is significant that the two earliest recorded international airline operations in Europe (and in the world) were performed on the same sector by the airlines of the two nations concerned. The custom in Europe was at that time and tends to be to this day to grant the most limited route rights possible in order to obtain the route rights sought for the national airline. This sort of a trade naturally resulted most often in an agreement that the airlines of the two countries should serve the same pair of points in their respective territories.

In considering how the European air policies developed, it is useful to look at the characteristics of the airlines to which they applied. They were an infant industry. They operated on a small scale and did not affect a large segment of the population. They were incapable of earning a normal business profit, so that they required subsidy or direct government operation. The equipment used was not radically different from the equipment used for military operations. They could provide services that were politically extremely useful to governments, particularly those with extensive overseas empires. Although passengers were often carried, the primary mission of the very early international air services was the carriage of air mail, which made the government itself the most important user, since the mails were a government monopoly.

The period between the first and second world wars, when the patterns of air transport regulations were being fixed in Europe (1918–1939), was a period of increasing economic nationalism throughout the world, and particularly in Europe. Most of the continental governments came out of the first world war with a bias toward protectionism and economic nationalism. In the decade following the war this general bias toward protectionism caused such traditional supporters of free trade as the British to enter protective tariff schemes and special marketing agreements with their overseas dominions.[7] This tendency fed upon itself to a point where by 1937, a French writer could claim to see in Europe a revival of the pre-Adam Smith doctrine of mercantilism.[8] At the same time, the governments of the European countries where international commercial aviation was developing had immediately before them in the experience of World War I the most drastic sort of evidence of the war-making potential of aviation. This potential undoubtedly led the governments of the major countries to consider it urgent to foster and control a national air transport industry, while at the same time maintaining the greatest degree of control possible over the air transport enterprises of other countries. The desire to protect the national airlines was intensified by the desire of the governments to protect their investment in the subsidy paid to them.

Thus, the Paris Convention of 1919,[9] which established for its parties the rules governing the technical aspects of air operation, was interpreted and subsequently amended (in 1933) to provide that special permission of the government concerned was required for the operation of scheduled international commercial service.[10] The bilateral "Air Navigation Agreements" that were signed to substitute for the technical provisions of the Paris Convention between parties where either or both of them were not at the time party to that convention all provided that scheduled commercial operations were subject to operating permits issued unilaterally by the government concerned, or to further agreement between the two governments. (Certain early agreements that were labeled "air navigation agreements" did provide for commercial service, and are treated herein as "air transport agreements."[11])

Between 1919 and 1939, many bilateral agreements for the establishment of commercial air services were signed between nations party to the

Paris Convention of 1919 and between those nations and third nations. Many of those agreements were reported in the Official Bulletin of the International Commission for Air Navigation (generally abbreviated by the initials of its name in French, "CINA"[12]). This type of agreement is referred to as an "Air Transport Agreement" in the CINA Bulletin, and this usage is still current.

The CINA Bulletin lists 34 air transport agreements between European nations. With few exceptions, these agreements bear witness to the desire of the parties to apply restrictive conditions to the operations of commercial airlines. That is to say in negotiations for air transport service, they sought to grant the most limited quid pro quo possible in order to gain their own ends, and to maintain a high degree of control over the competitive activities of the foreign airlines they allowed to serve their national markets.

One measure of restrictiveness is the degree of flexibility allowed the airlines in choosing the traffic points to be served in their operation. The more specific the description of the routes the more restrictive the agreement is likely to be. By this measure, 23, or 67 percent of the agreements reported, are very restrictive in specifying in detail the points that may be served.[13]

Another measure of restrictiveness is whether the routes grant traffic rights in third countries, either as intermediate points, or as points beyond ("fifth freedom rights"). Thirteen of these agreements are completely restrictive in granting only traffic rights between cities in the respective countries ("third and fourth freedom rights").[14]

Although the other 21 agreements contain fifth freedom rights of one sort or another, the scope of these rights is severely limited by the fact that in 15 of them the points that may be served in third countries are described restrictively in detail.[15] The right to serve intermediate points or points beyond in six agreements is more generally described and gives greater flexibility and scope for service to points in third countries.[16]

A further indication of the restrictive character of the bilateral air transport agreements among European nations during the period 1919–1939 is the fact that of the 34 agreements recorded in the CINA Bulletin, 28 either explicitly or implicitly allow each party to designate only one airline to operate on the routes granted.[17]

The provisions of most of these agreements relating to capacity also reflect a tendency toward restrictiveness. Only 11 of the agreements provide that the carriers (or their governments) may unilaterally fix their own capacity.[18] The remaining 23 agreements may be considered to be in one way or another restrictive in this respect: 12 agreements do not have provisions covering capacity, which in view of the provisions of the Paris Convention of 1919 amounts to providing that each government may regulate the capacity of the other's airlines.[19] Four agreements have the airlines' capacity fixed in the agreements themselves.[20] One agreement provided that each government may control the capacity of the other's airlines.[21] Six agreements provide that the capacity to be offered is to be established by agreement between the airlines or their governments.[22]

The pricing provisions in most of these agreements are similarly restrictive. The carriers are given the freedom to establish their own fares and rates in only six of the 34 agreements.[23] In 18 of the remaining 28 agreements, there is no mention of pricing, which leaves each government free to disapprove prices offered by the other's airlines. In one agreement, each government specifically has control of the prices to be charged by the other's airlines.[24] In nine agreements prices are to be set by agreement between the carriers or the governments. (In some cases the requirement for agreement is explicit,[25] in others it is to be inferred from such statements as "the method of operation is to be agreed by the carriers,"[26] or "by the aeronautical authorities,"[27] or from the fact that the service is to be operated in pool by the carriers of the countries concerned.[28])

Moreover, the European nations carefully exploited their geographical advantages in order to bring pressure on one another to achieve their own aviation goals. Concrete examples are hard to come by at this late date. Wagner[29] refers to an instance where the Germans were able to force the French to negotiate with them for air routes. Under the Versailles Treaty ending World War I, Germany was forbidden to have an air force, and for a temporary period, the aircraft of the victorious allies were allowed to land in Germany without obtaining permission of the German government. By virtue of the latter provision, the Franco-Roumanian Company, a French Company, was operating between France and Roumania via Germany. On January 8, 1923, this provision of the Versailles Treaty expired. The Germans thereupon notified the French that they objected to landings by aircraft in this service in Germany, although they would permit them to overfly German territory nonstop. The range of the aircraft did not permit nonstop operations, so the French, after unsuccessfully attempting a circuitous operation through Switzerland and Austria, were forced to negotiate with the Germans for the right to resume the service via Germany. Cooper[30] observes that it was through such negotiations that the Germans were able to nullify the provisions of the Versailles Treaty that forbade them to have an air force. By obtaining commercial rights for themselves which enabled them to establish airlines, they then used these as the basis for the clandestine development of an air force.

Wagner[31] also mentions a case where the British and the Italians harassed one another's airlines. In 1922, the British, invoking Article 15 of the Paris Convention held up operations by the Italians for three years on a route from Italy to Egypt (then a part of the British Empire). In 1929, when the British wanted to establish a route from England to India via Italy, the Italians imposed so many unacceptable conditions that the British ended up operating the service over a circuitous route via Central Europe.[32]

It can be noted that although the general tenor of the bilateral air transport agreements among the European nations in the period 1919–1939 was restrictive, certain nations, notably Great Britain and France, managed to obtain a measure of freedom for the operations of their airlines. The British and French also tended to a much greater extent than other European countries to permit private commercial companies to operate their international air services, although both ended up with a government-owned airline to perform the major portion of these services.

The British bilateral air transport agreements are the most liberal of those recorded in the CINA reports. All three of the British agreements with European nations recorded (with Greece, Italy and Austria) have loosely phrased route descriptions that allow the carriers considerable flexibility and permit them to carry third, fourth and fifth freedom traffic. In all three agreements, the carriers are free to fix their own fares and rates and their own capacity without control by the government granting the rights. Also, in all three agreements there is no limitation on the number of airlines that may be designated.

The very earliest British airlines were privately owned and operated without subsidy. Within a few months after these airlines inaugurated service in September 1919 it became apparent that they could not keep going without subsidy, and all British international airline service came to a halt in February 1920. Service was resumed in March 1921 when the British government decided to pay a subsidy to keep the airlines going. In April 1924 the four then existing subsidized private airlines were consolidated into a single company, Imperial Airways, with the British government as a minority shareholder. This company was given a monopoly of government subsidy.

Although Imperial Airways was nominally a privately owned company, there was never any doubt that its primary function was to act as a servant of the British Empire. During the period of Imperial Airways' growth, other smaller companies operated without subsidy and four of them merged into British Airways Limited in 1935. In 1936, this company managed to become eligible for payment of subsidy. In November 1938, it was decided that Imperial Airways and British Airways should be merged into a single government owned corporation with the name British Overseas Airways Corporation, BOAC, and this was done on April 1, 1940. During the war years, all British air service was at the disposition of the government.[33] Upon termination of the war, however, private airline competition for the national airline resumed.

The French, like the British, showed a certain ambivalence about the value of private enterprise in the air transport industry, and like the British, the French subsidized their national airlines. Four private French airlines survived from the earliest days until 1933 when they were consolidated into Air France, of which the French government originally owned 25 percent. During World War II, the Air France services were dedicated to the war effort until the fall of France, when all Air France personnel who could do so regrouped in North Africa. After the war, Air France was reconstituted as a nationalized company with the French government owning 70 percent of the shares. The French used their airline to establish communications with their overseas empire in Africa and in Indochina.[34]

The French, however, appear to have used their airline to a greater extent than did the British to spread French influence to points unrelated to their empire routes. They had an avowed interest in using the airline to spread French cultural influences, "to protect a cultural empire which is menaced by merchant empires."[35] The French route to South America, which was opened as early as 1930 and placed in service by 1935, is an example of a route that must have been operated for reasons other than to serve points in the French empire or to make money.[36] Presumably it was operated to enhance French prestige and to spread French influence.

It is interesting that in spite of the evidently nationalistic bent of French international air policy, it was the French who proposed the internationalization of air transport in 1930. This plan was part of a proposal to abolish air forces and prohibit bombing from the air. The French made the proposal in the League of Nations Disarmament Conference which started in 1930 and indicated that they were only willing to go forward with it if there should be established an international police force and if all air transport should be internationalized. The proposal failed and the disarmament conference broke down in 1934.[37]

The position taken by the French in these discussions appears to have been less the result of a conviction that a single internationalized airline was a good way to attend to the world's air transport needs than it was a logical recognition that if military air forces were to be abolished, it was also necessary to abolish national airlines to prevent nations from surreptitiously converting their civil airlines to military use as was being done at the time by Germany. When the conference debates disclosed the impracticability of "internationalization," the French dropped it.[38]

It is also to be noted that the Paris Convention of 1919 provided in Article 16 that each contracting state could establish "restrictions in favor of its National Aercraft in connection with the carriage of persons and goods for hire between two points in its territory." This concept is known as "Cabotage," after the term used to describe the trade on sea routes between domestic points. Such restrictions were established by the European nations party to the Paris Convention, and W.M. Sheehan, writing in 1950 in the *Harvard Law Review* observes that as of that date, "Practically all national legislation dealing with air navigation reserves air cabotage to the national carriers."[39] This is still the situation, although the United States shows some tendency to change its position.[40] No such tendency is to be seen in any European country.

Intercarrier pooling agreements among airlines have the effect of governmental regulations, and have been entered into almost without exception only by sanction of governmental authority. Details of pooling agreements are hard to come by. According to Lissitzen,[41] pooling arrangements were common in prewar Europe and the principal exponents were France, Germany and the Scandinavian states. Of the air transport agreements listed in the CINA Bulletin, the following contemplate pooling arrangements between the airlines of the countries concerned:

Pooling Contemplated

Italy-Spain	26 August 1929—Airlines to act "in conjunction as regards tariffs and the organization of the routes and traffic."
Italy-Austria	28 January 1930—Airlines to work out by common agreement "The method of operations referred to in Articles 1 and 2 (routes, frequency and overflights)"; also refers to possible "joint operation" on a new route (Article 3).
France-Italy	31 July 1929—Intercarrier agreements, both technical and commercial to be promoted.
France-Belgium	1 June 1930—Routes to be operated in collaboration.
Germany-Poland	18 May 1834—Companies required to sign an agreement for collaboration in time tables, pricing and charters.
Spain-Germany	9 February 1931—Airlines required to sign an agreement for a 50-50 split of the traffic.
Spain-Germany	7 January 1935—Germany to reserve 50 percent of its South Atlantic traffic for a Spanish airline.
Greece-Italy	15 January 1938—Air companies to "enter into an agreement as regards the common operation of the said lines."
Belgium-Czechoslovakia	3 February 1938—Airlines agreement for joint operations required.
Italy-Romania-Yugoslavia	19 September 1937—Pool called for.
Italy-Germany	26 April 1939—Airlines to agree on terms of a pooling agreement.

Italy–Netherlands	16 September 1935 — The companies "shall endeavor to come to an agreement as to the means of operating the air lines mentioned in Article 1."

As of 1936, the following pools were in operation on routes within Europe, by airline members of the International Air Traffic Association. (The carriers are listed by nationality, rather than by corporate name.)

Berlin–Cologne–Paris (German–French)
Berlin–Copenhagen–Malmo (German–Danish–Swedish)
Hamburg–Copenhagen–Malmo (German–Danish–Swedish)
Berlin–Munich–Venice–Rome (German–Italian)
Berlin–Halle/Leipzig–Frankfurt–Saarbruchen–Paris (German–French)
Berlin–Halle/Leipzig–Stuttgart–Zurich (German–Swiss)
Berlin–Poznan–Warsaw (German–Polish)
Berlin–Vienna (German–Austrian)
Amsterdam–Cologne–Frankfurt–Mannheim/Ludwigshafen/Heidelberg–Basel–Zurich (German–Swiss)
Berlin–Dresden–Prague–Vienna (German–Czechoslovakia–Austrian)
Vienna–Salzburg–Munich–Zurich (German–Austrian)
Halle/Leipzig–Chemnetz–Karlovy Vary–Marianske–Lazne (German–Belgian)
Cologne–Brussels–Paris (German–Belgian)
Vienna–Klagenfurt–Venice (Austrian–Italian)
Belgrade–Zagreb–Graz–Vienna (Yugoslav–Austrian–French)
Budapest–Vienna (Austrian–Hungarian)
Paris–Geneva (French–Swiss)
Paris–Brussels–Rotterdam–Amsterdam (French–Belgian–Dutch)
Brussels–Antwerp–Rotterdam–Amsterdam (French–Belgian)
Amsterdam–Hamburg–Copenhagen–Malmo (Dutch–Swedish)
Amsterdam–Copenhagen–Malmo (Dutch–Swedish)
Paris–Basel–Zurich (French–Swiss)
Stockholm–Turku–Helsinki–Tallinn (Swedish–Finnish)
Zagreb–Susak (Czechoslovakia–Yugoslav, although both points are in Yugoslavia)
Amsterdam–Frankfurt–Milan (Dutch–German–Italian)
Amsterdam–Halle/Leipzig–Prague (Dutch–Czechoslovakia)
London–Amsterdam–Berlin (Dutch–German)
Paris–Bordeaux–Madrid (French–Spanish)
Paris–Marseilles–Rome (French–Italian)[42]

Pooling automatically restricts competition. The widespread existence of pools in Europe in this period is another measure of the restrictiveness of the air transport policies being applied by these countries.

Early in the period of airline development in Europe, the International Air Traffic Association was established. This body was formed August 25, 1919. Its members were the airlines, and not the governments. The stated aim of this association, usually known by the acronym formed by its initials

IATA: was "the establishment of unity in the operation of air routes of affiliated organizations whose systems are of international importance." The by-laws stated that it was nonpolitical and that its members were to be entirely autonomous.[43] During the period 1919–1944, IATA was essentially a trade association for the European airlines.[44] Its committees were Legal, Postal, Radio Telephone, Cash Examination (Auditing), Combined Transport, Unification of Documents,[45] Time Tables, Accountancy,[46] Technical[47] and Agency. An example of IATA's trade association activity is the joint effort of the airlines under the IATA banner to break the monopoly of the railroads and the steamship companies in the carriage of mail.[48]

Although the members agreed informally at IATA meetings on fares, rates and pools, these activities "were neither authorized, sanctioned, registered nor enforced by IATA."[49]

The prewar IATA served as the basis for the postwar International Air Transport Association, also known as IATA, which came into being as a result of the Bermuda Agreement between the United States and the United Kingdom in 1944.[50]

During the entire period 1919–1944, there was no way an airline could provide service at a commercial profit. This meant that the airlines were necessarily either subsidized by governments, or directly owned and operated by governments. This automatically led to a certain bias toward government aims and purposes, as opposed to the aims and purposes that would be pursued by private entrepreneurs in the absence of government subsidy. In short, from the beginning the airlines were likely to fly where and when the geopolitical doctrines of their governments dictated, rather than where and when commercial judgment counselled.[51] In the end this did not make much difference so far as the overall route pattern is concerned, since irrespective of the motives the pattern of routes that emerged provides service on the sectors where people want to travel. The background is important, however, because in Europe and in much of the rest of the world, most governments continue to regard their airlines as instruments of national policy and to be ready to subsidize them if necessary.

During World War II, European commercial international air transport for all practical purposes ceased to exist. Commercial airlines were either militarized, or they went out of business entirely. Thus, there was no development of international air transport policy for the European countries during most of World War II. With the end of the war in sight in 1944, however, the European countries were forced to focus hard on the issue.

As early as March 1943 in the British House of Commons, speaking of the organization of postwar aviation, A. Sinclair said

> In the view of His Majesty's Government, some form of international collaboration will be essential if the air is to be developed in the interests of mankind as a whole, trade served, international understanding fostered and some measure of international security gained.[52]

Later in the same year, October 20, 1943, there was a further discussion of postwar aviation, in which many of the themes that were to dominate the discussions for the next few years were touched on.[53] Lord Beaverbrook said that the great air route of the world was going to be America–Europe. He also observed that Great Britain would be at a disadvantage in the postwar world because the United States was concentrating on building transport aircraft for wartime use which would be available for peacetime airline service whereas the British were building exclusively fighters and bombers which would have no peacetime use. Viscount St. Davids said that the wartime cooperation with respect to military aviation was so impressive that he felt it should be held together in the form of a single international company, along the ines of the Suez Company to operate commercial international services. Viscount Trenchard quoted from a *New York Times* article of October 1, 1943, wherein President Roosevelt was reported as having agreed that air transport within a particular country should be owned and run by the country.

Lord Beaverbrook reported that a Commonwealth conference on postwar civil aviation had been held at which it had been unanimously agreed that there should be an international air transport authority and that it should be intimately associated with and responsible to any United Nations Security Organization that might be established. Lord Beaverbrook also reported that there had been a discussion of "freedoms of the air" at the meeting between President Roosevelt and Prime Minister Churchill referred to in the *New York Times* story of October 1, 1943. He said the next step should be a meeting with the United States and the Russians.

3. AMERICAN INTERNATIONAL COMMERCIAL AIR TRANSPORT POLICY, 1919–1944

Regular commercial international airline operations did not start in the United States until 1927 when Pan American Airways (now called Pan American World Airways, and usually referred to herein as "Pan American") made its inaugural flight from Key West, Florida, to Havana, Cuba.[1]

Historically in the United States, as in Europe, the first air services were for the carriage of air mail. The first such service was by the United States Army Air Corps, which inaugurated regularly scheduled airmail flights from New York to Philadelphia and Washington on May 5, 1918. By August 1918, the Army gave up this service and turned it over to the United States Post Office Department. By 1920, the Post Office was operating a transcontinental airmail route from New York to San Francisco.[2] In 1925, it was determined that the carriage of domestic airmail should be turned over to private contractors, and in that year Congress passed the Air Mail Act[3] providing for airmail contracts with private operators for the carriage of domestic mail. There was no special enabling legislation for the carriage of foreign airmail by private carriers, although such mail could be carried under special appropriations.[4]

On May 17, 1928, the Kelly Amendment to the Air Mail Act was passed,[5] providing for a reduction in postage and the issuance of route certificates. In 1926, the first privately operated domestic airmail service in the United States commenced when Varney Air Lines (now merged into United Airlines) inaugurated service from Pasco, Washington, to Elko, Nevada, under contract with the Post Office. Private airline service grew rapidly and by 1929 transcontinental service was being offered with 14-passenger, trimotored Ford aircraft.[6]

Meanwhile, Juan Terry Trippe was starting his remarkable career as an airline entrepreneur and as a powerful influence on American international commercial air policy. In 1922, Trippe was 23 years old, having recently graduated from Yale University, where his career had been interrupted by service as an aviator in the United States Navy in World War I. In 1925, after a series of unsuccessful attempts to form an airline company, Trippe had got himself named managing director of a company called Colonial Air Transport, which held an airmail contract for service between New York and Boston. Trippe had as backers a number of the most wealthy men in the country, to whom he had access through his own family and his Yale connections.

During the latter part of 1925, Trippe flew to Havana with Anthony Fokker in one of Fokker's tri-motored aircraft on what has been referred to as a "barnstorming junket" thought up by Trippe.[7] While in Havana, Trippe had a Cuban lawyer prepare, and persuaded President Machado of Cuba to sign, a document granting Trippe the right to serve Cuba through Campo Colombia airfield. This document granted the rights to Trippe personally.[8] By March 1926, Trippe and his backers were out of Colonial. Thereafter a new company was formed under the name Aviation Corporation of America, with Trippe again as managing director.

In the meantime another company had been formed, with the name Pan American Airways, Inc. The original promoters of this airline were a group of United States military officers some of whom later became famous as aviators in World War II. They were Major Henry H. ("Hap") Arnold, Major Carl Spaatz, Major Jack Jouett and an Air Corps captain named John Montgomery. They had learned from Army intelligence reports that a group of German World War I aviators had set themselves up in Colombia shortly after World War I, under the direction of Peter Paul von Bauer, a former German officer, to operate an airline which they called Sociedad Colombo-Aleman de Transporte Aereo, or SCADTA (the name means Colombian-German Air Transport Society). According to the reports, von Bauer intended to extend his airline to Panama and eventually to the United States.

Apparently the group of American officers was moved in part by patriotic motives to protect the Canal Zone and the approaches to the United States from German aeronautical domination and in part by the hope of financial gain. They managed to get an airmail contract for Key West–Havana service, but they had trouble raising money after Arnold, Spaatz and Jouett were forced to withdraw from the project because of their involvement in the court-martial proceedings against General "Billy" Mitchell. At the same time, Pan American Airways was faced with a requirement that it start mail service within three months of the signature of its airmail contract, on penalty of losing the contract.

The document Trippe had obtained from President Machado proved crucial in enabling him to bring about a three way deal among Trippe's

Aviation Corporation of America, Pan American Airways, Inc., and a third company called Atlantic, Gulf and Caribbean Airways, which had strong backing but neither aircraft nor contracts. Trippe's Cuban document was crucial because it was something the promoters could exhibit to a bank to gain credibility for raising money and on October 13, 1927, just six days before the deadline to start operations under the mail contract, Trippe wound up as president and general manager of Pan American Airways, Inc., which was to be the surviving airline company.[9] The deadline was met and Pan American and Trippe were on their way.[10]

Although the United States did not establish extensive international air transport operations until the advent of Pan American in 1927, it had expressed itself officially on the subject of international air transport policy prior to that time. In 1919, in the negotiations for the Paris Convention for Aerial Navigation,[11] the United States took the position that although the treaty should provide that each nation has sovereignty over the air space above its territory, it should also provide for maximum freedom of commercial flight consistent with that sovereignty.[12] The United States refused to ratify the entire group of ancillary treaties arising out of the negotiations for the treaty ending World War I, with the result that it never ratified the Paris Convention of 1919 which formed part of these negotiations.

In 1929, the United States took part by special invitation (required because the United States was not a party to the treaty) in a meeting of the International Committee for Air Navigation, where it was one of only four nations represented that voted in favor of a clarification of the Paris Convention of 1919 that would have established freedom of passage for international air commerce.

In 1928, the United States became a signatory to and ratified the Pan American Convention on Commercial Aviation which appears to allow a degree of freedom of passage for commercial international air line flights. In practice however, this treaty seems to have little effect on the requirements of the parties for special authorization.[13]

Despite these indications of liberality, the United States passed in 1926 the Air Commerce Act.[14] This law provided:

> The Congress hereby declares that the Government of the United States has, to the exclusion of all foreign nations, complete sovereignty of the air space over the lands and waters of the United States, including the Canal Zone.[15]

The Air Commerce Act also included a provision reserving the carriage of cabotage traffic for American aircraft, including that between the continental United States and its overseas possessions.[16]

Section 6 of the Air Commerce Act of 1926 provided that foreign aircraft could only operate in the United States through authorization by the U.S. Secretary of Commerce, and that such authorization was contingent upon a foreign nation's granting a similar privilege in respect of aircraft of the United States.

Lissitzyn[17] observes that although the United States at the meeting of the International Commission of 1929 favored greater freedom for international airlines, it did not believe it could offer to practice such liberality on a unilateral basis. Thus, from the very beginning there was a certain ambivalence in the attitude of the United States toward operations by foreign air carriers. In principle the United States favored liberality in granting air routes; in practice, it adapted to the needs of the market place.

A similar ambivalence can be noted in the attitude of the United States toward competition among United States airlines on international routes. At this time a sine qua non for operations on any airline route was a contract for the carriage of mail. Airmail contracts with the United States Post Office Department required competitive bidding[18] and in 1928, the United States enacted the Foreign Airmail Act,[19] which provided for airmail contract rates that would subsidize the operations of the airlines holding them and required that such contracts be awarded by public bidding. The implication of this legislation was that the United States expected that there would be a number of airlines seeking to operate internationally. Similarly, in the domestic field, the United States in 1930 enacted the Watres Act,[20] which provided an element of subsidy for the carriage of domestic mail, and specifically required public bidding for airmail contracts.

On March 4, 1929, Postmaster General Walter F. Brown took office. Brown did not favor public bidding because he considered it detrimental to the establishment of a coherent air transportation system and he made an unsuccessful effort to achieve legislation that would authorize the awarding of airmail contracts by negotiation.[21] Despite this failure, Brown went ahead and in 1930 called a conference of domestic airlines at which he posted a map showing his proposals for what domestic airmail routes should be operated, and encouraged agreement among the airlines as to which should serve what routes. The carriers failed to agree, but did agree that Brown should be the one to determine how the routes were to be divided up.[22]

In the international field, Pan American's contract between Key West and Havana was awarded July 16, 1927, after a call for bids by the Post Office Department.[23] The next route to come up for bid was a route that went Cuba–Haiti–Dominican Republic–Puerto Rico and was designated by the United States Post Office as FAM6 (Foreign Air Mail [route number] 6). Trippe acquired this route for Pan American despite the competition of another U.S. airline, and thereafter acquired foreign air mail routes through Central America to the Canal Zone; and down the west coast of South America. The latter route was operated jointly with W.R. Grace & Company through Pan American–Grace Airways ("Panagra").

After a savage struggle with an airline named New York, Rio and Buenos Aires Airline, "NYRBA," Trippe won for Pan American the foreign air mail route down the east coast of South America via Caracas, Rio de Janeiro and Buenos Aires, after Postmaster Brown forced NYRBA to merge with Pan American.[24]

In 1931, Postmaster Brown told U.S. domestic operators to stay out of the international field and Pan American to stay out of the domestic field.[25]

In 1933 a Senate committee[26] undertook to investigate Brown's program because the airmail contracts had not been awarded by competitive bidding as required by law. In a sensational proceeding, this investigation led to the cancellation by Postmaster General Farley, Brown's successor in office, of the domestic mail contracts on February 9, 1934, and to the disastrous takeover of the domestic mail service by the Army Air Corps.[27] Although the Senate investigation had been directed to the foreign mail contracts as well as the domestic contracts, and although Postmaster General Farley in a report of the Post Office Department's own investigation insisted that he had the right to cancel Pan American's air mail contracts, he did not do so, saying:

> Either or all of the contracts under consideration in this report may be cancelled because they were awarded as a result of negotiation and not by competitive bidding as provided by law. It is not believed, however, that the cancellation of these contracts would be in the public interest, as such action would probably disrupt American air service to the Latin American Countries and might result in great harm to our trade relations with these countries. There is no other air company in the United States that has the experience, the equipment, the necessary concessions with the Latin American Countries and other facilities for service than the Pan American Airways System has for operation in the territory.[28]

It does not require any great effort of the imagination to surmise that this statement reflected pressure from the Department of State and that the Department of State had in turn been thoroughly lobbied by Pan American. At this point Juan Trippe was well on his way toward installing Pan American as the "chosen instrument" to perform international airline service on behalf of the United States, despite the indications that the direction of United States policy had been to encourage competition among American airlines both domestically and internationally. The policy established in 1931 of excluding domestic carriers from Pan American's international field was reaffirmed in 1937 when the United States Post Office Department refused to give Braniff Airways a contract for the carriage of mails to Mexico on the grounds that such a service would in effect be competing with the United States government, since service mail payments received by Pan American Airways from Mexico were turned over to the Post Office Department.[29]

Similarly, Oliver Lissitzyn, writing in 1942, could say

> The United States has not looked with much favor upon foreign efforts to compete with Pan American Airways on its Caribbean routes; the Secretary of Commerce turned down in 1937 an application of KLM, The Dutch Royal Air Transport Company for landing privileges in Miami.[30]

Apparently this was the only attempt at service between the United States and the Caribbean, South or Central America by a foreign airline until after World War II. Lissitzyn points out further that in 1938 "for military reasons" British and Dutch companies were denied landing privileges at Hawaii, thus foreclosing transpacific service to the United States by foreign airlines, since these two were the only foreign airlines that had applied for the route.[31]

In most areas where they operated in Latin America, Pan American and Panagra were welcomed by the local governments as providers of international transportation and even as providers of local transportation between internal points. Prior to the close of World War II, there were no significant international operations by South American Airlines and in most countries there were not even extensive internal networks operated by national airlines until after World War II. In Central America, there were more extensive local airline operations, but these were still of a relatively limited nature.[32]

The relative scarcity of Latin American international airlines is not surprising. For them to exist on a large scale, during this period, the governments would have to be willing to subsidize them, as the American and European governments subsidized their airlines, but the Latin American governments lacked one prime incentive for subsidy that the others had: there was no aircraft manufacturing industry in any Latin American country.[33] Moreover, the potential Latin American market for international service was small in comparison with the United States–Europe, United States–Pacific and the intra-European markets. The Latin American governments did not have empires which would lead them to develop services such as the British, French, Dutch, and the Italians did. Funds for such things as airline subsidies were scarce in Latin America. Where they were available, they were used to develop internal airlines where the need was more immediately apparent.[34]

Much of the Latin American air transport industry and all of the international operations were backed by foreign capital during the prewar period. A number of these companies were established by German nationals, who were driven to fulfill their aeronautical ambitions abroad by the terms of the Versailles Treaty after World War I.[35] These companies were used to an increasing extent by the Germans for the purpose of advancing their national interests in the area, to a point where the United States considered it necessary to act against them as World War II developed.

Pan American also had a number of affiliated companies in South America.[36] Most of these companies were acquired either to facilitate international operations to the country, or to give Pan American access to the cabotage market, or both.[37]

The development of Pan American's routes across the Atlantic and Pacific oceans forms an important part of the history of the United States commercial air transport policy. Trippe, on behalf of Pan American, signed an agreement as early as November 11, 1930, with the French Company Aerospatiale and the British Imperial Airways to operate jointly across the Atlantic, and not to operate in any other way. The parties agreed to split up the traffic 50 percent for Pan American and 25 percent each for the French and the British. This arrangement fell through, and the British blocked Pan American's efforts to reach Europe via a northern route through their control of Newfoundland, then a British Crown Colony, and the French blocked the southern route through a deal they had with the Portuguese for traffic rights in the Azores. Trippe in 1934 then turned his attentions to the Pacific. As early as 1933, Pan American had acquired an American company operating in China known then as China Airways and later as China National Airways Corporation (CNAC).[38]

In 1935, Pan American was engaged in a competitive struggle for a U.S. route across the Pacific with two United States companies, Inter Island, backed by the Matson Steamship Line, and South Seas Commercial, backed by Donald Douglas of the Douglas Aircraft Company among others. During 1935, Pan American made deals with Inter Island and South Seas Commercial which led to both of these companies' giving up their ambitions to operate transpacific service. Donald Douglas and a representative of the Matson interests joined Pan American's Board of Directors and both companies received options to buy Pan American stock. On October 21, 1935, Pan American was awarded an airmail contract by the United States Post Office for service across the Pacific. Pan American was the only bidder.[39]

Pan American was permitted by the United States government to have a free hand in dealing with foreign governments with respect to its operating rights, and it had firmly entrenched itself in the areas where it operated. Pan American negotiated its own operating rights throughout Latin America, except in Colombia, where an agreement was negotiated by the United States government to authorize Pan American's service.[40] Also in the Pacific, Pan American dealt directly with the governments on its own behalf. For example in 1935 and 1936, when Pan American encountered trouble persuading the British to permit it to serve Hong Kong, Pan American negotiated an arrangement with the Portuguese to allow service to Macao, which led to sufficient pressure in Hong Kong to bring about an agreement whereby Pan American was allowed to serve Hong Kong.[41]

Juan Trippe continued to deal with the British for a transatlantic route and on September 12, 1935, he signed with Imperial Airways a paper in which the parties promised one another a "square deal." In December of 1935, the British government negotiated with the United States for a transatlantic route, and on January 25, 1936, it was announced that agreement had been reached for reciprocal operation of transatlantic services. During those negotiations, the British asked for confirmation that the United States would accept Imperial Airways as the British carrier and announced that they would accept Pan American. The United States representatives said they must keep the route open to permit selection of any U.S. carrier and put out a notice requesting interested U.S. carriers to appear at the next day's meeting. Only Pan American showed up at the next day's meeting, but the United States nevertheless insisted on keeping the agreement sufficiently general to allow the permits to be transferred from Pan American or Imperial Airways to other companies. On January 25, 1936, Pan American and Imperial Airways signed an agreement promising that neither would operate on the route until the other was ready and assuring one another a "square deal." This agreement was understood to mean that Pan American and Imperial Airways were agreeing to freeze all other airlines off the North Atlantic at a time when it was becoming apparent that it could be a lucrative run. The result was a political uproar in the United States which delayed the issuance of any transatlantic permits for Pan American.[42]

When Pan American's British permit came through on February 22, 1937, it contained a provision that Pan American could not start service until Imperial Airways was ready to start.[43]

Under the new United States Civil Aeronautics Act,[44] Pan American applied for and on May 17, 1939, obtained from the Civil Aeronautics Board a certificate of convenience and necessity for two routes to Europe[45]: a Northern route to England via Bermuda and Canada, and a Southern route to Lisbon and Marseilles via the Azores. Pan American started service on the Lisbon–Marseilles route May 20, 1939, and on the London route June 24, 1939, the British having waived the requirement for simultaneous start up by Imperial Airways in February of 1939. (The British started service shortly after Pan American, but because of World War II, this service was discontinued in September 1939.)[46]

Thus, up to the entry of the United States in World War II, Pan American retained its position as the only U.S. airline operating international routes. It enjoyed the benefit of subsidy on those routes and was supported by the U.S. government in its dealings with foreign governments.

The passage of the Civil Aeronautics Act in 1938 marked a turning point in the trend toward a more open and "liberal" policy for the United States. The declaration of policy contained in the act as originally passed (and as continued in amendments to it substantially without change until passage of the Airline Deregulation Act of 1978[47] and the International Air Transportation Competition Act of 1979[48]) reads as follows:

> Section 2. In the exercise and performance of its powers and duties under this Act the Authority[49] shall consider the following, among other things as being in the Public interest, and in accordance with the public convenience and necessity—
>
> a) The encouragement and development of an air transportation system properly adapted to the present and future needs of the foreign and domestic commerce of the United States, of the Postal Service and of the national defense;
>
> b) The regulation of air transportation in such manner as to recognize and preserve the inherent advantages of, assure the highest degree of safety in, and foster sound economic conditions in, such transportation, and to improve the relations between, and coordinate transportation by, air carriers;
>
> c) The promotion of adequate, economical and efficient service by air carriers at reasonable charges, without unjust discriminations, undue preferences or advantages, or unfair or destructive competitive practices;
>
> d) Competition to the extent necessary to assure the sound development of an air transportation system properly adapted to the needs of the foreign and domestic commerce of the United States, of the Postal Service, and of the national defense.
>
> e) The regulation of air commerce in such manner as to best promote its development and safety; and
>
> f) The encouragement and development of Civil Aeronautics.

At the same time, the new act required U.S. carriers to obtain certificates of public convenience and necessity, after notice and public hearing before the Civil Aeronautics Board, in order to engage in commercial air transportation, including that between the United States and a point in another country,[50] and abolished the system of airmail contracts by providing that the Civil Aeronautics Board was to award the right to carry mail by aircraft and to establish the rates therefor.[51] The implication of all this was that there would be competing American airlines on the international routes serving the United States.

Meanwhile, beginning in 1937, American Export Airlines, a subsidiary of American Export Lines, the steamship company, had already begun efforts to start a transatlantic airline service.[52] In 1938, after the passage of the Civil Aeronautics Act, Pan American made an agreement with American Export to divide up the European territory. This agreement required approval of the Civil Aeronautics Board under Section 412 of the Civil Aeronautics Act, and the Board disapproved it as being against the public interest.[53] American Export continued its efforts to obtain a permit to serve points in Europe and also tried to compete with Pan American in Latin America by purchasing an interest in TACA airways, a Honduran carrier. Pan American managed to stave off the latter threat by persuading the Civil Aeronautics Board to disapprove the purchase of TACA on the ground that it had not been shown that control of an air carrier by a shipping company would be in the public interest.[54]

Nevertheless, throughout this period, American Export Lines enjoyed considerable support in the executive branch of the United States government, and on July 12, 1940, it was awarded by the Civil Aeronautics Board a certificate of convenience and necessity authorizing it to compete with Pan American between the United States and Lisbon.[55] This certification included the authority to carry airmail at rates which included subsidy. Pan American failed to block this decision in the Civil Aeronautics Board, and it also failed to upset it upon review in the United States Court of Appeals.[56] In the end, however, Pan American won the battle by persuading the Congress not to appropriate funds to pay American Export Airlines for the carriage of airmail, which deprived it of subsidy, and removed the financial incentive for operating the service.

Although Pan American was successful in persuading the Congress to block American Export Airlines from competing with it on the transatlantic route, this was not really a victory for the principle of having a single U.S. airline to perform international service. The discussion was more pragmatic in nature and the decision related more to the particular case than to the principle involved.[57] This episode undoubtedly generated considerable hostility toward Pan American in the executive branch, which viewed it as a defeat on its own territory by a representative of big business.[58]

Developing support for the idea of competition among U.S. international airlines is further evidenced by the text of a January 23, 1939, letter from R. Walton Moore, counselor of the Department of State, to W.H. Coverdale, president of American Export Lines, to this effect:

> It has been decided after consultations between this Department and members of the Civil Aeronautics Authority [later Board] that the question of obtaining transatlantic operating rights for American Air Transport Companies should be a matter of negotiations between the government of the United States and the foreign Government concerned.[59]

Hitherto, Pan American had been negotiating its own permits, with the assistance of the Department of State. With the institutionalization of the idea of competition, the United States government perceived that in order to avoid confusion with foreign governments the negotiations must be under the government's control.[60]

Despite the indications that the United States policy favored the idea of having more than one U.S. carrier on the transatlantic routes in the immediate prewar period, it is a fact that up to the entry of the United States in World War II, in December of 1941, Pan American (along with Panagra) was the only U.S. airline providing international commercial service of any sort other than that on the transborder routes between the United States and Canada. Pan American's predominance was due in very large measure to the efforts of Juan Trippe and the team he had put together at Pan American. Where he could not persuade the United States government to withhold operating rights for international service from competitive companies as a matter of policy, he overcame his competitors through economic power and political adroitness. During the pre–World War II period, the only inference one could reasonably draw from the facts is that it was the United States policy to have a single U.S. airline for international commercial air service, to support that airline through subsidy, and to deal with the route ambitions of other countries in such a way as to advance the fortunes of the U.S. airline. Such a policy is consistent with the policy being applied at the same time by the European countries. The United States government was not, however, fully consistent in enunciating that policy in its public statements.

By Executive Order No. 8974, of December 13, 1941, only one week after American entry into World War II, the Secretary of War was "Authorized and directed to take possession and assume control of any civil aviation system or systems, or any part thereof, to the extent necessary for the successful prosecution of the war."[61] Under this order the operations of United States airlines in the Atlantic and Pacific were fully militarized,[62] and in Latin America, the airlines were also at the full disposition of the government, although they were not directly under military control.

What took place in Latin America illustrates one of the most political aspects of the airline industry. In the South American area, German and Italian companies had expanded their own services and taken over local South American airlines to a point where they were regarded as a threat by the United States government. The reasons for the American concern were that (1) the airlines could be and apparently were being used for espionage, (2) they could be used to support commando-type invasions, (3) they were being used to spread propaganda against the United States, and (4) they presented a danger to the stability of South American governments because of their ability to give financial support to dissident groups planning coups.

The United States announced a program to eliminate German and Italian influence in South American airlines as early as 1939. The agents for carrying it out were Pan American and Panagra. To finance this program and a program for airport development overseas, the United States established the "American Republics Division" of the Reconstruction Finance Corporation (RFC) in April of 1941. The principle was to eliminate the German and Italian companies without materially reducing service. The two U.S. airlines performed as required and the program was in place by December 1941, when the last German airline, Condor, ceased operations in Brazil, after German and Italian influence had been eliminated in Argentina, Chile, Peru, Bolivia, Ecuador and Colombia.[63]

Despite their political role, the United States airlines in Latin America continued throughout the war to operate essentially as commercial enterprises, subject, however, to a high degree of direction by the United States government.[64]

As part of the war effort the United States domestic airlines operated contract services abroad for the military on a worldwide basis. United Airlines served Australia, Eastern went to Brazil, Northeast Airlines went to Iceland, Northwest Airlines went to Alaska, and American Airlines and TWA served Europe. American Export provided service to the United Kingdom. A total of 21 United States airlines provided some degree of international contract service in addition to Pan American.[65] These were not common carrier operations, however.

The trend exemplified by the passage of the Civil Aeronautics Act, by the granting of certificates for international operations to Europe for American Export Airlines and to Mexico for American Airlines, and by the decision of the Department of State to take over the negotiation of air transport rights in Europe was greatly accelerated after the American entry into the war.

The use of the domestic airlines to provide international service as part of the war effort undoubtedly had an influence in this acceleration. Both the United States government and the domestic airlines themselves had the opportunity to see that at least from an operational point of view, flying international services was not very different from flying domestic services. Since they were operating under contract to the United States government in wartime conditions, those airlines were not exposed to the different political aspects of international operations. In July of 1943, all of the domestic airlines except United signed a declaration on international air policy which they submitted to the Civil Aeronautics Board to supplement their replies to a previous CAB questionnaire. (Pan American was not a participant, since it was not a domestic airline.)

The 1943 declaration advocated free and open competition worldwide, subject to reasonable regulation by the appropriate government agencies; private ownership and management of airlines; fostering and encouraging by the United States government of a sound worldwide air transport system; freedom of transit in peaceful flight worldwide; and acquisition of the civil and commercial outlets required in the public interest. At the same time they advocated competition among American airlines operating abroad, saying

> without question, in air transportation where boundaries become meaningless, there can be no rational basis for permitting air transportation

> within the country to develop and expand on a competitive basis, and that outside the country, left to the withering influence of monopoly.

They also announced their intention of applying to the Civil Aeronautics Board for international routes.[66]

Although United States air transport as an industry has not been conspicuously successful over the years in influencing the course of United States policy, it has from time to time been extremely effective politically when it has been able to express itself in a reasonably unified manner. In the present case, the pressure from these 16 American domestic airlines for a liberal U.S. air transport policy and an end to the "chosen instrument" policy undoubtedly influenced heavily the already existing tendency in this direction within the United States government.

Pan American Airways tried hard to reverse the trend, but it was unable to do so. As early as 1943, Trippe, having seen that the days were drawing to an end when Pan American could hold its place as the single U.S. airline operating abroad, proposed the creation of what he called a "Community Company." This company would have a monopoly on the right to operate United States services abroad. Its initial assets would be those of Pan American, Panagra and American Export Airlines, which would be compensated by being awarded one-quarter of the shares of the new company distributed among them in proportion to the value of their contributions. The remaining ¾ were to be issued in a manner to be determined later to the rest of the United States air transportation industry. He got as far as having the plan embodied in legislation brought before the Senate,[67] but the executive branch was solidly opposed to it and Trippe was unable to convince a majority of the Senate. The bill failed.[68]

There were more than political influences at work, however. Conditions had in fact changed since the early days of American air transport. The size and range of the early aircraft were so limited that there was no way they could provide international service at a profit. The early airlines operating internationally had to provide and install their own ground facilities, which greatly increased their costs. Moreover, the available traffic was scarce. This meant that the airlines must be subsidized if they were to operate. Subsidizing the national airline made sense from a governmental point of view as a means to gain a toehold in an industry that showed promise of tremendous increase quite apart from any geopolitical reasons for fostering international air communications. Moreover, the growth of the air transport industry, including international services, was a necessary condition for the growth of the aircraft manufacturing industry in which the United States was a pioneer. Once the government decided to pay a subsidy, it was natural and reasonable from its point of view to conclude that there was no point in paying a subsidy to more than one airline to perform duplicative service.

By the start of World War II, and increasingly as it drew to a close, it was apparent that a fundamental change was taking place in the conditions in which the air transport industry operated. The available traffic was increasing as people became accustomed to air travel. The wartime air services demonstrated what worldwide routes could do. The size and range of the available aircraft had taken a remarkable leap forward with the introduction of four-engined equipment. The American aircraft manufacturing industry had expanded tremendously to take care of the demand for military aircraft required by the war. Many of these aircraft were adaptable with little change for airline service. The conditions seemed to be right for great expansion, including an end of the need for subsidy. Thus, the underlying economic and psychological conditions were present for a change in United States policy from a predominantly protectionist and "chosen instrument" tendency to a predominantly liberal and expansionist tendency, including the advocacy of at least some competition between United States airlines operating abroad.

It seems likely that these were the real reasons for the policy of the United States prior to World War II and for its abrupt change in direction during the war. Perhaps the prewar policy might have been different without the political skill and adroitness of Juan Trippe, but his skill and adroitness would have achieved nothing if the economic and psychological atmosphere had not been appropriate. Similarly, the agents of the change in United States policy were political events such as the passage of the Civil Aeronautics Act, and the manifesto of the United States domestic airlines, but the underlying reasons for the change, without which it probably could not have taken place, were economic and psychological.

4. THE CHICAGO CONFERENCE

As we have seen, as early as 1943 and increasingly as the end of World War II came in sight, the United States was coming to the position that the "chosen instrument" regime should be terminated and that the international air routes of the world should be thrown open to relatively free competition. This position came to be identified with the slogans "Open Skies" and "Freedom of the Air."[1]

The United States, in a 1948 report to the International Civil Aviation Organization[2] described its attitude in the closing years of the war as follows:

> *Development of Aviation During the War* By the time hostilities ended, a high degree of uniformity had been achieved among the allied military air services with respect to operating practices and the uses of instruments to facilitate navigation and to maintain communications. The preservation and further development of this standardization were of utmost importance, but there was no assurance that it would survive under civil management. Moreover, postwar air commerce on a global scale would require an even more extensive installation of instruments for navigational aid and radio communication, together with civilian staffs trained in their operation.
>
> The great technical progress made in aviation during the war was not, however, accompanied by any progress in solving legal and administrative difficulties which had plagued international operations before the war and threatened to do so again. Since every nation asserts sovereign rights over its air space, no aircraft can be flown across an international boundary without the consent of the country whose territory it enters. Before the war such permission was often difficult and sometimes impossible to obtain, and it was apparent that some method of negotiating and exchanging air transport rights between governments would have to be devised if post war air commerce was to meet the general need. A wholly unworkable situation would arise if each nation were to fix its own rules in total disregard of those in force in neighboring countries and if every airline pilot had to familiarize himself with a different set of rules for each country and change his operating procedure at every frontier.

The United States accordingly sent out an invitation to an international civil aviation conference to be held at Chicago November 1, 1944.[3]

The invitation referred to discussions with "a number of other governments" indicating substantial agreement

> on such topics as the right of transit and non traffic stops, the non-exclusivity of international operating rights, the application of cabotage to air traffic, the control of rates and competitive practices, the gradual curtailment of subsidies, the need for uniform operating and safety standards and the standardization of coordination of air navigation aids and communications facilities on a non-discriminatory basis, and the operation of airports and facilities in certain areas.

The United States said it was calling the conference

> for the purpose of agreeing on an increase in existing services and on the early establishment of international air routes and services for operation in and to areas now freed from danger of military interruptions, such arrangements to continue during a transitional period. The conference might also agree so far as possible upon principles of a permanent international structure for civil aviation and air transport and might set up appropriate interior committees to prepare definite proposals.

The invitation proposed the following specific objectives:

> 1(a) The establishment of provisional world route arrangements by general agreement to be reached at the conference.
> (b) Agreement on landing rights to make such routes possible.
> 2. Establishment of an interim council.
> 3. Agreement on the principles to be followed in setting up a permanent international body.

The invitation went to:

> A) All members of the United Nations
> B) Nations associated with the United Nations in this war (WWII)
> C) The European and Asiatic neutral nations, in view of their close relationship to the expansion of air transport which may be expected along with the liberation of Europe.
> The Danish Minister and Thai Minister in Washington will be invited to attend in their personal capacities.[4]

All of those invited accepted, including the Russians. Nevertheless, for reasons which were never made entirely clear, no Soviet delegates were present in Chicago, and the Soviet Union delayed until 1971 becoming a party to the Chicago Convention.

The Chicago Conference was extremely successful as a forum for agreeing on uniform operating and safety standards and the coordination of air navigation aids and communications facilities. It also succeeded beyond the hopes of the United States in reaching agreement upon a body for administering standards and coordinating facilities. It did not, however, manage to achieve substantial agreement on the commercial aspects of international air transport.

The Chicago Conference ran from November 1 through December 7, 1944. The substantive agreements reached were four: the Convention on International Civil Aviation ("the Chicago Convention"), the International Air Services Transit Agreement, the International Air Transport Agreement, and the Interim Agreement on International Civil Aviation ("the PICAO Agreement").

The "PICAO Agreement," which provided for a provisional council to meet concerning air transport matters until the International Civil Aviation Organization and its council should be established, came into force June 6, 1945, when the required 26 states had accepted it, and the Provisional International Civil Aviation Organization, PICAO, came into being on that date and remained in existence until April 4, 1947, when it was superseded by the International Civil Aviation Organization (ICAO), thirty days after receipt of the 26th ratification of the Chicago Convention which established it.

A great deal of the time spent in negotiating the Chicago Convention was spent in seeking agreement on provisions to govern the exchange of commercial air transport rights among states and the means to regulate the exercise of these rights. The United States urged the greatest possible freedom for commercial airlines of all nations to expand their services in the postwar world.[5]

The primary economic goal of the United States was to obtain approval for provisional routes for immediate operation.[6] The United States participated in the discussion of more elaborate schemes for complete economic regulation of air transport, but it was in the end unwilling to agree to turn over to the proposed International Civil Aviation Organization the economic regulation of air transport and it was primarily on this point that the economic aspect of the conference foundered.[7]

The British, like the United States, had begun to focus on postwar aviation as early as 1943. It was, at least in part, at their request, seconded by the Canadians, that the United States had called the Chicago Conference,[8] although the invitation made it appear that the conference was exclusively a U.S. idea.

It was quite evident even at that stage that the United States would come out of the war with its economy and manufacturing ability intact, whereas the British economy (along with that of the other European belligerents) as well as British manufacturing plants was seriously damaged by the war. In addition, by inter-allied agreement the United States had produced long-haul transport aircraft during the war which would be suitable for commercial use after the war, whereas the British had focused exclusively on fighter aircraft and bombers which had a very limited commercial potential.

Because of their concern with the probable weakness of their own position in competing for postwar traffic, particularly that across the North Atlantic, the British not surprisingly came to Chicago with proposals tending to place limits on the ability of individual airlines to expand and compete. The British position was characterized by the slogan "order in the air."[9] There were three separate proposals brought forward by various members of the British Commonwealth. The United Kingdom itself presented a proposal for the automatic granting of first, second, third and fourth freedom traffic rights, with the fifth freedom to be negotiated between states. The whole scheme was to be administered by an Autonomous International Air Authority which was to fix capacity and be in charge of licensing.[10]

The Canadians put forward a plan rather similar to that of the British, but the Authority was to regulate routes and capacity according to fixed formulas established in the agreement.[11]

Australia and New Zealand submitted a plan for international ownership and operation of all civil air services on trunk routes worldwide.[12]

The Australia-New Zealand proposal was rejected early in the deliberations when Brazil proposed an amendment to it to the effect that ownership of civil aircraft should continue to be by individual states and this motion was carried.[13]

Even the British voted in favor of the Brazilian amendment and against the Australia-New Zealand proposal, and one can guess that the proposal was introduced primarily to make the British and Canadian proposals appear less radical by comparison.[14]

The United States was the main objector to the British and Canadian plans. The ground of the American objection was that it was unreasonable to set up an international authority with such real economic power without having it responsible to any superior political authority. The United States also wished to allow much greater freedom than these plans permitted for commercial airlines to cary third, fourth and fifth freedom traffic around the world. The U.S. emphasis on the need for airlines to carry fifth freedom traffic was in particular a source of disagreement with the countries of the British Commonwealth.[15]

Although the record of the Chicago Conference does not show it, it seems reasonable to suppose that the United States must have had pretty much the same perception as did the British of the probable American advantage in the postwar world, and that this perception influenced the U.S. position in favoring free competition.[16]

When the Conference failed to reach agreement on the commercial aspects of air transport, the matter was referred to the temporary body PICAO for study.[17] The remaining commercial elements on which a measure of agreement could be reached were dealt with in various ways.

The "right of non-scheduled flight" was dealt with in Article 5 of the convention. The language of the convention makes it appear that commercial non-scheduled flights are granted a measure of freedom of operation, but by official interpretation of the ICAO Council and of the ICAO Air Transport Committee the "right to impose regulations, conditions or limitations" as provided in Article 5 included the right to require prior permission. The reason for the granting of such freedom and its subsequent withdrawal was very probably that when the Chicago Convention was drafted, there had been very few charter or non-scheduled operations and in the prewar period they did not constitute a threat to scheduled operations. In the postwar period, there were many such operations and they competed directly with scheduled operations, so the reason for considering them a negligible item that did not require regulation was no longer present.[18]

With respect to scheduled services, Article 6 of the Convention provides as follows:

> No scheduled international air service may be operated over or into the territory of a contracting state, except with the special permission or other authorization of that state, and in accordance with the terms of such permission or authorization.

This merely reflected existing law and practice,[19] and was the result of the failure to agree on a multilateral agreement to govern the exchange of traffic rights.

With respect to cabotage, the Convention provides in Article 7

> Each contracting state shall have the right to refuse permission to the aircraft of other contracting states to take on in its territory passengers, mail and cargo carried for remuneration or hire and destined for another point within its territory. Each contracting state undertakes not to enter into any arrangements which specifically grant any such privilege on an exclusive basis to any other State or an airline of any other State, and not to obtain any such exclusive privilege from any other State.

The second sentence of the quoted article is on its face somewhat obscure. Bin Cheng[20] says, "The net result is that States remain free to do what they like as long as they do not claim specifically that the privilege they are granting is exclusive." It seems likely, however, that the intention of the language was to address a practice described by the American representative in Chicago, Adolph A. Berle as follows:

> Clearly the right of reserved cabotage can be exercised by one country only; for if a number of countries were to pool their cabotage between each other, the result would be merely to exclude nations not parties to the pool; and it is the firm conviction of this government that discriminatory or exclusive agreements are raw material for future conflict.[21]

Such a proposal is by no means a dead issue in the modern world.[22]

In addition, the parties at Chicago proposed for signature the International Air Services Transit Agreement (the "Two Freedoms Agreement"), by means of which the parties grant one another the rights of transit and non-traffic stop. This agreement has enjoyed broad acceptance and has been of great benefit to the operation of international air services.

Also proposed was the International Air Transport Agreement granting first, second, third, fourth and fifth freedom traffic rights among its signatories (the "Five Freedoms Agreement"). This agreement had only 17 original signatories, most of which failed to ratify it. Because of the small number of parties, the United States denounced this agreement on July 25, 1946,[23] and the agreement now has very few adherents and it has little practical significance,[24] except as the source of the "Five Freedoms of the Air."

In addition, the parties at Chicago agreed to a Standard Form of Agreement for Provisional Air Routes.[25] This was agreed as a "recommendation," and provides the underlying structure for most bilateral air transport agreements in use today.

The purpose in making the International Air Transport Agreement and the International Air Service Transit Agreement separate agreements from the Chicago Convention itself, and in making the Standard Form of Agreement a recommended practice was to avoid numerous exceptions and reservations to the Chicago Convention, since there was not unanimous agreement on them.[26]

Because of their relevance to the discussions between the United States and the United Kingdom that led to the Bermuda 1 Agreement, it is useful to review in some detail the statements of chief U.S. representative Berle and Lord Swinton, the chief U.K. representative at Chicago. In his opening remarks[27] Berle said it is the United States position that each nation has sovereignty over the air space above its territory. He said that governments should agree to encourage air transport: "Nations have a natural right to communicate and trade with one another in times of peace; and friendly nations do not have a right to burden or prevent this intercourse by discriminatory measures." He said the United States believes that States should agree on a free exchange of air routes and that routes should be based primarily on the need of each country to maintain its own communications, observing

> in this respect the air routes of the world are far more like railroad lines than like free shipping; and indeed the right of air intercourse is primarily a right to connect the country in which the line starts with other countries from which, to which, or through which there flows a normal stream of traffic to and from the country which established the line... [and further that] In air commerce there appears at present to be little place for the tramp trade. ... The business we have in hand at present is the business of establishing

> the means by which communications can be established between each country and another, by reasonably direct economic routes with reasonably convenient landing points connecting the chief basins of traffic.

Berle said that the United States favored an international authority to cover the technical aspects of international aviation as was the case with CINA under the Paris Convention of 1919, but that it opposed giving that body power over economic and commercial aspects. He also said the United States opposes subsidies for international air services and would become a party to an agreement for minimum fares to prevent the use of the subsidy as a competitive device.

Lord Swinton in reply gave the United Kingdom position.[28] He said, "Every nation which aspires to be in the air will wish to have, and indeed will insist on it, in addition to its own internal traffic, a fair share of its external traffic as well," pointing out that before the war the United States and United Kingdom had agreed to run their transatlantic services on a fifty-fifty basis. Lord Swinton said that the number of services should be fixed in relation to the amount of the traffic offering in a "broad equilibrium." He said that each country's share in the services to be operated should be distributed in proportion to the traffic embarked in their respective countries. He also said that minimum rates should be settled in relation to standards of speed and accommodation.

With respect to capacity, the British offered in their Document 429[29] a synthesis of their own views and modifications acceptable to them of the views of the Canadians and the United States which foreshadow the formulas later agreed to by the British and the United States at Bermuda.

In view of the fact that the United States and the British managed to reconcile their views at Bermuda, it may seem remarkable that they were unable to reach an accommodation at Chicago. In a 1947 article, Peter Masefield, later eminent in British civil aviation, attributed the failure to reach a compromise to the personalities of Adolph Berle and Lord Swinton.[30] It is also worth noting that the compromise reached at Bermuda was workable on a bilateral basis, but it might not have served for a multilateral agreement which was under discussion at Chicago. It also seems likely that the passage of time made it easier to reach a compromise at Bermuda in 1946 than it was in Chicago in 1944, when the arguments were new and passions were fresh.

Bin Cheng cites an article by Sir George Cribbett[32] which attributes the impossibility of reconciling the British and American views to the differences in the background of experience that each brought to the negotiations. The United States was optimistic and favored expansion because it was conditioned by the ebullient domestic market for air transport and by the market in Latin America where the services of U.S. airlines had been welcomed by the local governments. The British were pessimistic and favored regulation and control because they were conditioned by the experience in prewar Europe where competition was chaotic.

Although at the time, there was a feeling that the Chicago Conference had "failed" because no agreement had been reached on a multilateral exchange of traffic rights,[33] the results have stood the test of time and the International Civil Aviation Organization has served admirably to administer worldwide technical and administrative standards. It has stayed out of the economic field because a majority of the more influential members of the organization have wanted it to do so, although there are at present signs that it may in future play a larger role in economic regulation.

5. THE BERMUDA AGREEMENT AND POSTWAR AMERICAN COMMERCIAL AIR POLICY

When the Chicago Convention was presented to the United States Senate for its "advice and consent" to its terms, the Senate requested that the Attorney General prepare a report concerning air transport policy. This report was addressed to the Senate and the House of Representatives and was dated February 28, 1945.[1] The report is interesting because it describes the policy that the United States took with it to the negotiations with the British at Bermuda. Moreover, with the modifications introduced by the Bermuda Agreement, the policy described in the report is in general the policy followed by the United States government during the next thirty years or more.

In broad terms the report recommends that the government set the nation's international air transport policy and that it be liberal; that the government conduct air transport negotiations; that in the agreements reached through such negotiations, bona fide national ownership should be required for the airlines sponsored by each government; that stability of operating rights should be promoted, blocs to discriminate against competitive airlines should be discouraged, and no limitations should be imposed upon capacity, aircraft types or pricing; technical standards should be observed, and each country should enforce its own immigration and customs laws, and otherwise the details of operation should be left to the regulatory authorities of each country.

The study goes on to say that the national policy should encourage the development and adoption of the newest types of equipment and the best operating procedures, provide incentives for efficient operation, reduction in costs and rates and for healthy financial conditions in the industry. The policy should also ensure "that United States airlines will carry a volume of world traffic commensurate with the importance of the United States as a market for air-transport services." Private operation of airlines should be encouraged. The United States should cooperate with other nations in developing airports and airways, which should be available generally without discrimination. The United States should seek an international agreement limiting airline subsidies and ensuring that the practice does not inhibit competition. The "chosen instrument" should be rejected, but unrestricted competition is not called for. Surface transportation companies should not own or control international air lines. The United States should promote the formation of an international civil aviation organization for aeronautical studies and for the resolution of common problems.

With few, but significant, exceptions the foregoing can stand as a broad description of the policy that can be inferred from the actions of the United States in this field and can be seen reflected in specific policy statements from the close of World War II, until the United States took a radical turn in the late 1970s toward "deregulation" and "freedom of the skies" in the international area.

The most important departures from the 1945 statement are, first, that the United States, under the Bermuda Capacity Clauses, accepted a form of limitation on airline capacity and, through its acceptance of IATA, agreed in the Bermuda Agreement to a form of limitation to be imposed on the prices charged by its airlines and, second, that the United States never achieved an international agreement concerning the payment of airline subsidies. It is worth noting, however, that although the United States agreed to the Bermuda Capacity Clauses and the IATA system of pricing control, there was throughout the postwar period a powerful bias against IATA and against capacity control within the U.S. government, which finally came fully to the surface in "deregulation." Moreover the capacity provisions of the Bermuda-type agreements to which it is a party have never been administered by the United States in such a way as to be seriously restrictive of the capacity offered by either foreign or American carriers. Where restrictions have been imposed, they have generally been in retaliation for unilateral action by a foreign party. The subsidy matter appears to have been a dead issue from the start.

The United States indicated its acceptance of the Interim ("PICAO") Agreement February 8, 1945, and deposited its ratification of the Chicago Convention on August 9, 1946.

In the meantime international civil aviation services were being reestablished around the world. The transatlantic services between the United States and the United Kingdom occupied stage center in this process, and there continued to be a large difference of opinion between American aviation authorities and the British, not only with respect to how international airlines should be regulated, but more immediately important, with respect to what specific American airlines should be allowed to do.

The *Aviation Daily* for November 27, 1945,[2] reported that the British were promoting a capacity theory which the United States was unwilling to consider.[3] The *Daily* reported "unless some agreement is reached, the chances are that some U.S. services may be cut back by the British."

The article reported that two United States airlines were then flying to the United Kingdom, Pan American Airways with two weekly round trips and American Overseas Airways with five. British Overseas Airways had two weekly transatlantic round trips to the United States.

The PAA and BOAC flights were authorized pursuant to a 1935 agreement between the United States and the United Kingdom.[4]

On November 23, 1945, Pan American had announced that it proposed to increase its services to five times weekly and had inaugurated a one-way fare of $275, New York–London. This fare was less than half of the fare of $572 hitherto charged by Pan American on that sector.

The British objected to this fare and the December 11 edition of the *Aviation Daily,*[5] under the headline "PAA Fare Tactics May Torpedo International Cooperation," reported that Pan American had been required by the British to raise its fare from $275 to $375. It also reported that the British had announced that they were willing to give up their insistance upon capacity controls in favor of rate controls.[6] In fact, PAA did raise the fare to $375.

Against the background of this controversy concerning particular services as well as against the background of the more theoretical discussions of the Chicago Conference, delegations representing the United Kingdom and the United States met in Bermuda from January 15 to February 11, 1946, to attempt to resolve their differences and to reach an agreement that would at least provide a temporary frame of reference for the operation of services between the two nations by their respective airlines.

Both countries brought to Bermuda the attitudes and opinions they had expressed at Chicago,[7] although as it appears in the news item referred to above the British had softened somewhat in their insistence upon capacity controls and were now in favor of rate controls.

Out of their deliberations, the parties produced the bilateral air transport agreement usually referred to as the "Bermuda Agreement"[8] or as the "Bermuda 1 Agreement" since July 1977 when the Bermuda 2 Agreement was signed.[9]

The American and British delegations at Bermuda agreed that they would use the Bermuda Agreement as a basis for future air transport agreements with other countries;[10] the United States signed some 54 such agreements.[11] Although the United Kingdom also based its later agreements on the Bermuda Agreement, the British were less consistent in this regard than the Americans. For example, shortly after signing the Bermuda Agreement, the British signed an agreement providing for predetermination of capacity and airline pooling with France.[12]

In June of 1946, the First Interim Assembly of PICAO was held. At that meeting a further, unsuccessful effort was made at reaching a multilateral air transport agreement.[13]

At the first session of the ICAO Assembly in May 1947, further unsuccessful efforts were made to achieve a multilateral agreement, and the matter was referred to a commission open to all member states, which was to meet in Rio de Janeiro no later than October 1947.[14]

The special commission actually met in Geneva in November of that year.[15] By this time the British and the United States were finally committed to the Bermuda system. They attempted to redraft the Bermuda language for multilateral use, but because of the peculiar nature of the Bermuda Agreement, this attempt failed.[16] In the end the entire effort to reach a multilateral agreement collapsed at Geneva, and there has never been a convincing attempt at achieving a multilateral air transport agreement since that time.

Thus, with the demise of the possibility of a multilateral agreement, the United States was left with the Bermuda Agreement as the central pillar of its policy with respect to air transport agreements.

Although the Bermuda 1 Agreement has now been superseded by the Bermuda 2 Agreement between the United Kingdom and the United States, and although the solutions it offers to the problems of rate and capacity competition among international airlines are now discredited in official United States doctrine, this agreement is well worth examining in detail, because it is essential to understanding the history of American air transportation policy from 1946 to the present day.

The agreement consists of a Final Act, with nine numbered paragraphs, an Appendix I, which is an Agreement with fourteen articles and an Annex with five sections, together with four exchanges of side notes related to route adjustments.

The "Agreement" contains the capacity provisions which are its most notable feature. The "Appendix I" follows generally the format of the Standard Form of Agreement for Provisional Air Routes, which was recommended in the Final Act of the Chicago Convention[17] and the Annex covers rates, routes and "change of gauge."[18] The side agreements are confined to matters of route description.

The usual description of the compromise reached at Bermuda between the United States and the United Kingdom is that the British gave up their insistence on strict *a priori* control of capacity in exchange for United States agreement to accept the control of rates through the medium of the International Air Transport Association ("IATA") and to accept a degree of *ex post facto* control of capacity.[19] This description appears accurate.

The Bermuda Agreement is an ingenious and pragmatic arrangement. The general idea is that the airlines are to set their own rates either unilaterally or by agreement in IATA subject to governmental approval, and to fix their own capacity unilaterally, subject to *ex post facto* review by the two governments on the basis of actual experience, and with reference to the general principles stated in the agreement, if one of the governments concerned has a problem with the capacity offered.

Since the discussion of the Bermuda capacity provisions necessarily requires close scrutiny of the text, the Final Act of the Agreement is reprinted in full in Appendix A hereto.

The Final Act in paragraphs 1 through 7 established the general principles that are to govern the provision of service pursuant to the agreement and in paragraph 9 it established how these principles are to be administered.

A reference to paragraphs 1 through 7 will show that the "principles" are in a sense contradictory.

Paragraph 1 favors expansion in talking about fostering the widest possible distribution of the benefits of air travel at cheap rates and stimulating international air travel.

Paragraph 2 in its reference to the preamble to the Chicago Convention looks to both expansion and regulation, since the preamble points out that the development of aviation can help friendship and understanding among nations yet its abuse can become a threat to general security and stresses the need for cooperation "in order that international civil aviation may be developed in a safe and orderly manner and that international air transport services may be established on the basis of equality of opportunity and operated soundly and economically."

Paragraphs 3 through 6 refer specifically to capacity and contain what is often referred to as the "Bermuda Capacity Principles."

Paragraph 3 can be invoked to justify a complaint that a given capacity is excessive, or it can be invoked to rebut such a complaint since there is room for argument about how close the "close relationship" to the "requirements of the public for such transport" must be, as well as about just what those requirements are.

Paragraph 4 allows either party to complain that its airline has been denied a "fair and equal opportunity" if it is dissatisfied with the results achieved by the airline. The other party can generally argue that the airline has been given a fair and equal opportunity, but has failed to take advantage of it.

Paragraph 5 leaves open for argument the degree to which air carriers are required to take into account one another's interests and how much effect is required before an air carrier has affected "unduly" the services of the opposite party's air carrier.

Paragraph 6, in its first sentence, requires that the services offered "shall retain as their primary objective" the provision of capacity for the carriage of third and fourth freedom traffic. ("Capacity adequate to the traffic demands between the country of which such air carrier is a national and the ultimate destination of the traffic.") It is worth noting that this refers to all third and fourth freedom traffic carried on the service, and not just the traffic between the two countries party to the agreement. The second sentence does not say explicitly that the carriage of fifth freedom traffic ("Traffic destined for and coming from third countries") shall be subordinate to the carriage of third and fourth freedom traffic, yet there is an implication to that effect in the previous requirement that the primary objective of the services shall be the carriage of third and fourth freedom traffic.

Nevertheless, the three "general principles" to which it is agreed that capacity should be related leave room for defending the practices of a carrier accused of carrying too much fifth freedom traffic, or of offering too much capacity for the carriage of such traffic. The first of these "principles" is similar to the requirement of the first sentence of Paragraph 6 in emphasizing the carriage of third and fourth freedom traffic. The second and third "principles," however, can be invoked to justify the carriage of fifth freedom traffic (or the offering of capacity for the carriage of fifth freedom traffic, which would appear excessive if the criterion were solely the capacity required for the carriage of third and fourth freedom traffic).

The second principle, which refers to 'the requirements of through airline operations," takes account of the fact that on a long multi-stop route, there is likely to be a great deal more third and fourth freedom traffic on the legs near the home country than there is on sectors near the outer extreme of the route. Thus the "requirements of through airline operation" refer to the need to use a single aircraft to serve the entire length of the route with the attendant likelihood that at the outward end of the route there will be an increased number of empty seats vacated or not yet filled by third and fourth freedom passengers travelling to and from intermediate points which must be filled by fifth freedom passengers.

The third "principle," that capacity should be related to the traffic requirements of the area through which the airline passes after taking account of local and regional services, allows the justification of otherwise excessive capacity on the basis that it is needed by the countries served. This argument can be rebutted by a showing that such traffic can be adequately served by local and regional services, or even that the local and regional services are prejudiced by the local seats offered by the through service. It should also be noted that this paragraph says that the parties agree that capacity should be "related" to the three elements mentioned, but it does not make precise how it should be related. This lack of precision and the inclusion of conflicting elements provide the framework within which the parties are expected to negotiate a mutually acceptable solution to capacity problems as they arise. Obviously, the actual negotiation takes into account the entire relationship between the parties, and is not necessarily confined to the elements mentioned in the capacity provisions of the agreement.

Paragraph 7 is a temporary provision to make allowances for the disruptions of World War II, and is of no current importance.

Paragraph 8 is also intended to cover a special situation arising out of the use after World War II of airfields constructed by the United States.

Paragraph 9, calling for "regular and frequent consultations" between the aeronautical authorities of the two countries, is the crux of the Bermuda Agreement. Although it is not stated explicitly, the idea is that the airlines of the two parties are free to establish their own capacity without *a priori* interference by the other government. If one party feels it is being prejudiced by the airlines of the other party, it is to call for consultation, and the two parties are then to negotiate a solution to the problem in the light of the "principles" enunciated in paragraphs 1 through 6. This consultation procedure is in effect the only method for reaching a final determination of problems arising under the agreement. Article 9 of the Annex to the Agreement contains a provision for an advisory opinion by the Council of the Provisional International Civil Aviation Organization, or its successor (i.e., ICAO). The ICAO Council, however, has been reluctant to take on judicial functions and less than helpful when it has done so.[20] No such advisory opinion was requested under the Bermuda Agreement.

The so-called "principles" of Paragraph 6 are in fact a list of competing considerations that are to be taken into account in negotiations intended to reach a mutually acceptable solution to capacity problems. The element of negotiation is essential to make the agreement work; the "principles" cannot be applied objectively as mathematical formulas.[21] For that reason, the Bermuda capacity provisions are simply not amenable to arbitration, or outside "advisory opinions," and in the forty years of effectiveness of the Bermuda Agreement, the United States never attempted to arbitrate a dispute under the capacity provisions of that agreement or under the similar provisions of the 54 United States agreements modelled on it. So far as I am aware neither the British nor any one else has ever attempted to arbitrate a dispute under a Bermuda-type capacity clause.

Barry Diamond, in an interesting review of the Bermuda Agreement,[22] makes the point that in modern law, certain treaty and municipal contract relationships are not meant to be subject to interpretation by third parties. He observes that such agreements, of which he says the capacity system of the Bermuda Agreement is one, are not mean to be subject to outside interpretation and are entered into without the hope or expectation of obtaining external enforcement of the agreement in the event of a breach by one of the contracting parties. Nevertheless, he says these agreements are still agreements between the parties, having as much validity as the parties wish to accord them. Diamond goes on to say that such treaties "differ from the traditional concept of a contract in that they can neither be enforced nor definitely interpreted because they are basically non-binding. What is left is self-interpretation of the treaty by the parties themselves."[23]

Although there is no doubt that the United States and the United Kingdom interpreted the Bermuda Agreement as providing for *a posteriori* capacity controls, which were to be negotiated between the parties in the light of the "principles stated in paragraphs 1 through 6 of the agreement," a number of varying opinions have been voiced through the years as to the meaning and effect of the Bermuda-type capacity provisions. For example, in Peru, under an agreement with Bermuda-type capacity provisions,[24] it has been contended by the Peruvians that the true meaning of the agreement is that it gives either party the right to restrict the capacity of the other's airlines *a priori,* with the other party's only recourse being to request consultation and to attempt to justify a lifting of the restrictions in the light of the stated principles.[25]

The French director general of aviation, Claude Abraham, speaking in 1976 at a meeting of the Institute of Air and Space Law,[26] criticizes the Bermuda-type agreement for not being sufficiently specific and for having conflicting provisions. He says the Bermuda discussions take place in a fog. He criticizes the concept of a "fair and equal opportunity" as being of no value when one party is weak and the other party is strong, claiming it is like sharing a bed with an elephant. He says the necessary goal is a rough equality of results, rather than an equality of opportunity. In a private conversation in his office, Abraham explained to the writer that the French authorities pursue the goal of achieving rough parity of results with all of their partners in air transport agreements, whether or not such parity is provided for in the agreements themselves. The implication was that where the French see or anticipate an inequality of results between American and French airlines, they will find an excuse to redress it.

In Japan, the United States has had a bilateral air transport agreement with Bermuda-type capacity provisions since 1952.[27] The Japanese have, however, rigorously controlled the capacity offered by United States airlines on an *a priori* basis throughout most of this period. At the other end of the scale, the Dutch have argued that the Bermuda-type capacity clauses in the U.S.-Netherlands agreement[28] enabled them to offer more capacity than the United States considered justified. The Scandinavians and the Belgians have taken similar positions.

In a number of other cases, exemplified by India, the United States has negotiated side agreements modifying the Bermuda capacity clauses to permit a degree of *a priori* capacity regulation. The Indian agreement is published,[29] but most of these side agreements are unpublished. The Indian arrangement provides that the United States will give India 90 days' notice of proposed capacity increases. If the Indians should seek governmental consultation on the proposed capacity increase, they would request it within 30 days of the notice, with consultations to start 30 days thereafter. If after consultation the Indians should continue to object to the proposed increase, they could prevent it from becoming effective. It was agreed further that if an increase in capacity should be made on the basis of American traffic estimates, it would be withdrawn if the estimates should not be fulfilled within a reasonable time.[30]

Similar arrangements with other countries are generally drafted on a reciprocal basis, although it is understood that the United States has had no interest in invoking such a provision. They vary in the degree to which they allow an objecting government to prevent a proposed increase from becoming effective, and in the details of the consultation and discussion required before action may be taken. These side agreements are few in number in relation to the total number of bilateral air transport agreements to which the United States is a party. They are often referred to as "screening agreements" in reference to the process of reviewing proposed capacity increases before they become effective.[31]

In addition, the United States has entered a number of side agreements to Bermuda-type bilateral agreements where the number of frequencies which may be operated by the airlines of each party is specified. Published agreements of this type have been made with Ecuador[32] and Peru.[33] A similar agreement was also negotiated with Argentina as a last resort when it proved impossible for the United States to reach agreement with the Argentinians on the terms of a bilateral air transport agreement.[34] Certain agreements with Communist countries also fix the airline capacity as part of the agreement, notably those with China[35] and the Soviet Union.[36]

Agreements for allowing a specified level of capacity have not been regarded with favor by the United States government, and were entered in every case to get over a specific problem, where the alternatives to reaching agreement on the level of service were to allow the other party to regulate the capacity of American airlines unilaterally, or to refrain from serving the particular country entirely, which in many cases, has been considered politically undesirable.[37]

In a number of instances, particularly in Latin America, the United States has been able to persuade its partners in Bermuda-type bilateral air transport agreements to sign supplementary agreements explicitly stating that they will refrain from *a priori* capacity regulation. Such an arrangement with Colombia was published in a Department of State press release.[38] Other similar agreements are with Peru,[39] Panama,[40] and Paraguay,[41] as well as with Chile.[42] Although these agreements are all perfectly clear, they have not been uniformly effective. For example, the Peruvians simply refused to recognize the existence of their agreement, even though it was part of the quid pro quo by means of which they acquired a route, and the Peruvians have imposed unilateral capacity restrictions on American airlines.

The United States managed to stay very close to the basic terms of the Bermuda provisions for traffic regulation in its agreements with most nations. The agreements with Egypt,[43] Iran,[44], Syria,[45] and Thailand[46] omit two or more of the elements of the Bermuda formula but retain the essential elements that capacity is to be related primarily to traffic to and from the home country and the provisions governing the right to carry fifth freedom traffic.

The agreements with Japan[47] and Pakistan[48] have a variation in the fifth freedom provisions, which provides[49] that capacity should be related:

> (a) to traffic requirements between the country of which the airline is a national and the countries of ultimate destinations of that traffic....

The Bermuda version of the same clause reads:

> (a) to traffic requirements between the country of origin and the countries of destination....

The difference is real, since the Japanese version does not allow the justification of capacity on the basis of fifth freedom traffic requirements, while the Bermuda language does allow such justification.

In summary, the Bermuda capacity clauses are unenforceable by any outside agency. The only judicial remedy available is an advisory opinion (or in some cases arbitration) and experience shows that no party to this type of agreement has ever been willing to trust the interpretation and application of these provisions to the judgment of a third party. This is logical because the essence of the agreement is that parties themselves are to negotiate a solution in the light of the agreed principles. Moreover, there is little agreement on the precise meaning of the "principles" themselves. They are deliberately intended as guidelines for negotiating, rather than as mathematical solutions to problems. Under these "principles" each capacity discussion is a separate negotiation, and the result of each need not be prejudiced by previous negotiations.

The "principles" do, however tend to favor the party to the negotiation that seeks liberal treatment, rather than the party that seeks to impose restrictions. In a world where there is little agreement on the degree to which competition between commercial airlines should be subject to governmental restrictions, this is no bad deal for a nation which favors liberal treatment as does the United States. This is especially so in the case of the United States because usually it is able to exert heavy negotiating leverage if it chooses to do so. The United States enjoys this leverage within the aviation field by virtue of its great traffic-generating potential, both as a source of traffic and as a destination for business and pleasure traffic. Outside the aviation field, the size and commercial vitality of the United States usually ensure that the United States has considerable external bargaining power to bring to bear in the aviation field if it cares to use it.

On balance, it can be said that the Bermuda capacity provisions were advantageous to the United States and to world aviation in general during the period of their ascendancy.

Appendix I to the Final Act contains the gist of the "Standard Form of Agreement for Provisional Air Routes" agreed as a recommended practice at the Chicago Conference.[50]

Article 1, in combination with sections III and IV of the Annex, constitutes the grant of routes by one party to the other.

Article 3 covers airport and user fees, customs duties on fuel, lubricating oil and spare parts introduced into the territory of one party by or for the use of the other and fuel, lubricating oils, spare parts and aircraft parts retained on board. With respect to airport and user fees the airlines are to receive national treatment; with respect to the other items the airlines are to receive national and most favored nation treatment. This language has been modified considerably over the years by the United States in its standard form of agreement for use in other bilateral agreements, but it has never been possible to develop a truly comprehensive form of agreement.

The problem is that there are so many ways to impose excessive charges on foreign airlines that it is difficult to stay ahead of them in bilateral agreements. Moreover, there are powerful incentives to impose excessive charges. In the first place, the cost of constructing and operating a modern airport is so high and the benefits are so widely dispersed that it is unreasonable to attempt to recover the entire cost from the airlines, although governments often attempt to do just that. In the second place, there is a temptation to use these fees as a method of discouraging capacity increases by foreign airlines, while providing disguised relief from the fees for the national airline. Moreover, where the national airline is government-owned, excessive fees for using a government owned and operated airport are not a real burden to it, since the transaction is in reality no more than transferring the money from one government pocket to the other, whereas the burden to a foreign airline is real.

Article 4, covering certificates of air worthiness, certificates of competency and licenses, provides for mutual recognition by each party of such certificates and licenses issued by the other, except those issued by a foreign state to its own nationals (i.e., to the nationals of the state refusing to recognize the credentials).[51]

Article 5, relating to the application of national laws to the entry of aircraft, passengers, crew and cargo, is consistent with the notions of sovereignty of most governments and has produced no controversy over the years. It continues unmodified in the Bermuda 2 Agreement, and in the current United States standard form of agreement.

Article 6 provides that if a party is not satisfied that ownership and control of a foreign airline are in nationals of the party designating it, or if a designated airline fails to comply with the laws referred to in Article 5 or "otherwise to fulfill the conditions under which the rights are granted," the granting party may withhold or revoke the exercise of the rights under the agreement. This article has not been a source of conflict between the United States and the United Kingdom, although the subject has come up from time to time in reported CAB cases with respect to the airlines of other nations.[52]

Similar provisions in other agreements and questions of ownership and control of airlines between the United States and other countries with which it does not have bilateral agreements have, however, been the subject of numerous hotly contested cases before the Civil Aeronautics Board and of a large number of intergovernmental consultations. The concept that airlines must be owned by nationals of the country that designates them is interesting. It is nearly universal in the air transport industry, but in the shipping industry "flags of convenience" are a perfectly normal device. Perhaps the root of the distinction can be traced in part to the early concern about aircraft as military instruments and in part to the concept that aircraft routes are granted by one government to another government, so that it is reasonable to expect the rights to be exercised by the nationals of that government, whereas under the concept of "freedom of the seas" the rights are not usually exchanged bilaterally, so there is less concern with the national identity of the vessel exercising the rights.

Article 7, requiring registration of the agreement with PICAO (now ICAO), has become standard in air transport agreements.

Article 8, calling for consultations between the aeronautical authorities of the parties to consider proposals to modify the agreement or its annexes, is consistent with the basic concept of the Bermuda Agreement. The idea of flexibility and freedom to amend the agreement seems to have been very much in the minds of the parties when they drafted the Bermuda Agreement, since the same idea is reiterated in the first sentence of Article 13. This freedom to amend is consistent with the provisions of Article 9 of the Final Act, which encourages "regular and frequent consultation" between the respective aeronautical authorities.

It is interesting, however, that despite numerous consultations, and a variety of route changes, the parties never agreed to changes in the capacity provisions, the rate provisions nor in any of the other provisions of the Bermuda Agreement which establish the terms under which the parties agree to regulate their airlines operating between the two countries, until 1977 when they agreed to a complete revision of the agreement for application on the North Atlantic. It appears likely that the reason for this is that both parties recognized that the fundamental part of the Bermuda Agreement was a verbal formula that could be agreed to by two parties that did not agree in principle, so that any attempt at clarification to satisfy one party would only result in the dissatisfaction of the other party.[53]

Article 9 provides for submitting disputes to the Interim Council of the Provisional International Civil Aviation Organization (now ICAO) for an advisory report. The United States and the British never submitted a dispute under the Bermuda Agreement to this or any other form of arbitration. Bin Cheng[54] points out that there is some doubt whether the ICAO would agree to accept jurisdiction conferred on it by bilateral agreements and whether it is in any case qualified to resolve disputes under international agreements.

Article 10 provides that existing operating rights shall remain in effect according to their terms. From the point of view of American and British airlines already resuming operations between the two countries after the war, it was extremely important that existing operating rights remain in effect. With the maturing of the world air route system and of the governmental machinery regulating it, the importance of this clause is greatly decreased and it is not reflected in the Bermuda 2 Agreement, nor in other modern United States bilateral air transport agreements.

Article 11, a provision that this agreement shall be amended to conform to a general multilateral air convention if one enters into force in relation to both parties, is a way of rendering lip service to the idea of a multilateral agreement, which was moribund at the time the Bermuda Agreement was signed, and dead after the Geneva Conference in 1947.

Article 12: The defintions contained in this article are now obsolete and have been amended and added to in the Bermuda 2 Agreement. The definitions of this article have never been considered controversial, however.

Article 13, which provides for consultation if one party wishes to amend the agreement, and also establishes twelve-months' notice for the termination of the agreement, is of a piece with the general scheme underlying the whole Bermuda Agreement. The parties agreed in Paragraph 9 of the Final Act to consult regularly about the application of the agreement, and in this article, to consult about possible amendment. The obvious implication of this article is that if the objecting part is unable to achieve an acceptable solution through either the consultations of Paragraph 9 of the Final Act, or the consultations for amendment provided for in this paragraph, it will give notice of termination pursuant to this paragraph. It was through this progression that the original Bermuda Agreement came to be superseded by the Bermuda 2 Agreement in 1977.

Article 14 is a provision that the agreement would come into force on the day it was signed. This was possible because it was signed in the form of an executive agreement, rather than as a formal treaty, which would have required the advice and consent of the United States Senate. All of the air transport agreements signed by the United States have been executive agreements on the American side, although they have been ratified as treaties in a number of countries where this was required by the constitution of the country.[55]

The Annex of the Bermuda Agreement has five sections.

Section I provides that at the agreed stopping places on the routes granted in Section III, the airlines of each party shall enjoy in the territory of the other the right to use airports designated as international airports and auxiliary facilities and to exercise the right of transit, stop for non-traffic purpose and of commercial international carriage of passengers, cargo and mail. This section also provides that the exercise of these rights shall be in compliance with the principles established in the Final Act.

Section II is the Rate Article. From a regulatory point of view, the importance of this section is exceeded only by that of the capacity provisions of the Final Act. The internal situation of the United States at the time the Bermuda Agreement was negotiated made it necessary for the rate article to be rather complex. As part of the Bermuda deal, the United States had announced that it intended to approve the IATA Conference machinery as a medium for establishing international rates, but it had not yet done so. Moreover, because of the ingrained antipathy in the United States to cartels and combinations in restraint of trade, it was evident that even if the United States should approve the IATA machinery there would always remain a real possibility that it might withdraw that approval at a later date. Therefore, it was necessary to cover in the rate article what was to be done when there was IATA machinery available, and what was to be done when there was no such machinery available. In addition, at the time of signing the Bermuda Agreement, the United States Civil Aeronautics Board did not have the power to fix rates in international air transport,[56] although it was seeking to obtain such authority from the legislature.

The most significant aspect of this article is its sanctioning of the International Air Transport Association, IATA, an association composed of commercial airlines operating international services.

Broadly speaking IATA operates by the airlines' agreeing on rates and accompanying traffic practices, which they then submit for approval to governments. The airline agreements do not become effective without government approval.[57] The IATA also has a number of the functions of a trade association, releasing financial and traffic statistics for the entire industry and speaking for the industry in matters where the airlines have a common interest. In addition IATA has established and operated a number of industry projects, such as a clearing house for the settlement of intercompany transportation accounts and technical services for the industry.[58]

Although conceptually airline agreements that require government approval to become effective are tantamount to agreements made directly between governments, the idea of competing airlines sitting down with one another to talk prices raises the deepest suspicions in the United States.[59] In addition, the United States position going into the Bermuda negotiations was that no limit should be placed upon airline pricing. Therefore, it is not surprising that the decision of the United States Civil Aeronautics Board to approve the IATA traffic control machinery was accompanied by a vigorous dissent.[60]

The majority in the CAB decision had no trouble approving so much of the IATA scheme as related to agreements that facilitate transportation, such as the format of tickets, interline traffic procedures and the like, but it was concerned about approving agreements on pricing. It did approve the entire proposal, however, giving the following reasons:

1. The Civil Aeronautics Act, Section 412 (a)[61] contemplated that rate agreements would be made among the airlines.
2. There is a precedent for agreed transportation rates in the shipping conferences.
3. Agreement on rates will tend to avoid the imposition of rates on United States airlines by foreign governments as had already happened in the United Kingdom and France.
4. If the CAB had the power to disapprove IATA rate agreements it would have more control over international rates than it would have in the absence of IATA, since it did not have the power to control international rates directly. Moreover the Bermuda Agreement calls for governmental review where IATA agreement fails.
5. Under the IATA provisions, where there is no agreement in IATA, each carrier is free to fix its own rates.

Civil Aeronautics Board member Josh Lee dissented. The grounds of his dissent were the following:

1. The comparison with the shipping conference is invalid because membership in the shipping conferences is voluntary whereas the airlines would be compelled by government pressure to belong to IATA.
2. The Association will eliminate competition because the rates will be the ones that all members will agree to, rather than the rates of the most efficient operator.
3. Service competition will be eliminated along with price competition.
4. The tenets of IATA are incompatible with United States aviation policy, which favors competition.

5. The "safeguard" that IATA agreements will require CAB approval is without value because the CAB will not have before it an adequate record of what took place at the traffic conference.
6. The pressure to approve the IATA agreements came only from the British and French. In the rest of the world the American airlines could have had free rein to establish their own rates.
7. There was no reason to fear rate wars.
8. The proposed safeguards were inadequate.

The reasons given by the majority for their decision all appear clear and valid on their face, with the exception of number five that in the absence of IATA agreement, each carrier would be free to set its own rates. Although this is true so far as the IATA agreements are concerned, in practice, governments usually stepped in to prevent the airlines from fixing rates to which they objected. Under the Bermuda Agreement itself, the United Kingdom had the right to fix the rates of United States carriers unilaterally if governmental agreement should prove impossible after consultation, since the United States Civil Aeronautics Board did not then have the power to fix rates in international air transport.[62] In other countries, where there was no agreement the government was free to fix rates unilaterally. The Bermuda-type agreements signed later contained various types of rate clauses. Some followed the Bermuda Agreement.[63] Others contained a general declaration that rates should be "reasonable," but lacked a requirement for consultation prior to unilateral action, or in some cases contained no rate article at all.[64] Moreover, as national carriers proliferated, the constituency for unilateral rate regulation grew.

The reasons adduced by CAB member Lee in his dissent were prophetic of the problems encountered by the United States Civil Aeronautics Board with IATA over the ensuing years.

Lee's first reason for dissent, that approval of steamship rate conferences is not a valid precedent for approving airline rate conferences because membership in the steamship rate conferences is voluntary whereas membership in IATA would be compulsory, does not seem to carry much weight. In fact, approval of IATA by the United States government did not make membership by United States airlines compulsory. There did exist, however, for airlines the same compulsion to belong to a rate conference as there was for shipping lines: namely, the pressure of foreign governments, plus their own desire to be protected from competition.

Lee's second reason assumes that a refusal to approve the IATA traffic conference agreements would bring about a situation where the rates of the most efficient operator would prevail in the market. This assumption is not warranted by the facts. As between the United States and the United Kingdom there had already been a case in the pre-Bermuda days where the British refused to let Pan American introduce low rates on the North

Atlantic.[65] Under the Bermuda Agreement itself, the British could act unilaterally after consultation to prevent a fare they objected to from becoming effective[66] in the absence of IATA agreement. The evidence available at the time, which was amply corroborated by later events, showed that when most governments considered the commercial well-being of their national airline to be threatened by low rates proposed by a foreign airline, they would contrive in one way or another to prevent the threatening rate from becoming effective.

The problem is not essentially with the IATA machinery, which in theory would allow the rates of the low cost operator to prevail in the absence of agreed rates, but rather with the basic attitude of most governments concerning the need to protect their national airline. Thus, most IATA rate agreements have in fact tended to be compromises between the proponents of high and of low rates, rather than being the result of technical economic studies on the basis of the costs of the low-cost operator.

Under these circumstances, the CAB was placed in a quandary when it came to approving a given rate agreement with rates higher than those which could be justified by the cost figures of the American airlines. Should the rates be approved as being the best that could be achieved in the circumstances, or were the United States carriers giving in easily to the pressure for high rates of the foreign carriers in order to take unfair advantage of the public? The problem of the CAB was compounded by its tendency to insist that IATA rates must be accompanied by adequate cost justification which was often obtainable only from the United States airlines.

Although it could not be said that IATA agreement on pricing completely eliminated service competition, Lee was certainly correct when he observed in his third reason that agreement on rates would also entail agreement on service conditions. The most entertaining example of this is the famous "sandwich war." The airlines involved originally agreed on the establishment of a tourist class service with low fares and relatively spartan service standards, including the provision of sandwiches for lunch, rather than the heavier entrees that were then the fashion. The management of the airlines that were serving normal sandwiches became indignant when they observed certain airlines serving as "sandwiches" such things as a half a chicken between two slices of bread and entire Scandinavian smorgasbords on a tray. The result was that at the next traffic conference they insisted upon and actually achieved an IATA resolution specifying the contents of the sandwiches that might be served in that class of service. Although this case amounts to a *reductio ad absurdum,* it is perfectly logical that when airlines agree on pricing they will also agree on standards for the service to which the price applies. This concept is implicit in the Civil Aeronautics Board's insistence that it be given cost justification for agreed rates: costs can only be established on the basis of known standards of service.

Lee's fourth objection, that IATA was incompatible with United States aviation policy, was certainly correct at the time, and throughout the years, IATA has been vulnerable to attack in the United States on the basis that it is contrary to public policy as a cartel. On the other hand, the reasons brought forth by the majority appear adequate to justify departing at that time from the underlying American policy to the degree necessary to approve the IATA traffic conference agreements.

The fifth objection, that the Civil Aeronautics Board would not have the safeguard it thought it would have against abusive IATA agreements, because it would not have an adequate record of what took place at IATA meetings, points to a recurrent cause for friction between the Board and IATA over the years. The problem has never been fully resolved and appears to involve a certain lack of understanding on all sides. The Civil Aeronautics Board (now the Department of Transportation) has appeared unduly suspicious of what goes on at IATA meetings and has demanded volumes of essentially useless papers. The IATA management has been composed principally of Europeans who have no feel for the depth of suspicion and antipathy aroused in the United States by IATA, which is called a cartel by its detractors and in any case engages in price fixing activities that would clearly be illegal in the absence of special legislation authorizing them. The managements of the foreign airline members of IATA, which play a large role in directing it, have the same lack of understanding as the IATA management and often feel in addition that the CAB's attempts to obtain IATA records are invasions of the sovereignty of the nations which they represent, particularly in the case of state-owned airlines. This has led them to take defiant attitudes in dealing with the CAB on this subject, which further antagonized the CAB.[67]

Lee was simply wrong in his sixth reason when he thought that the British and the French were the only countries that sought to control airline rates. The fate of the United States advocacy of "open skies" at the Chicago Conference and the scarcity of adherents to the International Air Transport Agreement should have made it clear that the majority of governments throughout the world desired to control all competitive aspects of foreign airline service. At any rate, subsequent developments have shown that most countries wish to control international airline rates.

There is no way of proving one way or the other Lee's assertion in his seventh reason that there was no cause to fear international airline rate wars. In the decades since the opinion was written, there have not occurred in the airline business major rate wars on the scale they are reported to have taken place in the steamship business, despite a number of breakdowns in the IATA system during that period. On the other hand, at the same time CAB member Josh Lee dismissed rate wars as a danger, he also dismissed government interference with airline pricing as a problem to be alleviated through approval of the IATA traffic conference agreements. In fact, it is arguable that if there were no serious rate wars during periods when there were no IATA rates, the reason was that governments tended to step in and control rates unilaterally.

Lee's eighth reason, that the "safeguards" proposed by the majority were inadequate, is prophetic of the efforts by the CAB during the ensuing years to impose further safeguards to ensure that it was fully informed of what took place at IATA meetings and to avoid abuses of the IATA system.

On balance, the Bermuda rates article, including the approval of the IATA traffic conferences, worked reasonably well for the United States over the years. Given the unwillingness of most other countries, including the United Kingdom, to allow full play to the forces of competition in this area, it is hard to imagine a better system for the United States to have adopted at that time to deal with rate problems.

Section III is the route schedule. The notable thing about this route schedule is that it states in detail the points that may be served on each routing. Other agreements describe routes with much more flexibility: For example the United States route in the most flexible agreements takes the following form: "From the United States via intermediate points to named cities in [country X] and beyond, in both directions." Thus United States airlines can choose their own intermediate and beyond points in their service and are also free to start the service from any point they might choose in the United States.

The more detailed route description in the Bermuda agreement was probably mainly the result of the worldwide extent of the British Empire at the time. It was necessary to describe the routes in some detail, in order to have a clear idea of what they were, since points in the British Empire were likely to appear as terminal points, intermediate points or beyond points on any given route.

The actual route trade between the United States and Great Britain appears to have been reasonably balanced, except that the United States obtained the right to operate more service beyond the U.K.'s major traffic point, London, to fifth freedom points (Amsterdam, Helsinki, Copenhagen, Stavanger, Oslo, Stockholm, Warsaw, Berlin, Frankfurt, Moscow, Leningrad, points in the Baltic countries, Brussels, Munich, Prague, Vienna, Budapest, Bucharest, Istanbul, Ankara, a point in Iran, Beirut, a point in Syria, a point in Iraq, a point in Afghanistan, Karachi, Delhi, and Calcutta). The British had as points beyond New York only Manila, Guam, Wake, Midway, Mexico City, Cuba, Panama, a point in Colombia, a point in Ecuador, Lima, and Santiago.

This advantage to the United States was one of the major issues pursued by the British in the negotiations that led to the Bermuda 2 Agreement

The British conveniently ignored the fact that they enjoyed the same advantage with respect to the carriage of traffic to and from points behind the home country as the United States enjoyed with respect to points beyond the territory of the United Kingdom. (For example, if the United States could offer London–Paris, the British could offer Paris–New York service on their flights from London to New York.)

In evaluating the trade of routes between the United States and the United kingdom, it is well to bear in mind, however, that on the U.K. side the agreement applied in addition to Ceylon, Cyprus, Ghana, Jamaica, Kenya, Malaysia, Nigeria, Sierra Leone, Tanzania, Trinidad and Tobago, all of which have since become independent, as well as to a number of Crown Colonies. Upon independence, these territories took on the status of separate nations in their dealings with the United States, and the United States in some cases had to pay a second time for the privilege of having American airlines serve them.

Section IV relates to changes in points served. Paragraph (a) merely states the obvious when it says that route changes in the territory of the other party may be made only after consultation. Paragraph (b) is unusual in allowing changes in other points by simple notification. What is unusual is allowing a precisely described route to be changed. Generally, when the parties intend to allow freedom to change points in the home country they describe the route "from points in X country"; when they intend to allow changes in intermediate points, they say "via intermediate points" and when they intend to allow changes in beyond points, they say "and beyond." As suggested above, the more precise route description of the Bermuda Agreement was probably required in order to describe the routes at all, in view of the worldwide scope of the British Empire at the time. This paragraph was evidently included to mitigate the restrictiveness of that route description, since the more general description would not have served.

Paragraph (c) follows the general scheme of the Bermuda Agreement in calling for the parties to exchange information concerning authorizations to their airlines to operate on the agreed routes.

Section V, "Change of Gauge," authorizes a practice that is still necessary in some cases for economical airline operation. The idea is that where operations are between two large areas, it may be desirable to use a large aircraft on the early stages, particularly long ones, and then use one or more smaller aircraft to carry the traffic to points beyond. Since the load to beyond points would be reduced by the volume of traffic from the home country to the earlier stopping places, it can be more economical to substitute a smaller aircraft than to continue the operation with empty seats on the original aircraft (and similarly in the reverse direction). This mode of operation also enables the airline to bring its operation more into line with the Bermuda capacity principles by reducing its capacity in proportion to the reduction in home-country traffic carried beyond the point where the change of gauge is made.

Sometimes, two or more smaller aircraft are used for the onward service, in order to consolidate on the early stages of the route traffic to points beyond the point where the route bifurcates. Under those circumstances it can happen that more seats are offered beyond the point where the change of gauge is made than are offered on the earlier stages from the home country. There is nothing specific to prohibit this in the Bermuda Agreement and it proved a source of irritation to the British. The point is much more firmly tied down in the Bermuda 2 Agreement, along with a number of other points related to the "beyond" service. The Bermuda 2 Agreement also makes its provisions relate to changes of gauge which occur in third countries.[68] In the Bermuda Agreement itself, such changes appear to be allowed, but they are unregulated by this clause of the agreement, although they would be subject to the capacity clauses.[69]

It is also interesting to note that this section of the Bermuda Agreement is drafted so as to refer only to the outbound service, although the intention is manifestly for it to apply in both directions.[70] This was corrected in the Bermuda 2 Agreement.

The Bermuda Agreement was the mainstay of United States policy in the regulation of international air transport from the time of its signature until the mid 1970s when the United States turned to a policy of deregulation. Nevertheless, throughout this period there was almost continuous discussion within the United States on the subject, and the emphasis within the Bermuda scheme changed from time to time. The constants and the varying elements present in the American attitudes are reflected in the formal statements of international air policy issued by the United States government during the period.

6. UNITED STATES POLICY STATEMENTS IN THE BERMUDA ERA

The period from 1946, when the Bermuda Agreement was signed, until 1977 when the Bermuda 2 Agreement was signed,[1] and the United States began in earnest to embark on a course of "deregulating" civil aviation, may be considered as a unit for conceptual purposes. The unifying element is that during this period, the Bermuda Agreement formed the backbone of United States commercial international air policy. If the Bermuda Agreement is regarded as a compromise between the desire of commercial nationalists to regulate and restrict the activities of international airlines, and the desire of free trade advocates to allow international airlines to operate in an unrestricted atmosphere, the United States may be seen to have oscillated during this period between the two attitudes, while remaining within the policy framework of the Bermuda Agreement, and while tending more often than not to favor liberal and unrestrictive attitudes.

United States international air transport policy may be inferred from specific actions by the American government, and it may be found in official pronouncements by various entities within the government.

From the time of the passage of the Civil Aeronautics Act of 1938,[2] there has existed a certain tension between the United States Congress and the executive branch of the government with respect to the regulation of civil aeronautics in general, and the setting of international air transport policy in particular. In passing the Civil Aeronautics Act of 1938, the Congress created the Civil Aeronautics Board as a quasi-judicial administrative agency under the thumb of the legislature, with the intention of sheltering the control of civil aeronautics from what it considered excessive political control on the part of the executive branch. By means of a series of reorganization plans, notably Reorganization Plan IV of 1940, the executive branch increased its power to affect actions in this field.[3] Nevertheless, there remained a certain ambiguity about just who was in charge of civil aviation, which showed itself, among other ways, in the pronouncements concerning international air policy that emanated from time to time from the executive branch (the president, the Department of State, the Department of Commerce, and later the Department of Transportation), the Congress (Senate and House) and the Civil Aeronautics Board itself.

The primary way for the Congress to express itself is through legislation, and it had already spoken on the subject of international air policy in Section 102 of the Civil Aeronautics Act of 1938. In addition, individual committees of the Senate and the House of Representatives held hearings on the subject and addressed themselves directly to the agencies charged with administering air policy. The effect of these pronouncements was mixed.

Presidents Truman,[4] Eisenhower,[5] Kennedy,[6] Nixon[7] and Ford[8] endorsed formal statements of international air transport policy during the period while the Bermuda Agreement was a major influence on United States policy. President Johnson did not issue a formal policy statement. The policy statement of President Carter was not based on the Bermuda Agreement. These policy statements can clearly be looked to as statements of intent on the part of the executive branch of the United States government. It is less clear, however, that they have the status of gospel with respect to the views and actions of the United States Congress. The discrepancy between the views of the president and the actions of the Congress is particularly noticeable in the case of the treatment of non-scheduled carriers, where the executive branch over a period sought to curtail their activities, whereas the Congress tended to encourage them through political pressure and through actual legislation.

The executive departments performed various studies of international air transport policy,[9] and some of these are interesting as expert opinions on the subject, but they do not have a great deal of force, in the absence of endorsement by the president.

Like the executive departments, the Civil Aeronautics Board from time to time issued air policy statements, but without the endorsement of the president, they do not appear to be entitled to great weight as international air policy statements. One must, however, look to the reports of cases decided by the Civil Aeronautics Board to discover what the United States actually did in furtherance of certain of its policies, such as the issuance of foreign air carrier permits to foreign air carriers for routes to the United States[10] and certificates of public convenience and necessity to United States air carriers for routes from the United States to foreign countries.[11] Nevertheless, the decision of the Civil Aeronautics Board with respect to such cases only became effective after review by the president and the president could alter or even reverse the Board's decision.[12] Thus, whatever may have been the original intent of Congress, the actual impact of the Civil Aeronautics Board on international civil aviation policy has not been a great deal different from that of the executive departments.

The first formal statement of civil air transport policy to be issued after the signature of the Bermuda Agreement came out of a temporary Air Policy Commission established by President Truman July 18, 1947.[13] The committee consisted of prominent private citizens and was generally known as the "Finletter Commission" after its chairman Thomas K. Finletter. The Commission's report came out on January 1, 1948, under the title *Survival in the Air Age; A Report by the Presidents Air Policy Commission.*[14] The pertinent portion of the report for present purposes is Section IV, "Civil Aviation." The relevant topics are as follows:

Air Mail Payments and Subsidy.[15] The Commission recommended that both domestic and international United States airlines continue to be subsidized through mail pay, with the objective of having them become self-sufficient in the future. The justification for such subsidization is based "on grounds of national security and economic welfare."[16]

Safety and Regularity.[17] The Commission recommended that new aircraft types be placed in passenger service only after a period of use on non-passenger schedules. The report also mentions a concern with the "lack of consideration for safety that has been shown by some contract carriers."[18] The Commission recommended that for the sake of safety and regularity of service there be established a nationwide system of air traffic control, navigation and landing aids, supplementing the existing system of navigational facilities and emergency landing aids. For international routes the commission recommended that the United States participate fully in the ICAO "joint effort" program to insure the installation of adequate aviation aids along the routes of the world.[19] The recommendation that called for putting new aircraft types into service first on all-cargo service was never implemented. The other recommendations of this paragraph became a part of United States policy and were implemented.

Economic Regulation.[20] The commission recommended that United States international airlines receive the subsidy required to allow them to compete with foreign subsidized airlines. The report recommended that there be "regulated competition" among American carriers operating internationally. It recommended further that full support be given to the efforts to eliminate burdensome regulations that constitute obstacles to international trade and travel. The commission took the position that routes should be exchanged bilaterally between governments, and that the principles for operating air services on such routes should be established on a multilateral basis. This was similar to the position taken by the United States in the negotiations for a multilateral agreement held in Geneva in November of 1947.[21] During this period, the United States was, in fact, exchanging traffic rights with other nations pursuant to bilateral air transport agreements that followed very closely the Bermuda Agreement.[22] Since the United States had a commitment to the British to follow the Bermuda Agreement in its agreements with other countries, one may conclude that this was the actual policy of the United States, and the reference to multilateral agreement on general principles was primarily to appear consistent with the position taken in the multilateral negotiations. The commission supported the Bermuda provisions allowing liberal exercise of fifth freedom traffic rights, and came out strongly against traffic restrictions.[23] It did not, however refer specifically to the Bermuda "capacity principles." The report recommended that air transport agreements should be effectuated through executive agreements, rather than taking the form of treaties, to ensure flexibility and avoid delay in their execution.

The commission also recommended that the Civil Aeronautics Board be given control of international airline rates. It was not until 1972 that Congress gave the Civil Aeronautics Board control of international airline rates, but the position of the executive branch consistently advocated such control throughout the period, albeit with varying degrees of zeal.

The commision recommended further that steps be taken to amend the American internal legislation and Article 5 of the Chicago Convention so as to obtain greater control over the activities of non-scheduled carriers operating internationally.[24]

As can be seen, the recommendations of the commission in the field of international air transport constitute a policy not very different from that enunciated by the attorney general in 1945, and quite similar to that followed by the United States until it was supplanted by the policy of "deregulation" in the late 1970s.

The Eisenhower Policy

The next formal statement of United States civil air policy appeared in a report issued in May 1954, under the title *Civil Air Policy; A Report by the Air Coordinating Committee by Direction of the President* (i.e., Eisenhower).[25] The items under the heading "International Aviation" are most directly pertinent to our present purposes.

Under "Routes and Rights," the following categorical statements of policy are made:

> 1. The exchange of air transport rights will continue to be by bilateral air transport agreement until such time as it is possible to achieve a multilateral agreement which contains principles generally in accord with those of existing United States bilateral agreements.[26] . . .
>
> 2. The United States will adhere to the policy of negotiating for air rights on the basis of all five freedoms.[27] . . .

> 3. In the negotiation of its agreements for the exchange of international air rights, the United States will continue to adhere to the Bermuda principles as the most satisfactory basis for relating capacity to traffic.[28] ...
>
> 4. In determining the routes to be included in bilateral air transport agreements, the United States will continue its objective of establishing, insofar as possible, an equitable exchange of economic benefits.[29] ...
>
> 5. The United States will seek interpretation and application of its agreements in a manner which will accord with the over-all objectives of an effective international air transport system.[30]

The first item, although it gives lip service to the idea of a multilateral agreement, is in effect a flat statement that the United States will continue to exchange traffic rights by means of bilateral agreements, since it was already evident that there was not going to be a multilateral agreement.

The second item echoes the statement in the Finletter report supporting the Bermuda provisions allowing the liberal exercise of fifth freedom traffic rights. Ultimately, however, the United States concluded that there were cases where adherence to the idea of refusing to accept a route that did not include all five Bermuda freedoms was keeping American airlines out of markets that could be served if the United States were more flexible in negotiating for routes with fifth freedom restrictions. The policy was changed to permit handling such routes on a case-by-case basis.

The third item squarely recognizes the Bermuda "capacity principles" as the basis for capacity provisions in United States bilateral air transport agreements.

The fourth item is the first statement in a presidential air policy of the determination of the United States that route exchanges should be based upon "an equitable exchange of economic benefits." This concept received its most elaborate gloss in an article by Frank Loy, United States deputy assistant secretary of state for transportation and telecommunications, which was prepared for delivery at the International Conference on the Freedom of the Air, McGill University, Institute of Air and Space Law, Montreal, November 3 and 4, 1967.[31] Loy says that in a route negotiation under a bilateral air transport agreement the economic benefits that are exchanged are rights to compete for the traffic generated in a particular country. In the case of fifth freedom traffic, it is obvious that a large country with an extensive market has more to put on the bargaining table than a small country with a small market. Loy cites the example of a route between New York and Luxembourg via London. The value of fifth freedom traffic New York–London would obviously be far greater for a Luxembourgeois carrier than would be the value of fifth freedom traffic London–Luxembourg for an American carrier.

Loy further says that the market potential of the home market is also relevant to the value of third and fourth freedom routes. He cites as an example an exchange of nonstop routes between the United States and

Austria: United States–Vienna for the American carrier and Austria–New York for the Austrian. Loy rejects the claim that the "market" is a route and since both ends are required to make a route, neither is entitled to greater bargaining weight than the other. He justifies rejecting that claim and giving greater bargaining weight to New York in the example given by saying that in a market analysis, the place of origin—the place where a paying passenger is and pays his money for the ticket—is more important than the place of destination. He also points out that in the absence of the agreement, the United States would still be able to transport a large part of these Vienna-bound passengers to Europe—some place near Vienna—whereas the Austrian carrier might never see them at all if it were not able to serve New York, or at best it would be able to carry them a short distance within Europe. Loy's view was attacked by Professor Bin Cheng of University College, London, at another conference at McGill University, in 1976.[32] Bin Cheng claimed that the American position is ill advised because it produces friction with countries that have a preponderance of terminating traffic. He also observes that a preponderance of originating traffic cannot be invoked as a justification for offering greater capacity, because the Bermuda Agreement refers to traffic between points as justification.

It should be noted that even if the value of third and fourth freedom traffic is equal for the two countries concerned, the United States will be able to claim the advantage in most cases, because the United States' large air transport market offers the airlines of most countries the opportunity to carry more fifth freedom traffic than they offer to American airlines.

The fifth item recognized that by 1954, the basic framework of the American system of bilateral air transport agreements was in place, and that future new agreements and amendments to existing agreements would be related to the development of existing routes. Underlying this position is the assumption that international competition among United States airlines is to be limited through regulation.

The study recommends that so far as possible, the payment of subsidy must be phased out for domestic services. With respect to international services, it provides:

> 3. It is recognized that foreign competition and other special factors will probably prolong the period during which subsidy will be required for international air transportation operations.[33] . . .
>
> 4. Where the public interest requires the continued maintenance of uneconomical services, increased emphasis should be placed upon the inclusion of such operations within route systems that are capable of absorbing their cost without subsidy. . . .
>
> 8. National interest factors require that many international routes be maintained, despite subsidy requirements. Route decisions in this area should recognize the necessity of avoiding or eliminating uneconomic duplication of service between United States carriers.[34]

As has already been observed, governments are seldom interested in subsidizing national carriers to compete with one another on international routes. It is one thing to pay a subsidy to ensure that a particular service is available. It is a great deal harder to justify paying a subsidy to make possible a duplication of that service solely in the name of competition. The policy statement is even more explicit in this sense in providing that cross-subsidization from profitable routes to unprofitable routes should be used.[35] To advocate this practice implies further that competition is to be limited, and that particular carriers are to be encouraged to develop strong route systems which enable them to absorb the cost of operating unprofitable route segments without requiring subsidy. Thus, although the 1954 policy has clearly abandoned the "chosen instrument" approach to international air transport, and although it does not explicitly come out in favor of regional monopoly, it is a long way from recommending unlimited competition among American airlines.

The international section of the report supports continued reliance upon the International Air Transport Association for the establishment of international fares and rates. It also supports the passage of legislation giving the United States Civil Aeronautics Board the power to fix international fares and rates to and from the United States.[36] It supports continued American participation in ICAO.[37] This section of the report also states that it is the policy of the United States to provide air navigational facilities in its territory in accordance with ICAO standards and to insist that other nations do likewise.[38] Finally, the report says that it is United States policy to extend technical and economic cooperation in civil aviation to friendly nations.[39]

Other sections of the report have importance for international air transport. Notable among them are the following:

Government Use of Air Services.[40] This subject has been a source of friction among various departments of the United States government and the U. S. international airlines from the time of this report to the present day. The conclusion in the report is that government departments should take the lead in making use of commercial air services, and that for travel abroad, they should use American airlines. The report also concludes that the military should deliberately refrain from competing with private airlines and that government agencies should abstain from using their superior bargaining power to exact unwarranted price concessions from private air carriers. The background of this was that most foreign countries with national airlines required government travel to be via those airlines. This policy statement was not especially effective for the American airlines, but it did provide a certain impetus toward United States government use of United States airlines.[41]

Non-scheduled Airline Operations.[42] The problem of non-scheduled operations under Article 5 of the Chicago Convention has already been mentioned.[43] Similarly, shortly after the Civil Aeronautics Act took effect in the United States in 1938, non-scheduled air transport services were exempted from the requirements of the Act so as to permit them to operate relatively free from economic supervision by the Civil Aeronautics Board.[44] Just as the economic threat posed by the non-scheduled operators of the newer and much larger aircraft that became available in the post–World War II era caused the governments in ICAO to redefine the ICAO regulations so as to rescind the apparent freedom of non-scheduled flights to operate without government regulation, the air coordinating committee in this report recommended that the United States adopt a firm policy against any general exemption status for common carrier transportation of individually ticketed passengers on large transport aircraft.[45]

At the time of this report, the non-scheduled carriers were a problem to the government regulators of American air transportation primarily in the area of domestic air transport. This report recommends that

> those operations of the large irregular carriers which represent a supplementary type of service, such as bona fide charter and contract operations should be encouraged. A new type of certificate should be developed for such operations, providing suitable flexibility in terms of areas to be served.[46]

The trouble was that the operators of the non-scheduled services were an extremely lively and resourceful group. If they were told they could not operate on a schedule, they coordinated their flights so as to produce the effect of a schedule, without publishing one. If they were told they could not operate individually ticketed flights, they operated charters that were plane-load flights only in form, with the passengers assembled individually by agents just like the passengers on scheduled flights. Moreover, the operators of non-scheduled services were able to generate a great deal of support in the United States House of Representatives and Senate.[47] Their operations became international in scope. Thus, although non-scheduled operations are dealt wiht in this report as a problem of domestic air policy, they soon became a problem for international commercial air policy, and future statements of American international air policy all deal with the relation between the scheduled carriers and the other class of carriers that is referred to in this report as non-scheduled.

Air Cargo.[48] The report recommends that the government promote the development of the air cargo industry both domestically and internationally and that it assist in the development of a suitable all-cargo aircraft.

Aviation and Mobilization Planning.[49] The policy statement is emphatic in calling for the integration of domestic and international airline capability with the military so as to be at a high state of readiness in case of war. The details of training and mobilization plans are of less importance to international commercial air transport policy than is the perception that the airlines form a reserve on which the military expects to draw in wartime. With that perception the government has a strong incentive to see to it that the airlines prosper and that they not be driven from the field by foreign competition. Conversely, if there is no such perception, a strong motive for protecting the national airlines operating internationally is absent. The changing perception of the relevance of civilian air transport to military planning undoubtedly had an influence on the progression of the stance of the United States government from being strongly promotional toward U.S. airlines to being a detached observer under a policy of "deregulation" in the late 1970s.

The Aircraft Manufacturing Industry.[50] Reflecting the perception that civilian airlines are a reserve for the military, the policy advocates continued government financial support for research and development of civilian transport aircraft.

The report makes evident a degree of conflict of interest in the United States between the international air transport and the aicraft manufacturing industries. The policy provides that

> if the manufacture and supply of aircraft becomes critical because of a shortage of materials, necessitating the use of a priority system, civil purchases of aircraft and parts in friendly foreign countries shall receive substantially equal treatment to that accorded United States civil purchasers.[51]

This was manifestly included in the policy at the behest of the manufacturers in order to protect their foreign markets. It would be to the American domestic airlines' interest if it said just the reverse.[52] In a final section, the report advocates that the Export-Import Bank make loans and guarantee loans by others for the purpose of financing sales by American aircraft manufacturers.[53] This provision is beneficial to the manufacturers, but it is in some ways detrimental to the U.S. airlines, since they have to compete with foreign airlines which obtain their aircraft at concessionary interest rates under the EximBank financing while they themselves have to pay the higher interest rates available in the open market for their own financing.

This civil air policy, and all subsequent statements of civil air policy, are highly political exercises. Everyone with a point of view tries to make sure that it is heard and if possible adopted by the group charged with preparing the study. For example, as shown above, the manufacturers are likely to have interests antithetical to those of the airlines. Individual airlines are likely to have divergent views and interests. The operators of non-scheduled services have interests that differ from those of the operators of scheduled services. Among the operators of scheduled services, those with extensive international route networks are likely to encourage measures that lead to a maintenance of the status quo, whereas carriers with small international routes but large ambitions are likely to advocate expansion of the routes available under bilateral air transport agreements. Similarly, carriers with routes where they see themselves threatened with what they consider excessive foreign competition are likely to advocate the adoption of restrictive measures which are quite contrary to the liberal measures advocated by other carriers that operate in an area where they find themselves the dominant carriers and fear unilaterally imposed restriction by the local governments. Users are apt to have views that are contrary to those of the providers of air transportation. In addition, academics, public interest advocates and ordinary citizens come forward with views that are essentially disinterested, but not necessarily well informed. All of these find their way into the mix that comes out as air policy.

The Smathers Report

In 1956, a subcommittee of the United States Senate Committtee on Interstate and Foreign Commerce issued a report that had a strong impact on the conduct of international commercial air policy by the United States in certain respects, although in other respects it was not especially effective. The Subcommittee on International Air Agreements, chaired by Senator George A. Smathers of Florida, stated its purpose as follows:

> The hearing has been called to inquire into the matter of policy in regard to the issuance of the foreign air carrier permit to a new German airline and the negotiation of a bilateral air transport service agreement.[54]

The German agreement [55] granted routes for the German airline that by any reasonable measure greatly exceeded in value the routes granted in it to the United States airlines. The committee report makes it evident that the impetus for the action of the committee came from certain American airlines which felt that they had been betrayed by the disparity in the value of the routes exchanged and by the failure of the U.S. government negotiators to consult the carriers before proceeding to an exchange of routes.[56]

The Senate committee agreed that the German route agreement was improvident and that the airlines had not been properly consulted. The committee made eight specific recommendations, the most important of which were:

> 3. The United States should not make grants which cannot economically be operated without violating Bermuda Capacity Principles. . . .
>
> 5. . . . The Committee recommends the following principles for government consultation with United States air carriers in connection with air transport negotiations:

> (a) Interested carriers should be advised by the Government prior to any discussions with respect to negotiations for air transport negotiations.
>
> (b) Full and complete opportunity for discussion between interested carriers, on the one hand, and the Government, on the other, should precede any negotiations respecting air transport agreements.
>
> (c) Prior to any discussions with foreign countries respecting air transport agreements, representatives of all interested carriers should consult fully with United States Government Representatives.
>
> (d) Prior to the formal negotiations on air transport agreements, a representative of interested carriers should be made a duly accredited member of any delegation appointed to negotiate such agreements. As a duly credited official representative of the delegation, a carrier representative should be included not only in all negotiating sessions but also in all United States delegation meetings, and be given a fair and reasonable opportunity to consult with his principals before any ultimate decision is made.
>
> (e) Also, throughout the negotiations, the interested carrier representative should be consulted. We cannot emphasize too strongly our view of the necessity of our Government's securing the benefit of the comment of such representatives at every stage of the negotiation.[57]

Recommendation No. 3, concerning grants that "could not be economically operated without violating the Bermuda Capacity Principles," was not fully observed in practice. The assumption underlying the requirement is that there is some sort of an objective standard that will tell you how much fifth freedom is too much under a Bermuda-type agreement, whereas the whole point of these agreements is that the solution to the problem can only be reached through negotiation. Therefore, it is not fully reasonable for an *a priori* judgment to be made by one party that a particular route will result in the carriage of excessive fifth freedom traffic. As it turned out, the fifth freedom traffic actually carried by Lufthansa beyond the United States on its route beyond New York to South America, which was the one primarily addressed by the Smathers Committee, was not great enough to warrant a challenge by the United States.[58] Moreover, if the United States had developed such a standard for application to foreign countries seeking routes to the United States, it would have had to accept the same standard for application to its own carriers when they sought routes in foreign countries, which would have been inconvenient, since there were several important routes where U.S. carriers carried a preponderance of fifth freedom traffic, which they sought to justify by "the requirements of through airline operation."

On the other hand, the committee was on the right track when it objected to the imbalance in the value of the routes granted to the American and German carriers. The Bermuda principles are intended for application to routes that are the result of hard trading. Where there is a serious imbalance in the value of the routes, the losing party not only suffers a loss of revenue, but it also is prejudiced in its dealings with third countries both by the lack of third and fourth freedom traffic it should have picked up under the particular bilateral agreement if the routes had been in balance, and by the effect of the competitive operations of the other party's carriers. Concretely, United States carriers operating to South America were prejudiced by Lufthansa's operations: because they lost to Lufthansa revenue they could have kept for themselves, because they lost to Lufthansa third and fourth freedom traffic (fifth freedom to Lufthansa) which they could have used in South American countries to justify their own capacity under Bermuda-type bilateral agreements, and because the South American countries were more likely to challenge the capacity of U.S. airlines as a result of the extra capacity thrown on the route by Lufthansa, since the U.S. carriers were the most conspicuous targets. The problem goes back to a failure to achieve "an equitable exchange of economic benefits," rather than to the Bermuda-type capacity clauses relative to a particular route.

The United States continued to pay lip service to the idea that routes should not be granted if they could not be supported under the Bermuda capacity principles, but it continued to sign bilateral agreements containing routes for foreign airlines that arguably could not be justified by the Bermuda capacity principles and the Civil Aeronautics Board continued to issue foreign air carrier permits for the operation of such routes.[59]

The position of the Smathers Committee in its fifth paragraph (above) concerning consultation with the carriers had a profound effect on the conduct of American air policy, although it has never found its way into a formal statement of U.S. policy. The tension between the various United States governmental agencies involved in the negotiation of bilateral agreements on the one hand and the American airlines on the other hand with respect to the right of the airlines to be informed about and to influence the outcome of negotiations leading to the signature of bilateral air transport agreements had existed from the time the United States government took over air transport negotiations. The airlines felt that these negotiations dealt with their vital interests to such a degree that they should be considered in effect the principals in the negotiations, and the government negotiators should be considered their agents.

The government agencies saw it differently. The Department of State tended to take the attitude that these agreements were simply a part of the foreign relations of the United States, and that although the airlines were entitled to their say, the overall interest of the United States was paramount.[60] This had the result that where the Department of State determined that the overall interest of the United States required, the views of the airlines were likely to be ignored, and information was likely to be withheld from them. The Civil Aeronautics Board was likely to share the more parochial aviation view of the airlines, but that did not necessarily lead to its taking the same position as the airlines. One can conjecture that in the German case, the American government determined that the national interest required the grant to Germany of a route that was excessively generous when viewed from the aviation point of view, and that this was what led to the route's being granted without adequate opportunity for the airlines to express themselves. In their turn, the airlines managed to gain the ear of an influential group of senators who helped to improve the position of the airlines for future negotiations by the issuance of this report.[61]

Since 1956, the degree to which American airlines have been consulted in the formation of positions for bilateral air transport negotiations and the degree to which their views have been taken into account when they were consulted have varied. Although formal statements of air policy have not addressed this subject, it is clear that it has always been a part of United States air policy to consult the carriers. The usual procedure at that time was for the airlines to be represented in negotiations and consultations with other countries by the Air Transport Association of America (ATA), the scheduled airlines' trade association. In dealing with the CAB and the Department of State with respect to such negotiations, the ATA representative spoke for the carriers when there was a consensus, and they spoke for themselves when there was a divergence of views, or when the airline concerned was not a member of the ATA.

In the actual consultations, the ATA representative usually sat in as an observer and afterward informed the carriers what had taken place.[62] The degree to which the ATA observer has been allowed to sit in on delegation meetings to determine strategy has often been a matter of controversy between the airlines and the government. During negotiations, individual carriers have often been given the opportunity to make their views known to the negotiators and American government officials have often met with airline personnel in Washington for that purpose.[63] In the German negotiation, the carriers were kept in the dark until the result was announced publicly.

The committee also endorsed the Bermuda principles and recommended that the United States "should see to it that they are enforced with respect to the operations of foreign carriers." Taken literally, this is nonsense because there is no way of "enforcing" the Bermuda principles against another nation, although, of course, it is always possible to take unilateral action outside the agreement. On the other hand the recommendation must have had a salutory effect in stiffening the backbone of American negotiators dealing with questions under the Bermuda-type agreements.

The committee further observed that the United States delegation was inadequately prepared for the German negotiation and recommended careful preparation in the future.

The committee pointed out that the CAB is the agency of the government vested with the responsibility "to develop an air transportation system properly adapted to the present and future needs of the foreign commerce of the United States,"[64] and urged that it be the principal advisor to the executive branch on international air agreements. In fact, the Department of State was at this time and has remained to the present date the lead agency charged with the negotiation of bilateral air transport agreements.[65] In the light of the responsibility of the Department of State for the conduct of the foreign relations of the United Staes this role appears inevitable. Although efforts were made by the carriers from time to time to upset it, they have in the main supported the Department of State as the lead agency in this field, probably as much on pragmatic grounds as any other, since the Department of State is the branch with expertise in international negotiations. It is not surprising, however, to find a Senate committee stressing the role of the Civil Aeronautics Board in this area, since the legislature had created it in part as a curb on the power of the executive to control civil aviation.

The committee recommended that the terms of the German bilateral agreement be applied strictly to minimize the effect of the unbalanced route exchange. Although it is hard to point to any concrete result of the Smathers committee on U.S. air transport policy, the process is instructive and it is apparent that it had an effect on the attitude of the executive branch of the government toward consulting with the airlines about air transport negotiations for a long time afterward. It also had an effect on attitudes toward the subject of air transport throughout the government. For example, the United States never again concluded such an obviously unbalanced route agreement until the whole pattern was changed under "deregulation."

The Bricker Proposal

By way of contrast, an example of a far-reaching proposal made in the United States Senate that had very little influence on American commerical aviation policy is the 1954 proposal of Senator John W. Bricker of Ohio that bilateral air transport agreements be required to be made in the form of treaties, rather than executive agreements.[66] The difference is that executive agreements become effective immediately, according to their terms, whereas treaties require the advice and consent of two-thirds of the Senate before they can be given effectiveness.[67] More importantly, under the Constitution (Article II), treaties have the force of law, whereas executive agreements do not have such force.

The proposal was made as part of an omnibus aviation bill and the Senate Committee on Interstate and Foreign Commerce published an aviation study concerning the issues raised by this bill, which included a section on Senator Bricker's proposal.[68] The conclusion of the study was that bilateral air transport arrangements should continue to be made by executive agreement and that there should be no requirement they be made by treaties. The reasons given were that there is a very large volume of such agreements and they require expeditious approval, which would put a burden on the Senate if it were required to act on them; that adequate supervision already exists through CAB supervision of the negotiating process and through CAB control of the issuance of foreign air carrier permits, as well as through direct Congressional oversight and consultation with the carriers. Although the study goes on to recommend that bilateral air transport agreements should be reviewed by the Senate, which should be empowered, but not required to act on them, no action was ever taken on this portion of the study. Senator Bricker's proposal, although it received considerable attention at the time, was never acted upon, and bilateral air transport agreements continue to be entered into through executive agreements. In view of the reasons cited in the Senate study, this appears to have been the proper result.

The Kennedy Policy

President John F. Kennedy devoted considerable attention to the subject of air policy. On March 3, 1961, he addressed a letter to Najeeb Halaby, whom he had appointed administrator of the Federal Aviation Agency, asking him to develop a statement of national aviation goals for the period 1961 to 1970. Halaby hired a task force for the job, which was named "Project Horizon." It delivered its report in September 1961.[69]

This report stated "continued U.S. preeminence in international air transport is unquestionably in the national interest," and accepted without question the military value of "an aggressive and expanding air transport system."[70] After expressing concern about the decreasing American share of transatlantic carriage, the report suggests the need to reexamine the policy of promoting direct competition among United States international airlines, and urges more vigorous government action in promoting U.S. aviation interests abroad particularly in negotiations under bilateral air transport agreements.[71] The study recommends that the president commission a "comprehensive study of our international aviation relations," which should use the Project Horizon study as its frame of reference.[72]

Following the recommendations of Project Horizon, President Kennedy appointed a commission to study international air transport policy in September 1961. This committee was referred to as the "Steering Committee" and was comprised of the heads of agencies having to do with air transportation, assisted by two outside consultants. The committee's report was issued by President Kennedy on April 23, 1963, under the title "Statement of International Air Transport Policy."[73]

The statement opens with a description of the goals and concerns underlying United States air policy. This begins with the optimistic statement that the future of the air transport industry "is as limitless as its past is brief." After reciting from the Federal Aviation Act the mandate to develop "an air transportation system properly adapted to the present and future needs of the foreign and domestic commerce in [sic] the United States, of the Postal Service and of the National Defense,"[74] the statement specifies that American policy must promote the welfare of United States air carriers, must be mindful of U.S. strategic and political interests, and must develop for the users a sound, efficient system of air transport. It provides further that the air transport system must be as free from restrictions as possible, must remain in the hands of private enterprise and must encourage competition.

The statement lists as changes that must be taken into account the "technological revolution" exemplified by the introduction of jet aircraft, and the development of competitive airlines by major foreign countries returning to the air transport marketplace after the devastation of World War II as well as by newly emergent countries, with resultant excessive capacity, and a decline in the United States' share of world air transport activities. It also mentions as a matter of concern decreased earnings for a number of United States international carriers, referring particularly to the adverse effect on the United States' balance of payments.

This preamble suggests a conservative and pragmatic policy to follow, and such was the case. A summary of the policy follows:

Item 1, the *Basic Framework,* calls for staying with the existing type of bilateral agreements, rejecting "freedom of the skies" as impractical, and rejecting as foreign to United States trade policies and harmful to U.S. carriers and passengers any restrictive agreements dividing markets or allocating shares of traffic. This paragraph is interesting in that it forthrightly rejects a multilateral approach to the exchange of air transport rights and the concept of "freedom of the skies." This is consistent with what the United States actually did throughout this period, but in most similar pronouncements, the United States felt called upon to make approving remarks about multilateral agreements and freedom of the skies.

Item 2, *Air Routes and Services,* says that the existing route network was rather fully developed and gives two rules that should govern the United States in negotiations for the exchange of routes: route exchanges should only be sought where they contribute significantly to the development or improvement of a service network, and the United States should seek to assure U.S. carriers the opportunity to gain as much benefit in the overall exchange as the foreign country's carriers. This paragraph in effect calls on the United States to be sparing in the granting of new routes, and continues the policy in favor of "an equitable exchange of economic benefits."

Item 3, *Capacity Principles,* says that the United States supports the Bermuda capacity principles and will resist efforts to distort the principles in the direction of arbitrary capacity restrictions, or in abusive provision of excessive capacity. The paragraph then says:

> If despite our best efforts we were to be confronted with abuses of the capacity principles, recourse will be had to the procedures available under our bilateral agreements. These include consultation, arbitration, and in the last analysis, denunciation and renegotiation of such agreements.

The quoted paragraph does not appear to be an accurate statement of United States air policy at that time or at any other time during the ascendancy of the Bermuda-type agreement. Of the procedures mentioned, the United States, so far as I am aware, availed itself only of consultation for the resolution of capacity problems. Arbitration was not a logical solution to such problems. The Bermuda capacity provisions assume a negotiated solution, which would be negated for both sides in the decision of an arbitrator; the United States was unwilling to risk the decision of an arbitrator concerning the meaning of the rather ambiguous language of the Bermuda capacity provisions, both as to the matter involved in a particular case and because of the danger of a precedent that might make unacceptable the entire body of Bermuda-type agreements it had already signed.

Denunciation would not improve the bargaining position of the United States with respect to an adversary who was restricting the operations of American airlines. With the agreement in existence, the United States can invoke the protection of its clauses for whatever value they may have. If the agreement is denounced, the opposite party can exercise its sovereignty to restrict U.S. airlines in any way it pleases.

It would be better for the United States to leave the bilateral agreement in effect, and to take such action as might be called for in the form of retaliation, or extraneous political and economic pressure, so as to obtain agreement on a satisfactory interpretation and application of the bilateral agreement itself.

Item 4, *Air Carrier Pooling,* provides that United States airlines will be permitted to participate in pools "only where the national interest so requires." The evident intention of this item is to send a signal that the United States government frowned on pooling, without entirely foreclosing the possibility of participation by an American airline in a pool where special circumstances warrant it. An example of such a case might be one where the United States had compelling political reasons to desire American airline service to a country that would only permit it if the U.S. airline would participate in a pool with its national carrier. The United States has got around the problem of having a certain flexibility without actually allowing pools by permitting on a case-by-case basis what it calls "blocked space agreements," which are agreements whereby one airline leases a block of seats on a scheduled flight to another airline which sells them as its own.

Item 5, *Rates,* says that the United States will continue to allow its airlines to belong to IATA, but that it will press IATA to adopt rates it considers reasonable and will augment these efforts by direct government-to-government discussions. This item also seeks authority to control international rates to and from the United States, subject to approval by the president.

Precisely at the time this statement of international air policy was being prepared and disseminated, the United States had a traumatic experience with pressing IATA to reduce its fares and with augmenting its efforts through direct government-to-government meetings. The Civil Aeronautics Board, after unsuccessful meetings with all of the European governments whose airlines were members of IATA with respect to increased North Atlantic fares which had been agreed by the airlines at a meeting of IATA in Chandler, Arizona, was forced in May of 1963 to back down after having disapproved the Chandler fares, and having told the American airlines to continue to charge the current lower fares, despite an order by the British government that they apply the Chandler fares. The British accomplished this by threatening to seize the U.S. carriers' aircraft.[75]

It is not hard to see that this controversy was behind Item 5, nor is it hard to see why the idea of government-to-government discussions of IATA rates was not pursued for a long time thereafter by the United States.

Item 6, *Competition Among U.S. Carriers,* says that the United States will continue to provide international service by more than one carrier. It states that

> we should continue to aim for a U.S. carrier system in which one U.S. carrier has access to world markets on a scale comparable to that of the flag carriers or combination of carriers of other major civil aviation powers, and other U.S. carriers continue to be authorized to serve one or more areas of the world in over all competition with this carrier.

The statement then points out that foreign airline competition has increased worldwide and hints at an intention to limit direct point-to-point competition between United States international airlines to cases of high-density routes, and routes where operating factors so require, such as logical terminal points on long-haul routes. The item ends with a statement that the principles governing the nature and extent of competition among American carriers will continue to require considerable study and evaluation in the light of changing factors.

Item 7, *Development of Air Cargo,* says that the United States would seek lower rates and flexible cargo routes that would stimulate the air freight industry and benefit the public. The need for routing flexibility is much greater for cargo than it is for passenger traffic, because cargo does not care how circuitous the routing is, so long as it arrives on time, whereas passengers are seriously inconvenienced by circuitous routings, back hauls and lengthy waits for connections between flights.

Item 8, *Supporting Facilities,* says that the United States will cooperate in the development of international air traffic control and navigation systems. The preferred means of financing them is for each nation to absorb its own costs, but where certain countries cannot pay the cost, the United States will consider joint multilateral financing. The United States will develop an equitable system of user charges for these services to apply to all international services, and in the meantime it will refrain from making such charges and will oppose unfair or excessive charges by other nations.

User charges have become in the years since 1963 a most heated topic in the relations between the United States and a number of other nations.

Item 9, *Aviation Assistance to Less Developed Countries,* says that in supplying aviation aid to less developed countries, the United States should focus on internal and regional programs. Presumably the idea behind this was that such programs would have an immediate impact on the economic development of such countries, while at the same time diverting them from competition on the main international trunk routes, where they would contribute to the further decline of the United States' share of world air transport activities.

The report concludes with a statement of American aims, which boils down to a declaration that the United States seeks a sound international system of air transportation and that it wants U.S. airlines to participate substantially in such a system.

With the passage of the Department of Transportation Act on October 15, 1966,[76] during the Johnson administration, a new cabinet department was created "to assure the coordinated, effective administration of the transportation programs of the Federal Government."[77] The Federal Aviation Agency was reassigned from the Civil Aeronautics Board to the new Department of Transportation.[78] The Secretary of Transportation was charged with leadership in transportation matters and in the development of national transportation policies and programs.[79] Numerous other transportation functions were also assigned to the new department. As a result of this legislation a new player was introduced into the air policy game.

Although the Secretary of Transportation is required by the Department of Transportation Act to be governed by the policy standards set forth in the Federal Aviation Act of 1958, as amended,[80] it is not without significance that the declaration of purpose of the Department of Transportation Act declares that

> the general welfare, the economic growth and stability of the Nation and its security require the development of national transportation policies and programs conducive to the provision of fast, safe, efficient, and convenient transportation at the lowest cost consistent therewith and with other national objectives, including the efficient utilization and conservation of the Nation's resources.[81]

The Declaration of Policy of the Federal Aviation Act of 1938 calls for reasonable charges (subsection c) and a qualified sort of competition (subsection d), but it does not call for low rates as such. This change may be seen as a harbinger of the developing thrust of the United States to press for low rates in both domestic and international air transportation.

The Nixon Policy

No formal presidential statement of United States air policy was subsequently issued until 1970, when President Richard M. Nixon issued a press release transmitting his "Statement of International Air Policy."[82]

The study that led to the statement was conducted under the leadership of the Department of Transportation. The committee that performed the study was composed of representatives of the departments of State, Justice, Commerce, Treasury and Defense as well as the Bureau of the Budget, the Civil Aeronautics Board and the Council of Economic Advisors.

The leadership of the Department of Transportation calls attention to the contest between the departments of State and Transportation for primacy in dealing with international air transportation matters. The Civil Aeronautics Board was not even a good third.

The preamble to the statement shows a certain ambivalence about the need to promote competition in international air transport. It says that the growth that accompanied the advent of jet aircraft had made further competition feasible, citing the development of the United States supplemental carriers and the existence of two American round-the-world airlines.[83] On the other hand, it observes that some people had noted the prospect of excessive capacity as a result of the introduction of wide-bodied and supersonic aircraft.

The statement of fundamental interests says that the United States' objective is specifically to promote an expanding system that gives passengers and shippers improved service and reduced fares, while assuring U.S. carriers a fair and equal opportunity to compete in world aviation.

After saying that hijacking must be stopped, the statement lists as "other objectives or principles": (1) United States strategic and political interests, (2) balance of payments, (3) legitimate interests of other countries, (4) retention of the traditional U.S. belief that economic and technical benefits can best be obtained through competition and by a relative freedom from governmental restrictions, and (5) concern for the quality of the environment.

The ambivalence between the prospects of growth in aviation and the perception that excessive capacity may result from the new types of equipment being introduced is new in the Nixon statement. The stress on the benefits of competition and low fares is greater in the Nixon statement than in previous statements. The reference to "a relative freedom from governmental restrictions" is prophetic of the move toward "deregulation" yet to come. The concern for the quality of the environment is a reflection of the general concern for the environment that became evident in the 1960s, and comes from the Department of Transportation Act.

Section I of the policy, "The Exchange of Air Transport Rights," advocates the continuation of the Bermuda-type air transport agreement for the exchange of air transport rights, but it returns to advocating a study of the feasibility of a multilateral agreement. It says that the rights exchanged under a bilateral agreement should meet the public needs and "assure U.S. Carriers the opportunity to achieve benefits no less than those available to the foreign carriers," but cautions against paying an excessive price for routes for which there is little immediate need. It goes on to recommend caution in granting rights on routes with limited potential, so as to avoid excessive capacity. The section concludes with the statement that the United States should "take appropriate measures" against the carriers of foreign countries that restrict American carrier operations in violation of the terms of bilateral agreements or of the principle of reciprocity.

This section reflects the same ambivalence evident in the preamble; the United States is to continue the Bermuda-type agreement and it is to seek for itself airline routes at least equal in value to those granted foreign airlines, but it is to avoid paying "an excessive price" for routes for which there is little immediate need and be cautious in granting routes with limited potential, to avoid excessive capacity. At the same time, it is to study the feasibility of a multilateral agreement, which appears to reach back to the "open skies" doctrine which the United States advocated in the discussions of the multilateral agreement.

The final reference to retaliatory measures reflects the then new Part 213 of the Civil Aeronautics Board's economic regulations. This regulation, which gave the CAB the power to retaliate for restrictive action by foreign governments, had been under consideration since 1961, but it was not until 1970 that action was taken on it.[84]

Part 213 was the brainchild of Joseph C. Watson, a veteran member of the CAB staff. Watson had observed that in a number of countries, particularly in South America, the local governments had simply ignored the *ex post facto* aspect of the Bermuda-type agreements and had unilaterally imposed restrictions on United States airlines. The only means available at that time for the United States to retaliate was to open a proceeding to amend the foreign air carrier permit of the airline of the country in question to impose counter-restrictions. To do that required a full evidentiary hearing,[85] which was not only time-consuming but would inevitably involve presentation of evidence and debate that would tend to inflame the issue. For those reasons, the United States had always been reluctant to respond in kind to unilaterally imposed restrictions on U.S. airlines. Watson felt that if machinery could be established to enable the United States to retaliate against such restrictions in the same unilateral and summary manner in which they were imposed, the exposure of American airlines to this type of harassment could be expected to lessen. It took him several years to engender sufficient enthusiasm at the Civil Aeronautics Board to warrant the opening of a proceeding to establish such legal machinery.

Finally, in January of 1961, the Civil Aeronautics Board issued an order opening the *Foreign Air Carrier Permit Terms Investigation.*[86] The idea was to issue a new Part 213 to the CAB's "Economic Regulations," amending the foreign air carrier permits of all foreign airlines serving the United States to make them subject to the CAB's power to require the filing of foreign air carrier schedules and to disapprove them with or without hearing. Although the Department of State did not become a formal party to this proceeding, it was evident at the time that it opposed the idea of issuing such a regulation. The basis of the Department's opposition was that such a regulation would be contrary to the spirit of the Bermuda-type agreements, which call for consultation rather than unilateral restrictions, and that if the United States should adopt such a regulation itself, it would weaken its ability to insist that others were precluded by Bermuda-type agreements from imposing unilateral restrictions on U.S. airlines.

Numerous foreign airlines filed formal opposition to the proposal. The CAB examiner (now known as an administrative law judge) who heard the case issued a decision recommending against adoption of the proposed regulation on the grounds that it "signaled a change in the United States historic Aviation Policy from one of bilateral negotiations to one of unilateral restrictions."[87] Thereafter the proceeding lay dormant, presumably because the CAB did not want to dismiss it, but at the same time had doubts about the regulation itself, as well as the possibility of obtaining the necessary presidential approval for its issuance.[88]

After a series of problems with restrictions imposed unilaterally by foreign governments and in response to the more hospitable atmosphere in the Nixon Administration, the proceeding was revived and in June 1970 the

CAB issued a new Part 213 of its economic regulations, which was duly approved by President Nixon.[89]

Part 213 provides that the foreign air carrier permits of all foreign carriers serving the United States shall be amended to make them subject to its terms. It empowers the CAB to require foreign air carriers to report traffic data to it and provides further: (a) That in the absence of provisions to the contrary in the permit and of Board action pursuant to Part 213, the foreign carrier may determine its own schedules; (b) that in the case of foreign air carriers whose governments do not have a bilateral agreement with the United States, the Board may require them with or without hearing to file their existing and proposed schedules with it; and (c) that in the case of foreign air carriers whose governments have a bilateral air transport agreement with the United States the Board may similarly require them to file their schedules, with or without hearing, if it finds that the government or aeronautical authorities of the permit holder, over the objections of the United States government, have taken action which impairs, limits or denies operating rights, or (by an amendment dated 1974)[90] otherwise denied or failed to prevent the denial of, in whole or in part, the fair and equal opportunity to exercise operating rights, provided for in such air transport agreement for a United States carrier designated under it to operate to such country.

Part 213 also provides that subject to the approval of the president of the United States, the Board may thereafter notify the carrier that operations under any proposed or existing schedule, or any part of them, may be contrary to applicable law, or may adversely affect the public interest, in which case service under the proposed schedule may not be operated or service under the existing schedule must be terminated.[91]

Part 213 really only gave the CAB a power which virtually all other aeronautical authorities have had from the start, yet it took nine years to bring it into being. The regulation has been attacked on a number of occasions as being inconsistent with the generally liberal approach to air transport regulations of the United States, and with the Bermuda Agreement scheme in particular.[92] Nevertheless, for the reasons stated by the CAB, it seems desirable that the United States aviation authorities should have this power, even though it may be used rarely.

Section 2 of the Nixon Statement on International Air Policy is entitled "Charter Operations and the Role of Supplemental Carriers in Relation to Scheduled Services." The section provides that scheduled and supplemental carriers should have a fair and equal opportunity to compete for the bulk transportation market, giving a narrow edge of primacy to scheduled service by providing that if substantial impairment to scheduled service appears likely, steps should be taken to prevent it "where necessary to avoid prejudice to the public interest." A similar provision covers the relation of charter service by both scheduled and supplemental carriers to the primary service performed by each class of carriers.

The section concludes with a paragraph advocating that separate bilateral air transport agreements be negotiated for charter and scheduled service and that there be no trade-offs between charter service rights and scheduled service rights.

This section was obviously the reconciliation of hard lobbying efforts by both the supplemental carriers and the scheduled carriers. One can note that the supplemental carriers have greatly improved their situation relative to the scheduled carriers over what it was under the Kennedy Policy, in which the supplemental carriers were not even mentioned.

Section 3 is captioned "Rates, Fares and the Role of the International Air Transport Association (IATA)." The section advocates retaining IATA for scheduled service, but encourages "developmental pricing." It provides that charter pricing for both IATA and non-IATA carriers be on a "free and competitive basis." Finally, the section recommends that the Civil Aeronautics Board be given authority to regulate international rates, subject to review by the executive department. This authority was in fact granted by Congress in 1972, by amendment to the Federal Aviation Act.[93]

Section 4 is captioned "Competition Between U.S. Carriers and Foreign Carriers." In this section, the policy statement favors competition, and again rejects the "chosen instrument," providing that the United States should maintain a flexible policy on certifying American airlines to compete with one another abroad, balancing the need for improved service against the commercial prospects of such service, including foreign competition and the likely effect of wide-bodied and supersonic aircraft.

The policy continues to oppose pools, while accepting blocked space agreements.

This section continues with a paragraph saying that unfair competition by foreign carriers must be controlled, referring specifically to "air services by foreign air carriers from points behind their home countries." This was a reference to the carriage of excessive "sixth freedom" traffic by a number of European airlines, notably the Dutch airline KLM, which became a heated subject of controversy with the United States, and was very probably the motivating force behind the 1974 amendment to Part 213.

The statement concludes with paragraphs referring to carrier liability (Rome and Warsaw conventions); insurance (should be required for foreign airlines serving the United States); facilitation (calls for United States support); user charges, fees and taxes (United States should seek equitable recovery of federal aviation facility expenditures from special beneficiaries), and balance of payments (effects of air transport on Balance of Payment Accounts should be watched).

The Ford Policy

The International Air Transport Policy issued by President Gerald R. Ford on September 8, 1976,[94] was the last presidential policy that presented the Bermuda-type agreement as the model of United States bilateral air transport agreements. This was also the most detailed policy statement to have been issued by a U.S. president. It is interesting because it expresses detailed views on a relatively large number of problems and because it tends to foreshadow the movement toward deregulation that was to follow. By 1978, the Ford statement had been superseded by President Jimmy Carter's "deregulation" policy. Nevertheless, the Ford statement merits attention.

The policy statement was prepared by an "interagency task force," cochaired by the Department of State and the Department of Transportation. The Civil Aeronautics Board was not even represented, which can probably be regarded as a victory for the Department of Transportation in its efforts to supplant the CAB as the lead agency dealing with commercial aviation.

A preamble or "overview" to the statement supports the use of private, as opposed to state-owned, airlines and says

> we will work to reform and modernize the international aviation structure in order to enable well-managed U.S. carriers to serve the public interest by providing economic air travel, to compete successfully with foreign air carriers and to earn a reasonable rate of return on investment.

It goes on to say that the policy must be consistent with United States objectives in national defense, foreign policy and international commerce.

Although the goals of the Ford policy are far from advocating deregulation of air transportation, this overview betrays the same naive faith in the ability of the United States to remake the world that has been apparent in the movement toward deregulation. To "reform and modernize the international aviation structure" is no small order, particularly when the rest of the nations involved are unlikely to come even close to sharing the goal of enabling U.S. airlines "to compete successfully with foreign air carriers and to earn a reasonable return on investment."

Under the heading "The Structure of International Air Service," the statement recognizes that the international environment differs from the domestic environment for conducting a commercial air policy. The following aspects are cited in particular:

Foreign airlines tend to be state-owned companies, and many governments tend to protect their airlines by imposing restraints against efficient practices by their competitors.

Foreign airlines are often supported by governmental subsidies, and they tend to engage in below-cost pricing for political reasons.

It is difficult to tailor the supply of international capacity to the demand, because of a multiplicity of airlines, the thinness of the traffic on many international routes, and the use of large aircraft for long-haul international services.

As "Principal Objectives," the statement lists the following:

1. To rely on competitive market forces;
2. To provide transportation where needed;
3. To support private United States airlines;
4. To act consistently with and to support U.S. national objectives in defense and security, foreign policy and international commerce; and
5. To encourage a safe efficient system of airports and airways and to protect the American environment.

Under the heading "Public Service Considerations," the statement lists the following goals:

> 1. Regularly scheduled international air transportation of people, mail and goods at as low a cost as is economically justified.
> 2. International air charter transportation of people and goods by charter specialists and scheduled carriers operating charter flights at as low a cost as is economically justified, recognizing that essential levels of scheduled service must be maintained.
> 3. Effective competition among carriers and among the classes of service offered, including a fair and equal competitive opportunity for the private enterprise air carriers of the United States.

It appears significant that the first of the "principal objectives" is to rely on competitive market forces, and that competition is listed among the goals without the qualification "to the extent necessary to assure the sound development of an air transportation system properly adapted to the needs of the foreign and domestic commerce of the United States, of the Postal Service, and of the national defense," which appears in the Federal Aviation Act of 1958.[95] Reliance on the market and competition, rather than governmental directives, to regulate the provision of air transport services became the rallying-cry of the proponents of "deregulation" who came into the ascendency after President Ford was succeeded by President Carter in 1976.

The careful balancing of the benefits accorded to "charter specialists" (i.e., non-scheduled or supplemental airlines) on the one hand and to scheduled airlines on the other, which appears in the goals noted above and in later sections of the statement, confirms the growing political strength of the "charter specialist" airlines, which have in this statement managed to shed the patronizing term "supplemental" and to come nearer to parity of treatment with the scheduled carriers, which were able to retain only a statement requiring recognition "that essential levels of scheduled service must be retained." This can be compared with the Nixon statement, which provided that if substantial impairment to scheduled service should appear likely, steps should be taken to prevent it where necessary to avoid prejudice to the public interest.

The Ford policy, under the heading "Policy; U.S. Flag International Route System," provides that

> Air transport interests are best assured for Americans by the presence of a strong, viable, privately owned U.S. flag international air fleet. Such a fleet is also an important asset to meet military requirements and non-military emergency situations.

This statement is worth noting particularly because of the contrast it provides to the views on the same subject that emerged in writings by the proponents of deregulation only a few years later. The statement assumes that it is a good thing to protect United States air transport interests and that it is important that they be assured for Americans by government action. It accepts the value to the government of a strong American-flag international air fleet as a military asset and as a means of dealing with non-military emergencies. This conclusion provides an incentive for government support for American airlines.

Under the heading "Extent of Route System" the policy statement says that the international routes of United States carriers should be as extensive as can be economically sustained, and that the impact of a particular route on the overall route system should be taken into consideration. If a particular route that is required for national interest reasons cannot be operated on a self-sustaining basis, it should be supported by the payment of a direct subsidy, rather than relying on cross-subsidization from other profitable routes. This difference from the Eisenhower statement, which encouraged cross-subsidization, is probably the result of the fact that at the time of the Eisenhower statement, the United States actually was paying subsidies and hence had a reason to seek to minimize them, whereas at the time of the Ford policy, no subsidies were being paid to American international airlines, so it cost nothing to be theoretically correct.

The statement echoes the Nixon statement in providing that

> it does not serve the interest of the United States to be put in a position where foreign governments can seek valuable rights for their carriers as a consequence of our granting uneconomic routes for our carriers.

The statement continues to support the idea of an equitable exchange of economic benefits in route exchanges, and provides further that this principle should govern both charter and scheduled bilateral agreements. The reference to charter bilateral agreements in this context is a new element and reflects the growing political strength of the charter carriers.

The statement calls for emphasis on negotiating major trunk routes that follow natural traffic flows, and observes that United States carriers should emphasize third and fourth freedom service, even while recognizing that fifth freedom traffic is important for economic reasons. It also calls for a greater integration of international and domestic route systems, specifically mentioning the opening up of internal U.S. gateway points for international service and calling for the operation of services to Canada, Mexico and the Caribbean as extensions of the domestic route systems of U.S. carriers. As part of the integration effort, the statement calls for the grant of authority to United States carriers to carry traffic on domestic segments of international routes and the use of blocked space and equipment interchange agreements among American airlines to achieve the same result.

It provides further that all American international airlines should have domestic systems to feed their international operations. With respect to opening up inland cities of the United States as international gateways, the statement suggests that different U.S. airlines might be used to provide service to different foreign destinations from single U.S. gateway cities, and also issues a note of caution that, in considering opening new American cities to international service, attention be paid to the need to gather traffic at a relatively limited number of gateway cities in order to achieve economic load factors on international routes, particularly with wide-bodied equipment.

Under the heading "Competition," the statement says in effect that competition is good, but it should not be overdone. It calls for recognition that on international routes there exists not only competition among United States carriers but between U.S. carriers and foreign carriers, and between foreign areas (i.e., foreign countries compete with one another as travel destinations). It says the United States should authorize more than one American flag airline in scheduled international markets only if they can operate profitably, taking into consideration the presence of competition from foreign scheduled airlines and from domestic and foreign charter airlines.

Under the heading "Relative Roles of Scheduled and Charter Passenger Operations," the statement calls generally for retention of the basic structures of the Nixon statement, observing that charters are for price-sensitive passengers and that for time-sensitive passengers the government has the responsibility to assure that essential levels of regularly scheduled service can be economically maintained. It observes further that the United States will use all appropriate means to prevent restrictions by foreign governments on the competitiveness of passenger charter operations by American carriers.

Under the subheading "Charter Services," the statement calls for regulations to promote more charter services, and gives details of the regulations desired. It also calls for application of the "country of origin" concept.[96]

Under the heading "Authority for Charter Services," the statement calls for the United States to grant charter authority on an area basis to scheduled carriers, abandoning the concept of "on route" and "off-route" charters as being no longer meaningful.[97]

The statement goes on to recommend that the supplemental carriers be made eligible to hold certificates of convenience and necessity for scheduled service and that a number of such certificates be issued, another indication of the rise in the political fortunes of supplementals.

With respect to cargo services, the statement calls for integration of the ground and air transport segments of carriage, and for the issuance of freighter-only certificates of convenience and necessity, separate from the passenger/cargo certificates normally issued for combination service. It provides that cargo-only authority be negotiated as part of existing bilateral agreements, rather than being negotiated separately. It provides further that split charters should be permitted for the carriage of passenger charter traffic and cargo charter traffic on the same aircraft.

Under the heading "Viability of the U.S. International Air Transport System," the statement recognizes as a national goal the maintenance of a "strong viable system of international routes." It calls for approval by the CAB of agreements between carriers limiting the capacity on international routes where the following standards are met:

> The public interest is served by assuring adequate service on the route by a U.S. Carrier.... Unilateral reductions or other less anticompetitive alternatives are shown by clear and convincing evidence of past practice to be unfeasible, and, undertaken in the current context, would put the carrier making them at a significant competitive disadvantage with respect to other carriers on that route.

On the subject of "Market Share," the statement calls for the retention of the Bermuda system of *ex post facto* review, while accepting that special procedures to deal with capacity disputes may be necessary in some instances, and recommending that

> when other countries advocate less flexibility in capacity competition, we may insist as a *quid pro quo* on greater flexibility in pricing competition, so long as forecast load factors are well below full utilization load factors.

The statement again recommends that the United States seek bilateral review of cases where foreign airlines carry excessive sixth freedom traffic to and from the United States.

Under the heading "Cooperative Agreements," the statement opposes pools between United States and foreign airlines, but approves flexibility on interline agreements, equipment interchanges and blocked space agreements. With respect to pools it says

> Pooling proposals should be disapproved unless there is clear and convincing evidence that the pool would achieve significant U.S. policy objectives and more competitive alternatives are not available.

The actual use of capacity agreements between U.S. and foreign carriers had commenced during the Nixon Administration, and continued into the Ford Administration.

Capacity agreements, blocked space agreements, pooling agreements and other basically anticompetitive agreements among carriers have always posed a problem for the United States, mainly because they are *prima facie* contrary to the whole concept of the U.S. antitrust laws.[98] The United States has never authorized a full-fledged pool between an American airline and a foreign airline, nor between two American airlines.[99] Viewed simply as a business device to maximize profits, it appears likely that agreements to limit capacity and share revenues would be so anticompetitive that United States carriers could never be allowed to participate in them.

It has been argued, however, that a pool between an American carrier and such an airline as the Russian Aeroflot would solve many of the problems that have beset U.S. airlines attempting to serve totalitarian countries with non-market economies. One of the main problems in trying to compete with Aeroflot is that it has used its position as the government carrier to force the lion's share of the traffic onto its own service. If the revenues from Aeroflot's service and those of its U.S. competitor were pooled, and then divided equitably between the two airlines, it would not matter on which airline the passengers actually travelled. Other United States airlines have opposed allowing pools for this purpose, because the lesson to other countries would be that if you want a pool with American airlines, all you have to do is to make their lives so miserable that entering a pool would appear to "achieve significant United States policy objectives." Recently, however, the United States did permit Pan American to enter an arrangement with the Russians to mitigate the effect of Aeroflot's competitive practices that has many features of a revenue pool, although it is not so labelled.[100]

Blocked space agreements are not unusual[101], and have provided a way of reaching an accommodation with countries that would otherwise refuse to allow entry by United States airlines unless they would agree to a pool.

Equipment interchanges between United States and foreign airlines are rather rare. The only case where such an interchange has been approved involved an agreement whereby Braniff Airways undertook to fly the supersonic Concorde aircraft from Washington, D.C., to Dallas as an extension of the service provided by Air France from Paris to Washington and by British Airways from London to Washington.[102] This service was eventually terminated because it was unprofitable. The arrangement was based primarily on the popular appeal of the Concorde and it ended because of the high cost of operating that aircraft.

Agreements among airlines limiting capacity had their original development in the United States as a domestic phenomenon. Like pooling agreements, they require approval by the CAB of the carrier meetings in which they are negotiated, and of the resulting agreement, in order for he parties to obtain exemption from the application of the United States antitrust laws.[103] The earliest of such agreements involved attempts to alleviate traffic congestion at Chicago, New York, Los Angeles and Washington, D.C. Although certain foreign airlines were involved in the agreements, they were essentially a domestic matter. The system employed under the agreements that were reached was that the Federal Aviation Agency set quotas of hourly aircraft movements at JFK, La Guardia and Kennedy airports in New York, at O'Hare International Airport in Chicago and at the Washington National Airport and that scheduling committees comprised of all of the airlines serving these airports allocated these quotas among the airlines serving them. The agreements were approved by the CAB, December 3, 1968.[104] A similar system was used nationwide to reduce schedules during a strike of air traffic controllers;[105] to transfer flights from Chicago's O'Hare to Midway Airport;[106] and to reduce congestion in United States Customs at the International Arrivals Building at JFK Airport at New York.[107]

In a more or less parallel action, capacity agreements were used to reduce carrier competition and to increase load factors on certain domestic sectors: in 1970 on intra-Hawaii flights;[108] in 1971 on transcontinental American sectors (New York/Newark–Los Angeles, New York/Newark–San Francisco, Chicago–San Francisco, Washington/Baltimore–Los Angeles)[109] and in 1972, on New York/Newark–San Juan, Puerto Rico, flights.[110]

Internationally, a series of capacity agreements between United States and foreign airlines was approved by the Civil Aeronautics Board between February 1974 and July 1975. The primary justification assigned for the approval of these agreements was to conserve fuel during the world fuel crisis, which arose out of the Arab oil embargo. Nevertheless, it seems clear that both the carriers and the regulators were strongly aware of the importance of the agreements as a means of reducing competition and improving airline load factors.[111]

The first of these agreements was between British Airways and the U.S. airlines Pan American and TWA. Later agreements with the British also involved National Airlines and British Caledonian Airways.[112]

Other similar agreements were between United States and Italian airlines,[113] Greek airlines,[114] Venezuelan,[115] Swiss[116] and Australian airlines.[117] All of these agreements were linked with intergovernmental negotiations with each country concerned.

Also part of the same tendency to support restrictive agreements among airlines which can be seen under the Nixon policy is the *Pan American World Airways, Inc.-Trans World Airways, Inc., Route Agreement,*[118] which approved a route swap whereby United States airline presence in Paris, Frankfurt, and a number of Pacific points was reduced from two airlines to one.

The policies that led to the approval of these agreements arose out of economic conditions which were causing distress among airlines throughout the world amidst complaints of excessive capacity. Also out of those conditions grew an increasing dissatisfaction with the Bermuda-type agreements within the United States. Those who favored restriction applauded the shift to airline capacity agreements; those who favored a free market approach called for an abandonment of the Bermuda-type agreement in favor of something less restrictive.[119]

Under the heading "Fares and Rates," the Ford statement calls for a continuation of the system of government oversight of passenger fares and cargo rates. It accepts the continued use of IATA, but calls for extensive revisions in its structure and gives detailed views as to how the rates for passengers, cargo and charters should be revised. It also calls for commission rates to travel agents to be determined individually by each carrier, rather than being set by agreement among the carriers belonging to IATA, subject to governmental control, as was currently the practice.

Under the heading "Government Procurement," the statement calls for greater use of American commercial airlines by the United States military and reduced competition by the military air transport command. It also calls for use of United States airlines for transportation financed by the U.S. government, as is called for in the Fair Competitive Practices Act of 1974.[120] The statement recommends that United States airlines continue to participate in the Civil Reserve Air Fleet (CRAF).[121]

Under the heading "International Competitive Environment," the statement refers to the International Air Transportation Fair Competitive Practices Act of 1974[122] and says the United States will first negotiate and then act unilaterally to oppose unfair, discriminatory or restrictive practices by foreign countries that limit the competitive capability of U.S. airlines and discriminatory or inequitable charges for the use of airways and airport properties.

The International Air Transportation Fair Competitive Practices Act of 1974 to which reference is made was an attempt somewhat analogous to Part 213 of the CAB's economic regulations to deal with discriminatory and unfair competitive practices and excessive or discriminatory user charges imposed on United States airlines by foreign governments. Examples of unfair competitive practices imposed by a government are such things as an order by the Korean government to Korean travel agents not to sell tickets via Braniff Airways on a service that competed with the Korean airline;[123] an attempt by the German government, which was in some degree imitated by the British and French governments, to establish a monopoly for the national airline in the provision of computerized reservations services; and a refusal by various governments to allow remittance of funds collected in payment of transportation at a rate of exchange reasonably related to the rate of exchange at which sales are made.[124]

Obviously no exhaustive list of such practices could be made, because new ones are being thought up all the time. Examples of excessive user charges are easy to recall, but difficult to document, because there is always a difference of opinion between the two governments involved about whether the charges are excessive. The United States has had a number of discussions on this subject with the British but there has not been agreement that the British charges are excessive.[125] Examples of discriminatory user charges are reduced prices for fuel delivered to the national carrier by the national fuel monopoly[126] and reduced landing fees for the national airline.[127] This type of restriction is more likely to be encountered in relatively unsophisticated countries, because it is so simple to remove the discrimination by charging the national airline the full price while paying it an increased subsidy to make up for the added cost.

The International Air Transportation Fair Competitive Practices Act calls on the Department of State, the Department of the Treasury, the Department of Transportation, the Civil Aeronautics Board "and other departments or agencies" to review and strive to eliminate all forms of discrimination and unfair competitive practices against United States airlines found to exist.[128] Upon a finding of excessive or discriminatory user charges, the Secretary of State is to inaugurate negotiations to reduce them and in the event of his inability to do so, the Secretary of Transportation is empowered to order compensating charges against the airline or airlines of the country imposing them.[129]

7. INTERNATIONAL AMERICAN NEGOTIATIONS IN THE BERMUDA ERA

Having reviewed the major statements of international commercial air policy during the Bermuda era, it may be useful to review how the United States dealt with a number of the problems that arose with respect to the regulation of international air transportation.

One of the more interesting items was the somewhat veiled struggle of the British and the Europeans to use IATA, through its control of fares, as a means of restraining what they evidently feared was the unbridled ambition of the United States to overrun the North Atlantic with airline capacity, and the efforts of the United States to counter what it evidently regarded as the unenlightened restrictionism of the European side by manipulating charters and non-scheduled air transport. Non-scheduled and charter carriers fell outside the scope of the bilateral agreements, and hence outside the compromise between the United States and the British, whereby the British agreed to accept the relatively unregulated Bermuda regime for the control of capacity in exchange for the undertaking by the United States to permit its scheduled airlines to participate in IATA.

The United States signed Bermuda-type agreements with very nearly all of the Western European countries, as well as with the United Kingdom.[1] Most of these countries took an even more restrictive view than the British of how air transport should be regulated, with the exception of the Scandivanians, the Dutch and the Belgians, who had a special problem with the Bermuda capacity provisions, related to their dependence on fifth freedom traffic for the prosperity of their airlines.

The tendency of the United States to press for low rates and increased capacity, against the resistance of many of the countries with which it had Bermuda-type agreements, may be seen as a natural consequence of the fact that the Bermuda Agreement itself was a means for the British and the United States to find an accommodation that would enable them to conduct their air transport relations despite a fundamental disagreement over the underlying commercial air policy.

We have seen how United States efforts to force low fares through IATA in 1963 in the Chandler fares dispute were thwarted by the British[2] who refused to allow U.S. airlines to land in the United Kingdom if they should charge the low fares the United States sought to impose. The United States, having been unable to put across its ideas through IATA, seems to have turned to charters and the supplemental airlines as a means of bringing pressure on the scheduled airlines to bring about lower North Atlantic fares. The supplemental airlines were expanding in the United States at the time and were pressing for international operations. They were useful for the purpose of introducing low fare competition because they fell outside the scope of IATA and the bilateral agreements. Although they could have been excluded from transatlantic service by the Europeans, as they were by many South American countries on the basis that there was no obligation to let non-scheduled services in under a bilateral agreement or otherwise, the Europeans seem to have been influenced by their own charter operators and their tourism interests to a degree where they did not find it convenient to exclude the United States supplementals altogether.

By 1963, the operators of non-scheduled service in the United States had increased their domestic flights and were branching out into international service. The non-scheduled carriers were fought every inch of the way by the scheduled carriers. Originally, the non-scheduled carriers (also referred to as "irregular carriers," "contract carriers," "charter carriers" and "supplemental carriers") were viewed with little enthusiasm by the American authorities. For example in the 1948 Truman air policy statement, reference is made to the "lack of consideration for air safety that has been shown by some contract carriers." The Eisenhower air policy statement of 1954 is more favorable to them when it recommends that the irregular carriers be granted certificates of convenience of necessity but such certificates were to be exclusively for charter and contract service,[3] whereas the scheduled carriers could operate both scheduled and charter service. The non-scheduled carriers had been operating in the United Staes under a 1938 exemption order for non-scheduled services and a 1947 amendment thereto requiring letters of registration for "large irregular" carriers (those using transport aircraft). The 1963 Kennedy international air policy statement makes no mention of the non-scheduled carriers, probably because at that time they had not become active internationally.[4]

Under the rather haphazard "regulation" of the original domestic exemption orders, the non-scheduled carriers managed to become extremely active and in fact thwarted the attempts of the Civil Aeronautics Board to prevent them from engaging in scheduled common carriage rather than confining themselves to plane-load charters, as the terms of their authorization required. At the same time, they also gained a measure of public and political support. From 1951 until 1962, the Civil Aeronautics Board, the United States Congress, the federal courts, the irregular carriers and the scheduled carriers were engaged in an almost continuous round-robin of legislative and administrative hearings and litigation to decide the proper role of the irregular carriers.[5]

In July of 1962, the Federal Aviation Act was amended to allow the Civil Aeronautics Board to issue certificates of convenience and necessity for supplemental carriers.[6] Supplemental air transportation was defined as

> charter trips in air transportation, other than the transportation of mail by aircraft, rendered pursuant to a Certificate of Public Convenience and Necessity issued pursuant to Section 401 (d) (3) of this Act to supplement the scheduled service authorized by Certificates of Public Convenience and Necessity issued pursuant to Sections 401 (d) (1) and (2) of this Act.[7]

The amendment did not, however, include a definition of "charter trips," so that the Civil Aeronautics Board had extraordinary latitude in deciding what sort of carriage the supplemental carriers might engage in under the heading of "charter trips."

The Board in 1964 authorized three of the applicants for international supplemental air carrier authority, Capitol, Saturn and Overseas National Airways (ONA), to enter the transatlantic market for five years.[8] At the same time, the CAB authorized those carriers to carry "split charters" in their transatlantic service (i.e., to carry two charter groups on a single aircraft).[9] The CAB's action was affirmed in 1965 in the United States Court of Appeals.[10]

After another series of cases in the Court of Appeals, concerning the CAB's authority to authorize the carriage of all inclusive tours on charters in supplemental air transportation,[11] the Congress in 1968 passed an amendment to the Federal Aviation Act, which authorized such charters for both scheduled and supplemental carriers.[12]

All of this, of course, had an impact on the cost of transatlantic travel. If the scheduled carriers wished to keep their fares high, they would see the passengers go on the services of the supplemental carriers and on their own charter flights, which they were not slow to develop. More significantly, the scheduled carriers competed with the supplemental carriers by introducing low excursion fares through IATA on their scheduled services.

The development of the supplemental carriers owes much to the enterprise and political skill of the men behind them, such as Edward J. Daly of World Airways, Inc., Howard J. Korth of Trans International Airlines (now Trans American Airlines) and Edward J. Driscoll, president of the National Air Carrier Association (NACA), the trade association of the supplemental airlines.

It appears likely, however, that the paramount influence on the development of the supplemental carriers was the fact that they were politically appealing to various segments of American opinion. They represented an outsider up against an established leader. Although by this time they were relatively big businesses, they had their genesis in the efforts of veterans of World War II to establish themselves with war surplus aircraft. Their main appeal to the public was cheap prices. All of these elements exert a great appeal to a populist trend in United States politics. At the same time, the supplementals provided a way of bringing pressure on the scheduled airline industry to remedy whatever causes for dissatisfaction the American political establishment might see in it. These elements contributed first to the growth of the supplemental airlines domestically in the United States, and later to their international growth.

The process by which the Civil Aeronautics Board encouraged the development of low-fare service outside IATA, and IATA responded with low fares of its own, resembled a sort of game. A play-by-play description of this game would serve no useful purpose here. In essence, the Civil Aeronautics Board broadened the definition of charters by progressive stages in its regulations, until by 1978 it had established "public charters," which were virtually indistinguishable from individually ticketed service, except that they had to be sold through a "public charter operator," who could not be a direct air carrier.[13] In a similar progression, the scheduled carriers sought to maintain their own competitive position through a series of cheap excursion and bulk travel fares and through operating their own charters on the North Atlantic.[14] In 1977 the pace of the game was accelerated by the arrival of Frederick Laker's "Sky Train" service between London and New York,[15] and by the decision of the United States to have an all out go at deregulating civil aeronautics.

During the period from the 1963 confrontation over the IATA transatlantic fares with the British until the United States embarked on a course of deregulation, IATA remained as the primary fare-setting mechanism for scheduled travel over the North Atlantic. Although the CAB expressed hostility to IATA on numerous occasions,[16] and brought pressure on the IATA fares through the supplemental carriers, no direct attack on IATA as a fare-making body was launched by the CAB until 1978, when it issued a "show cause order," which would have had the effect of terminating IATA's role in setting airline rates to and from the United States.[17]

During the same period, the efforts of the American authorities to build up the supplemental carriers were not notably successful in themselves, but they can be considered to have been successful in bringing pressure on the scheduled carriers to lower their fares, and presumably to develop the transatlantic market. Whether the United States carriers would have attempted to do so on their own can never be known, but it appears likely that they would not have been allowed to do so by the European governments in the absence of the pressure created by the CAB through the supplemental carriers.

Regional Associations

International air transport politics has manifested itself in the creation of regional civil air organizations. The first of these was the European Civil Aviation Conference, "ECAC". This body was established under the aegis of ICAO, and ICAO provided the secretariat, but it is essentially an independent body, in the sense that it establishes its own agenda and fixes its own times of meeting. Nevertheless ECAC continues to maintain a close liaison with ICAO.[18] The membership of ECAC is limited to European nations, including Great Britain, Ireland and Turkey. The objects of the body are "generally to review the development of intra-European air transport with the object of promoting the coordination, the better utilization, and the orderly development of such air transport"[19] and "to consider any special problem that may arise in this field."[20] The conference functions are consultative and its conclusions and recommendations are subject to the approval of governments.[21] The European conference has met regularly, and has served as a forum for the consideration of numerous intra-European problems,[22] and has also acted as a means of reaching agreements on the operation of charters and on pricing between its members and the civil aeronautics authorities of the United States and Canada. The ECAC has shown some tendency to act as a means for the European aeronautical authorities to unite against the United States.

There have been two Latin American regional associations. The first of these was the Conferencia Regional de Aviación Civil ("CRAC"), which met in 1959 in Rio de Janeiro, in 1960 in Montevideo, and in 1962 in Bogotá.[23] Thereafter CRAC fell into disuse, and was finally replaced by the Conferencia Latino-Americana de Aviación Civil ("CLAC"); in English, this body is known as the Latin American Civil Aviation Conference, "LACAC". The CRAC was a rather informal body to which all of the nations of the Western Hemisphere including the United States were invited to send representatives. The chief delegates were the directors of civil aeronautics, and they acted by majority vote, to reach agreement on recommendations which thereafter became effective upon approval by the respective governments. The most notable achievement of CRAC was to pass a recommendation over the strenuous objection of the United States, that 80 percent of "regional" traffic should be carried by the airlines of the two nations between which it moved. "Regional traffic" was originally not clearly defined. Later it was defined as traffic moving within South America. The CRAC had no connection with ICAO and had no permanent secretariat. It was never convened after the Bogotá Conference in 1962, and it gradually went out of existence until it was superseded by LACAC.[24]

The Latin American Civil Aviation Conference was formed in Mexico in December of 1973. Countries of the Caribbean, Central and South America are eligible for membership. The LACAC, like ECAC, operates under the aegis of ICAO, and ICAO provides a permanent secretariat for it. The Latin American conference does not appear to have been able to achieve a sufficient unification of views to enable it to become a strong force in aviation matters, although it has served as a forum for expressing coordinated views to the United States,[25] and for the discussion of fare policies among the airlines of the entire Western Hemisphere.

In addition to ECAC and LACAC, there is a similar African Organization, AFCAC (African Civil Aviation Conference), which also operates under the aegis of ICAO, with a secretariat provided by ICAO.

Arbitrations and Negotiations

In addition to the relatively unstructured maneuvers that involved IATA and the so-called "nonskeds," there were a large number of formal consultations under individual bilateral air transport agreements between the United States and nations all over the world, as well as a very small number of formal arbitrations pursuant to bilateral air transport agreements with European countries. Since the latter are few in number and involve rather narrow issues, it appears practical to describe them first, and then go on to a sampling of individual consultations with nations from various parts of the world.

Arbitrations

Although the United States has been unwilling to arbitrate the capacity provisions of the Bermuda-type agreements, it has on three occasions arbitrated certain other aspects; twice with the French and once with the Italians, all involving transatlantic transportation.[26]

The first of the two French arbitrations[27] concerned the question whether four weekly flights operated by Pan American via Paris to Rome, Beirut and Teheran (Iran) were justified under a route description that read in part:

> ... to Paris and beyond via intermediate points in Switzerland, Italy, Greece, Egypt, the Near East, India, Burma, and Siam to Hanoi and thence to China and beyond; in both directions.[28]

The question was whether Iran was properly included in the route under the description "Near East." The French authorities had expressed their opinion that Teheran was in the Middle East and not in the Near East, and that it lay too far north to be on a reasonable route between Paris and India, but they had nevertheless allowed Pan American to operate the route between 1955 and 1962, when the French suspended Pan American's traffic rights between Paris and Teheran.

A subsidiary question related to service between Paris and Istanbul and Ankara, Turkey, which the French had permitted only on a blind sector basis, alleging that they would not allow traffic rights between Paris and Turkey, because service to Turkey was not permissible under the heading "Near East" in the route description.

The Istanbul service had been the subject of an exchange of diplomatic notes between France and the United States, pursuant to which France and the United States had exchanged certain operating rights and had agreed that there would be "no interrruption of Pan American World Airways' existing service between Paris and Istanbul."[29]

The arbitral tribunal agreed with the French that neither Teheran nor Istanbul was properly included in "the Near East," but it also said that the conduct of the parties led to the conclusion that the French had authorized the four flights per week between Paris and Teheran with traffic rights outside the bilateral agreement and similarly that by having agreed not to interrupt Pan American's blind sector service between Paris and Turkey, the French had agreed to this operation and could no longer contest it.[30]

The second arbitration with the French took place in 1978.[31] It concerned a service which Pan American sought to operate between the West Coast of the United States and Paris, via London with a blind sector on the London–Paris leg,[32] and a "change of gauge" on the London–Paris leg from a wide-bodied Boeing 747 on the U.S.–London leg to a narrow-bodied Boeing 727 on the London–Paris leg. Concerning changes of gauge, the bilateral air transport agreement between the United States and France contained the following provision.

> *Section VI* (a) For the purpose of the present Section the term "transshipment" [i.e., change of gauge][33] shall mean the transportation by the same carrier of traffic beyond a certain point on a given route by a different aircraft from those employed on the earlier stages of the same route.
>
> (b) Transshipment when justified by economy of operation will be permitted at all points mentioned in the attached Schedules in territory of the two Contracting Parties.
>
> (c) However, no transshipments will be made in the territory of either Contracting Party which would alter the long range characteristics of the operation or which would be inconsistent with the standards set forth in this Agreement and its Annex and particularly Section IV of the Annex.[34]

The French claimed that since the quoted clause referred only to changes of gauge made in the territory of one or the other of the parties, Pan American was precluded from effecting one in London. The United States claimed that no special agreement with France was necessary for a change of gauge made outside of France, but rather, it was exclusively a matter to be dealt with between the United States and the country where the change of gauge was made. The arbitral tribunal decided that the change of gauge in London was authorized by the Franco-American bilateral air transport agreement, so long as the service was continuous, and was not inconsistent with the capacity clauses, thus, in effect, agreeing with the United States. The arbitrator appointed by France dissented on this point.

In the skirmishing that preceded the agreement to arbitrate, the French had (on May 2, 1978) physically prevented Pan American from operating the service with the change of gauge in London. The United States thereupon proposed that the matter be arbitrated on an accelerated basis and that Pan American be allowed to operate the service. When the French failed to reply to this suggestion, the United States (May 8, 1978) filed an order under Part 213 of the CAB's economic regulations ordering Air France and UTA (the other French carrier serving the United States) to file with the CAB their schedules for transportation to and from the United States.[35]

Finally, the French Government agreed to abritrate, but refused to allow Pan American to operate the service proposed by it, whereupon the United States government, through the Civil Aeronautics Board, issued on May 31, 1978, an order under Part 213.3(d) of its economic regulations directing Air France to cancel its services between Paris and Los Angeles,[36] on the grounds that disapproval of Air France's three weekly 747 frequencies "should deprive a French carrier of operating rights roughly equivalent to the rights being denied Pan Am, without escalating or widening the dispute." Before the order could receive presidential approval, as required in Part 213, the Americans and the French had made a deal as part of the compromis of arbitration that the United States would vacate the 213 order and the French would allow a number of flights by Pan American on the disputed sector over the next six months. The CAB rescinded its order[37] and the question of the right of the United States to retaliate was made a part of the arbitration. On this point the arbitral tribunal decided unanimously that the United States did have the right to impose these counter measures, on the grounds that they were proportional to the injury.

The arbitration between the United States and Italy, which took place in 1964,[38] concerned the rather narrow question whether the Bermuda-type air transport agreement between Italy and the United States permitted the operation of all-cargo services. The American-Italian bilateral air transport agreement provided in its granting clauses[39] that the designated carriers will enjoy in the territory of the respective parties:

> rights of transit and of stops for non-traffic purposes, as well as the right of commercial entry and departure for international traffic in passengers, cargo and mail at the points enumerated on each of the routes specified in the Schedules attached.

The Italian contention was that all cargo service was excluded because the quoted language referred to "international traffic in passengers, cargo and mail," which they claimed meant that only combination service was allowed. The arbitration panel held that all-cargo service was permitted under this language, pointing out that although in normal grammatical usage the word "and" does not have the same meaning as the word "or," to read the quoted language with "and" taken in its normal cummulative sense does not imply that cargo-only service may not be operated, but only lists the types of traffic that may be carried. To discover the intention of the parties the tribunal looked to the Bermuda Agreement, on which the U.S.-Italian agreement was based, and concluded that neither it nor the 1948 Italian-American agreement expressly excluded all cargo service and that

> if it had been intended to exclude all-cargo service from this regime, this would certainly have been stated clearly, since this form of air transport was already known and practiced.... At all events, all-cargo services were already known and being operated at the time the Bermuda Agreement and the 1948 Italo-American Agreement were concluded, and this fact is decisive.

There was a dissenting opinion by the arbitrator appointed by Italy.[40]

Negotiations

Although it would be impossible to summarize in a work of this scope all air transport negotiations and other dealings between the United States and other countries that have influenced the developemnt of the international air transport policy of the United States and that illustrate its application in practice, or even to describe a single negotiation in great detail, it appears useful to provide a brief summary of a number of negotiations and other dealings of the United States in various parts of the world during the "Bermuda era" to give a feel for how the United States has dealt with the problems of international air transport in widely varying contexts. Such an exercise also appears useful to illustrate what the United States is up against when it attempts to formulate a coherent policy to cover the multiplicity of commercial aviation problems it must face throughout the world.[41]

Negotiations with European Countries

The three arbitrations referred to on pages 214 to 220 were part of larger disputes between the United States and the French and Italians. The disputes appear to have been related to, if not part of, the maneuver in which the British attempted to use IATA to produce high fares which in turn would restrain the capacity offered by U.S. airlines. In this case, the French and the Italians conducted separate attacks on the right of American airlines to carry fifth freedom traffic beyond the European gateways on their flights. Although these attacks occurred during the same general time frame (1950s and 60s) it is not clear that they were coordinated.

Lowenfeld points out that during this period the European aviation authorities were meeting regularly in the European Civil Aviation Conference,[42] where the French and the Italians had the opportunity for coordination. He observed further that the initial doubts of these countries about the Bermuda compromise were aggravated by the advent of jet propelled aircraft in the late 1950s and early 60s, which led to a temporary excess of capacity and to greatly increased airline costs related to the acquisition of the new equipment.[43] (The same condition obtained in the 1970s with the introduction of wide-bodied equipment.)

It can also be observed that the Europeans probably felt a certain animus against the United States because they had to turn to U.S. manufacturers to obtain jet aircraft, since the British Comet jet had proved unsatisfactory, and also because the American airlines were able to finance and obtain jets earlier than the Europeans were. On the other hand, the United States could feel that it had entered the Bermuda compromise at the cost of giving up its own far more liberal views, and it was unhappy about attempts to reduce the rights of its airlines to operate behind the European gateways and to restrict the capacity offered by U.S. airlines.

Restrictions on beyond rights and capacity at European gateways affect more than the traffic to and from the particular gateway involved. United States airlines serve a global network of routes, including points in Eastern Europe, the Near and Far East. Service to these points requires the support of a multistop service, even where the technical characteristics of the aircraft permit nonstop service, because the traffic between the United States and such points as Istanbul or Delhi is not sufficient to support frequent nonstop service. Thus, when United States airlines lose the support of the European gateway cities on such services, they lose not only the fifth freedom traffic between the gateway city and the beyond point, but they also lose the ability to provide adequate service between the United States and the points beyond the European gateway. Moreover, when the United States airlines are unable to serve this traffic, which for them is third and fourth freedom traffic, the opportunity is opened for the European airline to carry it and for the European airline it is fifth freedom traffic (i.e., "sixth freedom").

The French dispute in 1963 involved a number of elements centered on United States service to the "Near East," which was the subject of the first French arbitration. The French sought to limit Pan American's ability to operate beyond Paris to Teheran, Ankara and Istanbul. As it turned out the tribunal decided in favor of the United States, but in the meanwhile, the French had prevented service by Pan American to those points via Paris. The subsequent French dispute concerning the change of gauge by United States airlines at London in 1978, which was the subject of the second arbitration with the French, also constituted an attempt by the French to limit the ability of a U.S. airline (again Pan American) to operate an efficient service to France. Although the French ultimately lost the arbitration, they managed to keep Pan American from operating the service long enough so that in the end it was never operated.[44] In both cases, it can fairly be said that in a practical sense the French were the winners.

In general, the French appear to have abided by the letter of their Bermuda-type agreement with the United States, but they have been quite frank in saying that they think very little of it as a means for regulating competitive relations between airlines. Where the agreement provides the opportunity to exercise control, they have done so. The French also exercise a measure of domination through their ability to control the travel market by virtue of their control of travel outlets and computer reservation systems, but this aspect has not produced a confrontation under the bilateral agreement. The reason for this is probably that the United States has never felt it was able to produce clear enough proof of what was going on to enable it to make an open accusation.[45]

The arbitration described above between the Americans and the Italians concerning cargo services formed part of a larger dispute between the United States and Italy of which it was only a tangential aspect. The real dispute concerned attempts by the Italians to restrict unilaterally the beyond rights and the capacity of United States airlines in passenger service, and it continued long beyond 1963, when the arbitration took place. Even at the time of the arbitration, the dispute involved a refusal by the Italians to allow United States service beyond Rome to Africa and restrictions imposed on the frequency and capacity of United States airlines between intermediate points and Rome, and from Rome to points beyond.[46] In 1966, the Italians denounced the Bermuda-type agreement with the United States,[47] and it was not until 1970 that a new agreement was signed.[48] The new agreement, which was a Bermuda-type agreement, evidently included an unpublished "screening agreement."[49] After a five-year respite, consultations with the Italians on various capacity and route matters took place regularly in 1975, 1976, 1977, 1978, and 1979.[50]

The issues involved in the disputes with Italy were typical of those that underlay many of the problems the United States had with other European countries, but they emerged in more stark form in the dealings with Italy. The Italians objected to the capacity of United States airlines, both because they claimed it was excessive and unduly affected Italian airlines and as a means of exerting bargaining leverage on the United States to induce it to grant improved routes for Italian airlines. They also sought to impose far-fetched interpretations of the bilateral agreement to prevent United States airlines from competing with Italian airlines for traffic between Italy and points on the routes intermediate to the United States and between Italy and points beyond Italy. Their denunciation of the U.S.-Italian bilateral agreement in 1970 appears to have been based primarily on their belief that it did not give them sufficient *a priori* control over the capacity of United States airlines. The substitute agreement signed in 1975 was not on its face very different from the agreement it replaced with respect to capacity regulation, but the Italians evidently felt that the accompanying route concessions and whatever side agreements went with it were sufficient to make it acceptable.[51]

One of the disputes with Italy concerned traffic statistics. The United States has traditionally reckoned the true origin of the passenger to be the point where transporation commences under his ticket, and the true destination to be the ultimate point where transporation terminates under his ticket. Under this definition, the true origin and destination of the passenger remain unchanged, even though he might make intermediate changes of flight, aircraft or airline, or if he should make a stopover at an intermediate point.

For example, according to the United States' interpretation, the true origin and destination of a passenger whose ticket reads New York–Rome on TWA and Rome–Cairo on TWA or any other airline would be New York and Cairo. On the Rome–Cairo leg, the passenger would be classified for TWA as "primary justification" traffic, nor would this classification change if the passenger made a stopover in Rome of if he travelled New York–Rome on Alitalia, and Rome–Cairo on TWA. This rankled the Italians, who would have classified the TWA passenger as a primary justification passenger on the New York–Rome leg and as a fifth freedom passenger on the Rome–Cairo leg.

Conversely, if the same passenger had travelled New York–Rome and Rome–Cairo on Alitalia, the United States would continue to say that his true origin was New York and his true destination was Cairo, and it would have classified him as a fifth freedom New York–Cairo passenger when applying the Bermuda capacity provisions. The Italians would have called him a New York–Rome passenger insofar as the United States was concerned.

The difference is that the United States insisted upon looking to the ticket to determine origin and destination, whereas the Italians and much of the rest of the world insisted upon looking to the particular flight to determine origin and destinations. The latter system is sometimes referred to as "on flight" origin and destination, or "coupon" origin and destination (referring to the fact that generally each coupon of the ticket covers a single flight segment, operated under a single flight number), or "manifest" origin and destination (referring to the fact that the passenger manifest, where used, usually lists the passengers carried on a single flight by their origin and destination on that flight. This term has lost currency since the abolition by ICAO of the requirement for the passenger manifest as an official document).

The Italian dispute has never really ended. The situation goes through periods of quiescence, but the Italians have never given up on their desire to control the capacity of American airlines and have in fact controlled it to the extent they can under the agreements they have with the United States. The United States, on the other hand, undoubtedly feels that a controlled market is an anomaly in an era of deregulation and open skies.

The dispute about traffic statistics had great practical consequences for the United States that were by no means limited to Italy. A major controversy for the United States arose with the Netherlands concerning the practice of KLM to carry traffic between the United States and major traffic centers of Europe via Amsterdam. According to the United States, such traffic was for KLM fifth freedom traffic which may not be relied upon as primary justification for capacity under a Bermuda-type agreement. If, however, "on flight" or "coupon" origin and destination statistics are used, the traffic on the U.S.-Amsterdam leg is primary justification traffic and beyond Amsterdam the passengers are irrelevant to the United States-Netherlands bilateral agreement, so that the dispute would automatically be resolved in favor of the Dutch.[52]

In fact, there never was agreement on what statistics to use, so the United States used its own statistics and the controversy became very heated. Various distinctions were attempted to resolve the problem at least partially, such as giving weight as third and fourth freedom passengers to "sixth freedom" passengers who made a stopover of at least 24 hours in Amsterdam, but the volume of "sixth freedom" traffic carried by KLM was too great for this to be a cure. The problem is one that appears inherent in the Bermuda capacity principles when the parties both have very vigorous airlines, but have widely disparate capacity to generate international airline traffic. Notable among countries with which the United States has this problem are the Netherlands, the Scandinavian countries, Belgium and Switzerland. All of these countries are small in area, have relatively small populations and hence do not generate a great deal of traffic either as points of origination or of destination. Nevertheless, each of them is extremely sophisticated in the areas of business skill and technical development and is very aggressive commercially, so that they can and do operate national airlines that are competitively the equals of the airlines operated by much larger countries, including the United States.

By the bilateral agreement with the United States, KLM was authorized to operate between the Netherlands and New York, Houston and Chicago;[53] KLM had a large capacity across the Atlantic, and most of the traffic by far that it carried had as its origin or destination points in European countries behind Amsterdam. Such traffic is sometimes referred to as "sixth freedom traffic," and is considered by the United States as being simply a type of fifth freedom traffic, and hence not traffic between the country of which KLM is a national and the countries of ultimate destination of the traffic—which, according to the agreement, is required to be the primary objective of the capacity provided pursuant to it.[54]

The United States took on the Dutch in a number of capacity consultations on the basis of their excessive carriage of "sixth freedom traffic," notably in 1973[55] and in 1975.[56] In the 1973 consultations the United States again failed to reach an agreed solution with the Dutch and feelings of frustration ran high. It was primarily to deal with the Dutch situation that the 1974 amendment to Part 213 of the CAB's Economic Regulations was passed. This provision empowers the CAB to restrict the operations of a foreign airline whose government has denied or failed to prevent the denial of the fair and equal opportunity to exercise operating rights granted to United States airlines.[57] In November of 1974, the CAB issued an order under Part 213, as amended, requiring KLM to file its schedules, in contemplation of a later order requiring it to reduce its flights to the United States.[58]

After a period of intermittent negotiations, the Department of State announced, on May 6, 1975, that the United States and the Netherlands had failed to settle their differences on sixth freedom traffic carried by KLM and the CAB submitted for presidential approval an order requiring KLM to reduce its schedules. At the same time, the Dutch issued a statement saying

> The Netherlands Government has no wish to exacerbate the air transport problems on the North Atlantic and has requested KLM, in view of the over all present air transportation situation to reduce its Boeing 747 frequencies on its Amsterdam–New York route from 14 to 11 frequencies per week....[59]

This of course was purely a token reduction.

According to the *Aviation Daily,* the Dutch foreign minister had discussed the matter with the United States Secretary of State, Henry Kissinger, who had observed,

> The problem is that looked at from a strictly technical point of view there

> is considerable merit in the view of our technical agencies. Your leaders have convinced me that it is not simply a technical issue. And I have therefore agreed to open the negotiations from a wider perspective.

Other sources[60] indicate that the Dutch managed to convince Kissinger that the United States should back off to avoid having the Dutch withdraw from a NATO project involving their purchase of U.S.-manufactured F-16 aircraft. The order to KLM to reduce its schedules lapsed because President Ford never approved it.[61]

Presumably the reduction from 14 to 11 weekly flights by the Dutch was a face-saver for the United States. The use of Part 213 by the United States against the Dutch has been called contrary to the spirit of the Bermuda principles[62] and evidence of the changing attitude of the United States. Nevertheless, it is hard not to have a certain sympathy with the position of the United States in this case. The United States was confronted with air policies in other countries, notably France and Germany, which stressed the restrictive side of the Bermuda-type agreements against U.S. airlines, and even beyond that, sought by market manipulation to see to it that American airlines carried no more traffic to and from the United States than the national airline.[63] When the Dutch airline drained off a significant share of the U.S. traffic from these markets, the United States airlines were affected not only competitively, but by direct government intervention in the market in third countries.

At the same time, the United States was itself called to account by its partners in other Bermuda-type agreements where U.S. airlines carried what they considered a disproportionate amount of the traffic. There is considerable force to the argument that the United States would create an intolerable situation for itself if it should acquiesce in the restriction of the capacity of U.S. airlines under Bermuda-type agreements in some countries while at the same time failing to insist on its own rights in other countries in such a flagrant case as was presented by KLM. The situation was exacerbated by the obdurate attitude taken by the Dutch.

On balance, however, the United States would have been better advised to have dealt with the problem through a negotiated solution as provided for in the bilateral agreement, rather than attempting to resort to self-help. If the United States' action had been a case of retaliation, as it was in the second French arbitration, the U.S. position would have been stronger. Here, however, the action against KLM was based on a "denial of a fair and equal opportunity," which in turn rested in part upon a disputed interpretation of the bilateral agreement (i.e., whether "sixth freedom" traffic is a form of fifth freedom traffic, or a combination of third and fourth freedom traffic), as well as upon the debatable question, how much fifth freedom traffic is too much. The United States was thus put in the position of attempting to impose unilateral restrictions in order to enforce its views of what the Bermuda capacity provisions mean in a given context. This was probably a mistake.

In the first place, attempting such an action could be seized upon by another country as a justification for imposing its own unilateral restrictions on U.S. airlines on the basis of interpretations of the Bermuda capacity provisions with which the United States did not agree. This should have been predictable, since American airlines have often been subjected to pressure by foreign governments to restrict their capacity. It took very little time for one such nation, Peru, to invoke the KLM case as justification for restrictions imposed unilaterally on United States airlines. Another reason it was probably a mistake for the United States to have imposed Part 213 in this instance was that the United States did not have the internal resolution to make the order stick once the Dutch threatened to cancel their order for F-16 aircraft. It appears likely that the United States was sensitive to this threat as a result of lobbying by the manufacturers of the F-16 aircraft. The lessons seems to be that in dealing with bilateral air transport relations as in many other matters it is well to think one's position through before acting.

Negotiations with Communist Countries

The Bermuda type of bilateral agreement had no real relevance to dealings between the United States and the principal Communist countries. Those countries have no interest in increasing the play of free market forces, and it was readily apparent that the United States would have to adapt to their rather rigid views on market control if it wished to establish air transport relations with them. The first air transport agreement with the Soviet Union came in 1966.[64] The agreement established the number of weekly flights and the routes for the airlines of each party, as well as naming the airlines of each (Aeroflot and Pan American). Any increase or decrease in the number of flights or their routings was accomplished by further governmental agreement. In short, the agreement adopted a rigid system of *a priori* capacity control, and left no leeway for entrepreneurial judgment in either scheduling or aircraft routing. Nevertheless, Article (3) (1) of the agreement, presumably to salve the free market conscience of the United States, provided an echo of the Bermuda Agreement as follows:

> The capacity to be provided by each designated airline on the agreed services shall be related primarily to the requirements of the traffic having its initial origin or ultimate destination in the territory of the contracting party whose nationality the airline possesses. Such origin and destination is determined by the ticket or air way bill. Traffic which transits the territory of a contracting party, with or without stopover, shall not be considered to have its origin or destination in that territory.[65]

Although the agreement contained an article calling for a fair and equal opportunity to operate and promote the agreed services[66] and a further article providing that passengers were to be free to choose which airline to ride and to pay in the national currency of the origin of travel if airline tariffs are published in such currency,[67] the Soviets subjected Pan American to various forms of harassment, such as making it easier for United States tourists using Aeroflot to get visas and hotel accommodations in the U.S.S.R. than for tourists on Pan American and apparently denying Pan American any real access at all to the Russian market.[68] Ultimately, Pan American gave up service to Russia entirely, as part of a general retrenchment program.[69]

The Soviet agreement was a throwback to the pre–ICAO "air navigation agreements" which covered the technical aspects of international service, as well as certain commercial aspects. This was because the U.S.S.R. was not at the time a member of ICAO, so that the technical standards that apply automatically among ICAO members had no application to the Soviets.[70]

Aeroflot continued to operate between the Soviet Union and the United States after termination of Pan American's service. In 1979, the CAB by exemption order allowed Aeroflot to operate three weekly flights to the United States, one more than was authorized in the bilateral agreement and in the Aeroflot foreign air carrier permit.[71] This was on the understanding that the Soviets would facilitate charters by American carriers and provide a fair opportunity for United States airlines to carry traffic to the 1980 Olympics which were to be held in Moscow.

The CAB terminated Aeroflot's exemption authority to operate three weekly flights, in January of 1980.[72] According to the CAB's 1980 *Annual Report,*

> This was done in the wake of the Soviet invasion of Afghanistan and at the request of the Department of State, which cited "overall foreign policy considerations." Civil aviation negotiations which had been scheduled for February 1, 1980 were cancelled.[73]

This action was consonant with the generally political tone that has surrounded United States-Soviet air transport relations. At the same time American participation in the 1980 Olympics was cancelled.

From February 1980 until February 1986, air transport relations between the United States and the U.S.S.R. remained suspended. In 1983, the United States imposed further restrictions on interline connections between U.S. and Soviet airlines in protest over the shooting down of a Korean Airlines plane that had inadvertently entered Soviet air space with American citizens aboard.[74] In February of 1986, in a general lessening of tension between the United States and the Soviet Union, a new aviation agreement was signed between the two countries, giving each the right to operate four weekly round trip flights between them.[75]

To alleviate the problem of Soviet restrictions on Pan American's ability to generate traffic to and from the U.S.S.R., through the use of such devices as withholding visas to divert traffic to Aeroflot in the American market and restricting sales outlets in the Soviet Union, the new agreement contains what amounts to a revenue pool. The agreement is described in the *Aviation Daily* as a "balancing mechanism," which is to be applied

> only to the number of one-way passengers carried by either designated airline that exceeds 12,000 per year, with a round trip counted as two passengers. One half the revenues calculated by multiplying the number of one-way passengers over the 12,000 mark by $350, the agreed revenue unit, will be paid by one carrier or the other. Infants and up to 450 passsengers with free tickets or tickets with a 75 percent discount or more can be excluded from the revenue calculation.

Although it is unlikely that it would have been possible to induce Pan American or any other U.S. airline to serve the Soviet Union without some such provision, this agreement greatly weakens the ability of the United States authorities to refuse to allow pooling by American airlines as a matter of principle, and it appears likely that the existence of this agreement will cause problems for the United States in dealing with other countries.

Service by American airlines to other Iron Curtain countries has been sporadic. Pan American suspended service to Yugoslavia, Romania, Hungary and Czechoslovakia at the same time it suspended service to the U.S.S.R.[76] Service to Yugoslavia and Romania was resumed in June of 1979 and was again suspended in April of 1980.[77] Service to Poland was suspended by Pan American in 1980. In 1981, the United States "suspended" the American-Polish bilateral air transport agreement and the foreign air carrier permit of the Polish airline LOT, in the wake of repressive action by the Polish government against its own people.[78] In 1984 the United States gave LOT permission to operate 88 charters per year[79] and in 1985 this was extended to permission to operate scheduled service.[80]

Between 1983 and 1986, Pan American resumed service to Yugoslavia, Romania, Hungary, Czechoslovakia and Poland. It remains to be seen whether this service will be more profitable than it was in the past, in the absence of some sort of an arrangement such as the one between Pan American and Aeroflot to control predatory marketing practices by the national airlines and governments of these countries.

Air transport relations with the People's Republic of China are following the same general pattern as those with the Soviet Union, although the airlines serving the routes seem to be making out somewhat better. Before the government of China would sign a bilateral air transport agreement with the United States, it insisted that the United States cancel the agreement it had with the government in Taiwan. This was done, without disrupting air transport relations through the device of an "American Institute in Taiwan" and a "Taiwanese Coordination Council for North American Affairs," which established the concept that they were nongovernmental entities, so that a bilateral air transport agreement could be established between these two "insititutes" to cover air transport operations between the respective territories, ostensibly without direct government intervention. An agreement was signed on November 16, 1979, between the American Institute in Taiwan and the Coordination Council for North American Affairs and this constitutes the currently effective bilateral air transport agreement between the United States and Taiwan.[81] The agreement itself is a "post-Bermuda" type agreement, following the United States' standard form agreement in effect at the time.

Negotiations for an agreement with the People's Republic of China took place in the fall of 1980, and the agreement was signed on September 17.[82] The body of the agreement contains a capacity article that sounds like a typical Bermuda capacity article, except for the last paragraph, which implies that the parties intend to split the traffic more or less equally between their respective airlines.[83]

The annexes to the agreement, however, provide for a strict *a priori* regulation of capacity. Annex I provides for a route to be operated by one airline of each party, with a promise for agreement on a route for a second airline to be designated by each party after two years of operation by the first airline. If the parties are unable to agree on a new route, the second airline may operate on the first route. Annex V provides that each designated airline shall have the right to operate two frequencies per week, with a further proviso relating the number of frequencies to the capacity of the aircraft used.[84] If a second airline is not designated, two more frequencies may be operated by the first airline. Any variations in capacity are to be negotiated between the two governments.

Annex V also contains specific procedures that make it clear that the last paragraph of the capacity article refers to an equal division of the traffic to be carried by the airlines of the two countries. Thus, the annex calls for *a priori* capacity regulation, just as the Soviet agreement does and goes beyond the Soviet agreement in calling for an equal division of traffic. It is possible that the latter provision was acquiesced in by the United States to prevent the Chinese from using their total control over their national economy to carry the lion's share of the local origin traffic, as seems to have occurred in Russia.

Annex II concerns charter transportation, and covers the formalities of applying for charter permits, but it does not set standards under which charter permits are to be granted, beyond requiring the parties to state their reasons for disapproving particular charter applications.

Although the Chinese agreement may have started out mainly as a political exercise, it appears likely that the agreement will provide good commercial opportunities for the airlines of both China and the United States, in view of the apparent interest of the Chinese in promoting tourism. It does not appear likely, however, that the Chinese will soon relax their insistence on strict *a priori* control of the capacity offered by the airlines of the two countries, so that development of the services under the agreement could suffer if the Chinese attitude toward tourism should change or fail to develop.

Western Hemisphere Negotiations

The United States managed to get Bermuda-type agreements with almost all of the Western Hemisphere countries, but few of them administered these agreements in a way that was satisfactory to the United States. Although the United States airlines managed to keep their services going, they have been subjected to unilateral restrictions in most Western Hemisphere countries at one time or another.[85]

Argentina has been one of the most difficult countries for the United States to deal with. The Argentines have a well-developed and tenaciously held body of air transport doctrine, based on the theories of the late Dr. Enrique Ferreira, of the University of Córdoba.[86] Ferreira took the position that traffic between each pair of countries was the joint property of those two countries, and was theirs to divide up as they might choose. Ferreira considered that air traffic is actually the physical property of the two countries concerned and that it forms part of the "national patrimony" of the country, just as do mineral and petroleum resources. This analogy to minerals and petroleum lent an emotional tone to the consideration of air traffic that continues to influence the debate on this subject in a number of countries.

Ferreira recommended that states keep 80 percent of such traffic to be divided equally between their own airlines and that they allow the airlines of third countries to carry the remaining 20 percent as fifth freedom traffic, He made a special case of "regional traffic," defined as the traffic between contiguous countries, which he said was analogous to cabotage traffic and should be carried exclusively by the two countries concerned. The views of Ferreira have not been applied literally, but they have greatly influenced the air policy of Argentina as well as that of a number of other countries, in particular Peru, Bolivia, Ecuador, Uruguay and Paraguay. In Argentina, they resulted in a system of traffic quotas which the Argentines have applied from time to time to foreign airlines.[87]

Ferreira's views were reflected in the Argentine air policy law.[88] The provisions of this law are so sharply opposed to the United States views on the regulation of air transport that it appears worthwhile to set out certain of the sections of the law dealing with reciprocity and airline capacity in detail:

National Policy in the International Field:
Basic Principles:

Article 9—For the purposes set forth in Article 2 (which provides that the Executive Branch of the Argentine Government shall promote the development of air transport links between Argentina and the rest of the world, either through bilateral air transport agreement, or through the direct issuance of operating permits), the following basic principles are established:

a) That the national airline be assured the free exercise of the right of overflight (1st freedom) and of technical landing without commercial purposes (2nd freedom).

b) That the demand for air transport between the Argentine territory and that of a particular country is to be attended to primarily by operators of the two flags. The capacity to be authorized for the said operators must conform to an equal distribution, fixed on the basis of the requirements of the traffic embarked in the national territory and disembarked in the other country and vice versa (3rd and 4th freedoms). Any increase in this capacity, through increases of frequency, substitution of equipment or modification of its internal configuration, must conform to this principle and will only be considered when in the carriage of this traffic (3rd and 4th freedom), the load factor, taken as an average of the last twelve months for the carriers of both countries, exceeds 55% of the total capacity authorized, or when because of reciprocity it is appropriate to apply the exception provided for in subparagraph C of this article. When such load factors are not achieved, the change of equipment or modification of its configuration may be authorized only on condition that the authorized capacity not be increased in any flight in either direction.[89]

c) That the total traffic carried by any foreign carrier from third countries to the Argentine Republic and vice versa (5th freedom) shall not exceed what it carries from the country of its flag destined to Argentine Territory and vice versa (3rd and 4th freedom) except in unusual cases in which because of reciprocity it is appropriate to grant the right to carry fifth freedom traffic greater than that shown for third and fourth freedom, when the Argentine flag operator must perform an operation like the one described. Consequently, the capacity will be increased only when it is absolutely necessary for the proper operation of the service.

d) That regional traffic shall be carried primarily by Argentine flag operators and those of the contiguous country concerned and, if necessary, a regime of special protection must be established.

e) That the granting of any right to a foreign company, in addition to being based on the requirements that justify it, shall be conditioned on reciprocity on the part of the country of its flag toward national air transport companies and the real and effective need and convenience of its exercise by them.

f) That similarly to the preponderant participation which is the right of national air carriers in the carriage of passenger traffic, the growth and development of air cargo shall be promoted toward the same end.

g) That the carriage of mail by air from the national territory to points abroad shall be performed primarily by Argentine flag carriers to the points on their services that assure the arrival of the mail at its final destination in the most appropriate way. The assignment of mail to foreign flag carriers will be subject to the provisions of subparagraph (e) of the present article. The reciprocity to which reference is made in the said article shall be measured in terms of the economic value of the service.

Article 18—International services provided by foreign air carriers which link the exterior with our country shall conform to the following:

a) When there is in effect a bilateral air transport agreement with the country of the flag of the foreign carrier, the services shall conform to the clauses of said agreement;

b) When there is not in effect a bilateral air transport agreement, the principles set forth in subparagraph (e) of Article 9 shall be applied. Any authorization granted shall be subject to the regulation of frequency, capacity and traffic as well as any other regulation which the State must impose through application of the principles established in Article 9 of the present law.[90]

As can be seen, this law is extremely nationalistic in favoring the Argentine airline and it is based upon virtually total unilateral government control of frequency and capacity on an *a priori* basis.

The provisions of Article 9 (e) with respect to reciprocity are particularly interesting in that they reject the Bermuda 1 formulation of equality of opportunity[91] and call for "real and effective" reciprocity. This means that if for one reason or another the Argentine airline is impeded from exercising the rights of reciprocity accorded to it by another state, there is no basis, so far as the Argentines are concerned, for the airlines of that state to seek similar rights in Argentina.

In concrete terms this doctrine has led the Argentines to refuse to permit United States airlines to increase their capacity in Argentina, and to reject U.S. arguments that because the United States would allow the Argentine airlines to increase their capacity at will, the Argentines should allow U.S. airlines to increase their capacity. The Argentines said there was no "real and effective" reciprocity because they did not have the equipment to make increases themselves. In this legislation, the concept is carried even further: it makes reciprocity subject not only to the "real and effective" possibility of its exercise, but also to the *convenience* of its exercise by Argentine carriers. This means that even though there was a "real and effective" possibility of the exercise of reciprocity by the Argentine airline, no new operating rights would be granted to the foreign airline until it should suit the Argentine airline to exercise reciprocal rights.

Although the concept of "real and effective" reciprocity does not fit the United States' idea of reciprocity, it, along with the idea of the ownership of air traffic fits in with the Third World insistence upon the doctrine that the new economic order must lead to an equitable share in the benefits of economic activity, rather than to an equal opportunity to compete. The United Nations Charter of Economic Rights and Duties of States[92] provides that economic and political relations among states are to be governed by "Mutual and equitable benefit" and that "every state has and shall exercise full permanent sovereignty, including possession, use and disposal over all its wealth, natural resources and *economic activities*" (emphasis supplied). Ferreira's "real and effective reciprocity" and his concept of air traffic as a national resource, although they sound outlandish in the United States, do have some support around the world.[93] Nevertheless, the idea of a reciprocity that is applicable only when it is convenient to the Argentine airline appears to negate the whole idea of reciprocity.

The incompatibility of the Argentine air transport doctrine with the ideas of the United States on the subject prevented the conclusion of a formal bilateral air transport agreement between the two countries, and their airlines have operated under a series of ad hoc arrangements. At first, Argentine and United States airlines operated under operating permits issued unilaterally by the U.S. and Argentine aeronautical authorities. In 1966, Braniff, Panagra and Pan American were the three U.S. scheduled airlines serving Argentina and Aerolineas Argentinas was the scheduled Argentine airline serving the United States. In 1967, Braniff and Panagra merged, with Braniff the surviving carrier. At about the same time, Pan American revised its schedules to operate primarily nonstop and one- or two-stop service between Argentina and the United States. Braniff, however, continued to operate a multistop service, with the result that it carried a great deal more fifth freedom traffic to and from Argentina than did Pan American.[94] The Argentine authorities unilaterally imposed a series of increasingly harsh restrictions on Braniff to compel it to decrease its proportion of fifth freedom traffic. These restrictions continued despite attempts by the United States to negotiate a solution to the problem with the Argentine authorities, until on October 10, 1972, the U.S. Civil Aeronautics Board issued an order under Part 213 of its economic regulations[95] ordering Aerolineas Argentinas to reduce its flights to the United States from 14 per week to 9 per week, in retaliation for the restrictions imposed upon Braniff. The Argentines replied by ordering Braniff to reduce its 9 weekly flights to 3 and Pan American from 8 weekly flights to 6, for a total reduction from 17 weekly flights by United States carriers to 9 weekly flights. Thereafter, on December 15, 1972, delegations of Argentina and the United States reached an agreement covered by a "Memorandum of Consultation" effective until December 31, 1974, which provided roughly as follows: Aerolineas Argentinas would receive certain new route authorizations and it was authorized to operate all of the frequencies it wished.

Braniff was to reduce its frequency from 9 per week to 8 per week and would resume 9 frequencies per week on July 1, 1973. In addition Braniff was to reduce from 5 to 4 weekly frequencies between Buenos Aires and Santiago and from 9 to 8 weekly frequencies between Buenos Aires and Lima on July 1, 1973. Braniff was also to increase expedited service between Buenos Aires and the United States by operating two one-stop services northbound; one one-stop service southbound; and one round trip non-stop service. On January 1, 1974, it was to reduce to a maximum of 7 round trip services per week between Buenos Aires and Lima. Braniff was also subjected to local traffic quotas on the Santiago–Buenos Aires and the La Paz–Buenos Aires sectors. At the same time Braniff received relief from certain restrictions on the routing of its aircraft between Argentina and the United States.

Pan American was to resume its 8 weekly frequencies, and was to operate two new scheduled cargo services on January 1, 1974, and a ninth combination service on July 1, 1973, and a tenth combination service on January 1, 1974.

All restrictions on the sale of seats on the aircraft of Pan American and Braniff were lifted.

This agreement was partially implemented on both sides, but before Braniff could resume its ninth frequency in July of 1973, Argentina had repudiated the agreement. Thereafter, until September 1977, the United States and Argentina operated on the basis of the schedules that were originally approved under the 1972 agreement, but the Argentines subjected the United States carriers to a series of harassments consisting of refusals to approve the renewal of Braniff's ninth frequency and to allow Pan American to operate the new frequencies that had been granted it, as well as refusals to allow certain relatively minor schedule changes filed by the United States airlines.

The United States responded by withholding authority for Aerolineas Argentinas to serve Brasília, Caracas, Bogotá and La Paz in accordance with the 1972 memorandum, since that authority had not been granted at the time Argentina repudiated the agreement. Thereafter the United States consistently rejected requests for schedule increases filed by Aerolineas Argentinas. After a series of hopeful sounding contacts between the two governments in 1975 and 1976, the government of Argentina imposed notably harsh quotas on the traffic Braniff was to be allowed to carry between Buenos Aires and Santiago and La Paz and at the same time imposed a large fine on Braniff for having carried more fifth freedom traffic than third and fourth freedom traffic to and from Argentina in 1975 and advised Braniff that similar action was being taken for 1976. The United States responded to this by again invoking Part 213 of the CAB's economic regulations to disapprove the schedules of Aerolineas Argentinas insofar as they provided for any traffic stops at Mexico City and for more than two flights per week between the United States and Lima.[96] This disapproval was withdrawn when Argentina agreed to further aeronautical negotiations with the United States and temporarily suspended the regional quotas that had been imposed upon Braniff, as well as the proceeding against Braniff for the carriage of more fifth freedom traffic than third and fourth freedom traffic.

In September 1977, Argentina and the United States reached a memorandum of understanding which was to run until October 31, 1983.[97] This agreement described the routes to be operated by the airlines of the two countries and specified the number of weekly frequencies that might be operated by each of them, with a series of frequency increases phased in over the life of the agreement. There is a provision for the operation of wide-bodied aircraft, which might be placed in service at will by the carriers, subject to a conversion table.[98] The carriers of each flag might operate up to six scheduled all-cargo narrow-bodied aircraft frequencies per week and all-cargo charters are to be freely admitted by each country in accordance with country of origin rules. (Passenger charters are subject to unilateral control).

Although there is no overlooking the fact that the United States–Argentina agreement was an *a priori* agreement on capacity, it was pretty clearly the best agreement that could be reached in the circumstances, and it worked to the great advantage of both Argentine and United States airlines. There was no possibility of reaching agreement with the Argentines on a set of principles to govern the offering of air transport capacity. Experience had shown that under a system of unilateral regulation, in the absence of some sort of an agreement on capacity, the Argentines tended to act in an unpredictable manner and to prevent United States airlines from adjusting their schedules and capacity so as to take best advantage of the market. This capacity agreement with its built-in increases over a six-year period provided for all of the capacity required by United States and Argentine airlines during that period.

Moreover, the agreement provided for a degree of operating flexibility which United States airlines had never had in Argentina. Under the Argentine regulations each fequency was treated as a separate element of the carrier's operating permit. This meant that in the absence of the agreement, the carrier had to go through a formal procedure to amend its operating permit, not only to add or subtract a frequency, but even to add or subtract a single point, or to switch points among frequencies. The 1977 agreement contained a provision that enabled the airline to put together the schedules for its route according to its own managerial discretion, just as it was able to do in the United States and in most other countries, thus freeing U.S. airlines from the necessity of amending their Argentine operating permits in order to make changes in routing. The flexibility and predictability that this produced were of great value to the United States airlines.

After 1977 U.S.-Argentine air transport relations remained relatively tranquil until 1987. Although the 1977 agreement was scheduled to expire in 1983, it was extended until 1985, at which time a new agreement along similar lines was signed.[99] In March 1987, the Argentines, although they had permitted increases above the level of the 1985 agreement by both Pan American and Eastern, determined that United States carriers must reduce their frequencies to the levels operated in 1985. The United States Department of Transportation was forced to conduct a lottery to determine how to allocate a reduction of two weekly frequencies between the two carriers.[100] The result of the lottery was that each of the two airlines had to give up one flight.[101] This is manifestly a bizarre way to conduct the air transport industry, but if it buys time for the United States to work out a more stable arrangement with the Argentines, the action will have served its purpose.

Agreements establishing a specific number of frequencies for the airlines of each party were also entered into with Peru and Ecuador. The United States had Bermuda-type air transport agreements with both of these countries,[102] but both of them had nevertheless insisted upon imposing unilateral capacity controls on the United States airline serving the country and had subjected it to considerable harassment.

The agreement with Ecuador[103] was dated December 31, 1975, and ran through December 31, 1980. The Ecuadorean agreement was particularly timely because it established an orderly schedule of capacity increases at a time when the Ecuadorean authorities were refusing to allow any increases in frequency and were trying to force capacity cutbacks on the United States airline. They were also attempting to require payments by the United States airline (Braniff Airways) "in lieu of reciprocity." At the time, the Ecuadorean authorities tried to force Braniff to enter a contract with the national airline pursuant to which it would make a payment to that airline to compensate it because the Ecuadorean authorities alleged that Braniff was gaining more from the United States–Ecuador air transport agreement than the national airline.[104] Article 10 of the 1975 understanding constitutes an undertaking not to impose such charges on U.S. airlines and reads as follows:

> 10. In view of the mutual benefits accorded by this understanding, neither government will require from the airline of the other country benefits other than those specified in this understanding and the permits attached thereto.

Under this agreement, U.S.-Ecuadorean air transport relations enjoyed a five-year period of peace and tranquility. Since 1980, when the agreement expired, the parties appear to have been careful not to put the underlying Bermuda-type agreement to the test, and there have been no confrontations between the two countries. It appears likely, however, that if the United States should attempt to increase the capacity of its airlines in Ecuador to any marked degree the Ecuadoreans would refuse to allow it, despite the underlying Bermuda-type bilateral agreement.

Peru, after many years of tranquility, has given United States airlines an even more difficult time than Ecuador or Argentina. The full story is too long and complicated to be given here in detail, but essentially it is as follows. In 1946, when the Peruvian-U.S. Bermuda-type bilateral air transport agreement was signed,[105] there was a Peruvian airline; it was not really Peruvian but was primarily backed by Canadian and United States capital. This airline, Peruvian International Airways, had some support from the Peruvian government, but because of its essentially foreign ownership, it could not command the government's full backing, either in the form of a subsidy or in the form of regulations that would discriminate decisively in its favor against United States and other foreign airlines. This airline engaged extensively in rate cutting, and was not well managed. In 1949 it declared bankruptcy and went out of business. Thereafter, until 1956, there were no significant international operations by Peruvian airlines, and the Peruvians did not harass United States airlines.

In 1956, Aerolineas Peruanas ("APSA") was formed, again with United States captial.[106] Although APSA was able to generate some support within the Peruvian government, its foreign ownership worked against it so it never could count on full support and in the end it went out of business. Since there had never been a legitimate national airline operating internationally, Peru did not adopt a body of highly nationalistic measures to discriminate against foreign airlines. Nevertheless, certain such measures were adopted to favor APSA, and after the demise of APSA, a 20 percent charge "in lieu of reciprocity" was levied on the fifth freedom traffic carried by foreign airlines serving Peru.[107]

In October of 1973, a new Peruvian airline, Aero Peru, was formed. This airline was wholly owned by the Peruvian government, and it was administered by the Peruvian Air Force, although it had a corporate form and its employees were mainly civilians, under a Peruvian Air Force general as president. The route of this airline paralleled that of Braniff Airways, the United States airline then serving Peru, all the way from Buenos Aires to Miami and later New York. The Peruvian aeronautical authorities soon abandoned the 20 percent "reciprocity charge," at least so far as it concerned Braniff, and by unilateral order required Braniff to reduce its capacity in Peru radically, in order to make way for the operations of Aero Peru. The United States government responded with counter-restrictions, which in turn were answered by Peru, so that at one point the Peruvian and United States airlines were ordered to reduce to one flight each per week.[108]

In the end an agreement was reached in July 1975,[109] under which Braniff was allowed 15 frequencies between the United States and Peru and 10 frequencies beyond Peru, and comparable rights were allowed for Aero Peru. This represented a significant reduction in capacity for Braniff (down approximately 25 percent between Peru and the United States, and approximately 50 percent beyond Peru), and an increase for Aero Peru.[110] Upon expiration of the 1975 agreement in 1978, the parties reached a new agreement that would have allowed new frequencies for both sides and increased flexibility in the scheduling of airline service, as well as expanded charter authority. Although both Braniff and Aero Peru had expanded their service in reliance upon the effectiveness of this agreement in December 1978,[111] the Peruvians reversed themselves in April 1979 and repudiated the agreement, forcing Braniff to go back to the capacity in effect under the 1975 agreement, which had expired in 1978.[112] The United States also required Aero Peru to cut back its services in the light of Peru's refusal to implement the terms of the 1978 understanding. Although Peru permitted Eastern Airlines to substitute for the services of Braniff after it had purchased the route from Braniff, no agreement between the two countries was possible, and restrictions were imposed on Eastern's ability to operate south of Lima.

On November 10, 1982, Peru gave notice of termination of the Peru–United States bilateral air transport agreement, effective November 1, 1983. Thereafter things went rapidly down hill. Peru steadfastly refused to allow Eastern Airlines to extend its service beyond Peru to Buenos Aires, and it also refused to allow the United States airline, Challenge Air Transport, to serve Panama as an intermediate point on its service between the United States and Lima, although Peruvian airlines were operating between both of those cities and the United States.

The CAB issued orders cancelling the permits of the Peruvian carriers serving the United States as of November 11, 1982, and allowing them to continue operating at the existing levels of service on the routes they were then serving.[113] This authority lasted until April 30, 1984, at which time the CAB issued an order giving Peru until May 21, 1984, to allow the United States carriers to carry traffic between Peru and Buenos Aires and Panama, to which the United States considered itself entitled through reciprocity, and advising that otherwise the U.S. operating authority of the Peruvian airlines would be allowed to expire.[114] When the Peruvians continued firm in their position, the permits of the Peruvian airlines were allowed to expire, and the Peruvians cancelled the permits of Eastern and Challenge.[115]

The Peruvian and U.S. governments were unable to achieve a new agreement until December 1986.[116] This agreement provided for resumption of service six months after signature (i.e., June 1987) and runs for three years. It is similar to the agreement the Peruvians repudiated, but provides for less service on both sides. In particular, it provides for 15 weekly narrow-bodied frequencies (with a conversion table for wide bodies), which was the number allowed United States airlines by the Peruvians after repudiation of the 1978 agreement, versus the 19 weekly frequencies allowed in that agreement. The December 1986 agreement does, however, contain no further restriction on the number of flights that United States airlines may operate between Peru and La Paz/Asunción, Santiago and Buenos Aires.[117]

United States air transport relations with Venezuela have also had a rather stormy course. Venezuela frankly insists upon exercising unilateral control over the capacity offered by foreign airlines and has in fact managed to control the capacity offered by U.S. airlines despite a Bermuda-type agreement with the United States.[118] Presumably on the basis of the precedents set in Argentina, Ecuador and Peru, as well as in the Pacific and in China, the United States in 1982 entered an agreement with Venezuela setting *a priori* capacity levels, accompanied by a formula for allowing increases. The formula is described in the *Aviation Daily* as follows:

> The capacity agreement assures carriers that they may continue operating current schedules because those schedules are attached to the agreement as the base level. The pact sets up four scenarios for capacity increases in markets where U.S. and Venezuelan carriers operate. If carrier A operated at load factors above 70% and carrier B at loads below 60%, then carrier A may increase capacity only to bring its load factors back to 70%. If carrier A operated at over 70% loads, while carrier B operated at loads between 60% and 70%, then carrier A may gain capacity relief to reduce its loads to 70% or may increase capacity to allow for growth, but may not allow for both capacity relief and growth. Carrier B may increase flights to accommodate growth. If however, both carriers are operating with load factors between 60%-70%, both may increase flights to allow for growth to 65%. If both carriers are above 70%, they may increase frequencies to allow for both capacity relief and growth.[119]

This agreement was for one year and it was extended in 1983 until September 1984.[120] Although the agreement appears somewhat bizarre, in the sense that the capacity formula seems likely to give unpredictable results, it can be justified as an experiment.

Brazil had a Bermuda-type agreement with the United States[121] which was modified by a "screening agreement" that allowed the parties to get along without unsurmountable difficulties until 1981, when Brazil became so upset over the capacity being offered by U.S. airlines and the possibility of even more through the exercise of rights of multiple designation by the United States that it cancelled the agreement with effect April 20, 1982.[122] At present, United States and Brazilian airlines are operating without an agreement, on the basis of comity and reciprocity, after a temporary arrangement expired in September 1985.

There is in effect a Bermuda-type bilateral air transport agreement between Colombia and the United States,[123] supplemented by an agreed minute that provides a means for terminating the agreement automatically in the event of an unreconcilable dispute concerning the capacity offered by a party's airlines and provides further:

> (2) Pending the conclusion of the procedures invoked by any notification under Article 15 pursuant to Paragraph 1 above (i.e. termination of the bilateral agreement)
> A. Neither party will impose any unilateral restrictions on a designated airline or airlines of either party with respect to capacity, frequencies, or type of aircraft employed over an agreed route or routes.
> B. Any restrictions on the carriage of Fifth Freedom Traffic previously imposed by either Party on the designated airlines of the other party will remain lifted and no new restrictions will be imposed.[124]

Since the effectiveness of this regime, United States airlines have been able to operate to Colombia relatively free of overt restrictions. This is probably owing primarily to the fact that Avianca, the Colombian airline, has generally carried far more traffic between the United States and Colombia than have the U.S. airlines serving the country.[125] Avianca has also carried a large amount of fifth freedom traffic between the United States and South America. The Colombians have, however, subjected United States airlines to discriminatory fuel and other charges, which the United States has been unable to prevent, except on a temporary basis.

Air transport relations between the United States and Chile have varied greatly throughout the years. The Chileans have had an ambivalent point of view toward protecting the national airline, Línea Aérea Nacional de Chile ("LAN"), by means of restrictions on foreign airlines. Wholly owned by the Chilean government, LAN has been supported by subsidy. Thus the Chilean government, like other governments in the same situation, has had a strong motive to protect it, and has done so by imposing quotas on the amount of "regional" traffic (i.e., traffic to neighboring countries) that might be carried by foreign (including United States) airlines, and by imposing other indirect restrictions intended to reduce the participation of foreign airlines in the Chilean market.

On the other hand, the Chilean authorities have recognized for many years that the geographical situation of Chile, and in particular the capital city, Santiago, does not favor the inclusion of Chile in the major travel routes between the United States and Europe on the one hand and Buenos Aires and Rio de Janeiro on the other hand. Because of the fear of being deprived of access to the major sources of air transport, the Chilean authorities have from time to time encouraged foreign airlines to improve their service to Chile.[126] With the advent of the Pinochet regime, under the tutelage of the "Chicago School" economists who have been advising the Chilean fiscal authorities, the latter tendency has been augmented by a doctrinaire belief in the efficiency of a free market, and the Chilean aeronautical policy seems rather similar to the U.S. policy under "deregulation." Nevertheless the United States has not signed with Chile a post–Bermuda bilateral air transport agreement and the Bermuda-type agreement signed with Chile in 1947[127] remains in effect. The reason for this appears to be the reluctance, for internal political reasons, of the United States executive branch to make agreements with the present Chilean regime.

Air transport operations between the United States and Mexico and Canada have been regarded by the United States as extensions of the domestic routes of United States airlines.[128] Although the United States has tended to describe the routes to most countries as originating in "the United States" for U.S. carriers and in the national territory of the other country for the foreign carrier, it has been necessary to specify the U.S. points involved, as well as the foreign points in order to convey a description of the route between the United States and a contiguous country. For this reason, both the Canadian[129] and the Mexican[130] agreements specify the points to be served in each country at both ends of the route. (The Canadian agreement covers only routes between the United States and Canada. The Mexican agreement contains for the United States two routes beyond Mexico, one to Panama and beyond and one to Central America and beyond.) For Mexico, the agreement contains a route beyond the United States to Canada and a route beyond the United States to Europe. Nevertheless, it is clear that the main thrust of both agreements is to provide for transportation between the respective countries, rather than to accommodate the structure of international trunk routes, as is the case of the agreements with countries in most other parts of the world.

The Mexican agreement is a Bermuda-type agreement and was supplemented by a "screening agreement," which gave the governments of each country the ability to impede, but not to prevent entirely, capacity increases proposed by the airlines of the other.[131] The latter agreement was cancelled in 1977. The Canadian agreement is of the Bermuda type,[132] but the route agreement contains limitations on the number of airlines that may be designated on particular routes, which in effect give the Canadian and American governments the right to veto the designation of more than one airline on most routes.[133]

The United States also has charter arrangements in effect with both Mexico and Canada. The Mexican charter arrangement is contained in the agreement dated January 20, 1978.[134] It provides for a "country of origin" regime of regulation (i.e., if a charter conforms to the charter regulations of the country where it originates, it will be accepted by the country of destination). The Canadian arrangement consists of a separate charter bilateral air transport agreement.[135] Although the agreement provides for a "country of origin" regime, it specifies what types of charters are allowed in each country, evidently to quiet Canadian fears that the United States might later change its regulations so as to allow new types of charters hitherto unheard of in Canada. The agreement provides that for markets characterized as "unidirectional," all of which originate in Canada, with a destination in United States winter resort areas, the larger percentage of the seats to be offered by the airlines of the two countries shall be offered by Canadian carriers.

Other charter flights are subject to a limitation that the number of charter flights between the two countries performed by an airline of one country which originate in the territory of the other country must not exceed by more than one-third the number of flights performed by it which originate in the territory of its own country. (This is known as an "uplift ratio.")

Both Canada and Mexico have underlying policies that call for strict governmental control of international airline capacity.[136] It cost the United States long years of patient negotiating to achieve the degree of liberality it has in its air transport agreements with each of these countries, and it seems likely that under serious provocation both would revert to unilaterally restrictive policies. Canada has, however, recently expressed interest in a limited form of "deregulation."

Pacific Area Negotiations

The most significant of the American negotiations in the Pacific Area under Bermuda-type agreements have been those with the Japanese and the Australians. There have also been numerous and difficult negotiations with the Philippines. These are not described herein because of their similarity to the dealings with South American countries.

The United States signed a Bermuda-type air transport agreement with the Japanese on August 11, 1952, which entered into force September 15, 1953.[137] Despite the fact that it has had a Bermuda-type air transport agreement with the United States, Japan has contrived by one means or another to inhibit the expansion of American airlines in Japan. In 1961, the Civil Aeronautics Board recommended in the "Trans Pacific Route Case"[138] that United States service to the Orient be increased by duplicating service by American carriers, particularly to Japan.

President Dwight D. Eisenhower disapproved the CAB recommendation, saying:

> Greatly increased capacity—always of considerable concern to other nations engaged in international commercial aviation—should not in my judgement be approved unless traffic forecasts for the routes in question plainly show that the additional capacity can be absorbed without engendering a

> legitimate fear abroad that United States flag carriers will collect so much of the traffic as to make service on the route by a foreign carrier economically untenable or marginal at best. The evidence in the case at hand, including particularly the traffic forecasts does not establish the circumstances I have described. It is reasonable therefore to predict that approval of the Board's major recommendations in this case would unsettle our international relations—particularly with Japan which would be faced with an additional U.S. carrier on all but one of the now existing four routes from the U.S. to Tokyo.[139]

It does not appear ever to have been the policy of the United States to require that a U.S. carrier proposing a capacity increase have the burden of showing that

> forecasts for the route in question plainly show that the additional capacity can be absorbed without engendering a legitimate fear abroad that the United States flag carriers will collect so much of the traffic as to make service on the route by a foreign carrier economically untenable, or marginal at best.

It appears likely that what happened was that the United States policy called for an expansion of Japanese aviation and the Japanese managed to persuade the United States executive branch that the designation of new carriers would inhibit such expansion. Presumably, whoever was assigned to write the letter to the CAB invented a principle to justify the result. In any case, there is no hint of such a policy in the Eisenhower civil air policy nor in any subsequent U.S. air policy. The fact that the Japanese managed to stall off the capacity increase is, however, significant.

Throughout the history of American-Japanese air transport relations, the Japanese have had a surprising degree of success in thwarting the efforts of U.S. airlines to expand their presence in Japan. At times, they alleged extraneous problems that prevented them from permitting capacity increases by United States carriers that were fully in compliance with the agreement.

Although the Civil Aeronautics Board found in 1961 that another U.S. airline was warranted by the traffic between the United States and Japan, it was not until 1982 that the United States managed to convince the Japanese to accept the designation of a third American airline to operate passenger service between the Continental United States and Japan. Despite the provision of the U.S.-Japan bilateral agreement that permits the multiple designation of airlines, the Japanese refused to allow United Airlines to operate on the Seattle/Portland–Tokyo route for which it had been designated by the United States. In refusing to accept the designation of United, the Japanese invoked an imbalance in the agreement. An article in April 1981 in the *Wall Street Journal* says that the U.S. aviation officials had replied that if there was an imbalance it existed only on paper:

> Despite broad language in the aviation treaty allowing American carriers to serve Japanese points, Washington officials contended, the airlines are

> allowed to land only at Tokyo's Narita Airport, Osaka Airport and Naha on Okinawa. Officials maintained that US expansion has been hindered by noise and environmental controls and a lack of adequate fuel supplies at Narita. Moreover, they added, Japan has resisted allowing new US carriers to fly to Japan.... Japan has thrown up road blocks to new service by United Airlines which was granted rights to Japan by U.S. regulators.[140]

Talks in 1981 ended without agreement,[141] and to increase pressure on the Japanese, United Airlines filed a complaint with the CAB calling for the suspension of Japanese Airlines flights between Tokyo and New York in retaliation, pursuant to the International Air Transportation Fair Competitive Practices Act of 1974.[142] In September 1981, the Civil Aeronautics Board reopened its "Trans Pacific Low Fare Route Case," sending out a press release that said it sought to qualify more carriers to serve Japan, with the idea of designating them under whatever agreement might come out of negotiations with Japan, or if the negotiations should break down, of designating them under the existing bilateral agreement, since it permits multiple designations.[143]

On December 14, 1981, the CAB issued orders, in response to United's filings,[144] turning down a number of requests for improved service conditions by Japan Airlines (JAL), and ordering JAL to file its schedules with the CAB. An accompanying press release says that at the same time a confidential order was sent to the president providing for additional sanctions against JAL, if required.[145] The Japanese imposed countersanctions on United States airlines and after the parties agreed to negotiate, the U.S. sanctions, and presumably the Japanese sanctions also, were suspended.[146]

The airline matter by this time had apparently assumed such proportions that it was interfering with a high level meeting between President Reagan and Premier Suzuki in June of 1982. In order to clear the decks for the meeting a deal was worked out in Washington and signed in Tokyo.[147] The agreement, dated June 4, 1982,[148] provides that a new airline (i.e., United) may operate 7 weekly round trip combination flights Seattle/Portland–Tokyo. For this Japan got a new route Tokyo–Seattle/Chicago, on which it was permitted to operate 5 weekly round trip combination flights.

At the same time the American carrier, Continental/Air Micronesia, got the right to operate 7 weekly narrow-bodied combination trips Saipan–Nagoya, and JAL got the right to operate two weekly narrow-bodied cargo services between Tokyo and Chicago. In addition JAL got the right to operate two weekly round trip combination flights Tokyo–Los Angeles–São Paulo/Rio de Janeiro, with full traffic rights.

Thus, in order to make effective the right that it already had to designate United Airlines under the bilateral agreement, the United States found it necessary to bring heavy pressure on the Japanese and to give JAL a new route between Tokyo and Seattle/Portland.

Earlier, the United States had experienced similar problems with Continental/Air Micronesia's service between Saipan and Tokyo, where it had to agree to capacity limitations and grant Japan a similar route in order to make effective the route the United States already had under the bilateral agreement. This was done as part of a note exchange dated November 12, 1969, amending the U.S.-Japan bilateral agreement.[149]

Although the United States obtained the right to serve Osaka in the November 12, 1969, agreement, the Japanese were still keeping American airlines out of Osaka "for environmental reasons" in September 1980.[150]

In addition Pan American and Northwest chronically had trouble making capacity increases and routing changes in Japan.

In December of 1985, it was reported that JAL was losing its right to be the exclusive Japanese airline.[151] This could lead to some liberalization of the Japanese attitude toward suppressing competition by foreign airlines, but the record suggests that one should not believe in such liberalization until it actually appears.

Although the Japanese managed to impose on United States airlines controls that were unwarranted by the bilateral agreement, and to extract concessions from the United States that it was not contractually required to yield, this does not necessarily mean that the United States was stupid to allow itself to get into that position, or that the Bermuda-type agreement was at fault. Given the relative positions of the United States and Japan at the end of the Second World War, and up until relatively recently, it appears reasonable to believe that the United States could have forced onto Japan just about any interpretation of the Bermuda language it might choose. It appears likely that the United States' overall policy called for a strong Japanese commercial aviation industry, and that what looked like irritations and frustrations to the American airlines that saw their ambitions thwarted were regarded with a great deal more complacency within the higher levels of the United States government, as steps toward rebuilding the international presence of Japan. Such a belief is consistent with the observations of President Eisenhower in the Pacific route case, and may be compared with the route grant in the German air transport agreement that caused an uproar in the Smathers Committee in 1956.[152]

Although the Australian negotiations have great economic importance, their contribution to a study of air transport policy is largely cumulative. Australia is a strong believer in protecting its own airline, and it has done so despite a Bermuda-type agreement with the United States.[153]

Consultations were required in 1970 to get American Airlines Incorporated into Australia[154] and in 1971 the United States found it necessary to invoke Part 213 of the CAB's economic regulations imposing restrictions on Qantas Airways to persuade the Australians to permit a schedule increase proposed by American.[155] When American Airlines gave up service to Australia in 1974, it took the United States a year and a half to persuade the Australians to accept service by Continental Airlines.[156] United States airlines serving Australia have had trouble throughout the years with capacity increases.

The Bermuda 2 Agreement

The denunciation of the original Bermuda Agreement and its supplanting by the Bermuda 2 Agreement mark a watershed in United States commercial air transport policy, although paradoxically the Bermuda 2 Agreement was not destined to play an influential role in the development of that policy.

The British denunciation of the Bermuda 1 Agreement was brought about primarily by dissatisfaction with the share of the transatlantic market British airlines had been able to achieve under it. The British wanted some assurance that British carriers would achieve a 50 percent market share. They were also concerned that the United States' opportunity to carry fifth freedom traffic under the Bermuda 1 route plan, particularly to destinations beyond London, was enabling American carriers to offer what the British considered excessive capacity between the United States and London and to divert from British airlines traffic between London and points East.

The British felt that the capacity provisions of the Bermuda 1 Agreement were inadequate to prevent the offering of excessive capacity. They also complained that the Bermuda 1 provisions for the establishment of airline fares were inadequate and that the agreement should contain provisions to limit the number of airlines that could be designated to serve a particular route.[157]

The United States was unable to impress the British in the negotiations with arguments in favor of allowing market forces to control the fares and capacity of the airlines nor was it able to persuade the British that over the course of time, the share of traffic carried by British airlines would stabilize at a satisfactory level.[158]

For some reason the United States was unwilling to propose an ad hoc solution that would alleviate the immediate distress of the British, while leaving the rest of the Bermuda 1 Agreement intact, as had been done for example in the case of the Italians, the Brazilians, the Mexicans and the Ecuadoreans.

The negotiations leading to the Bermuda 2 Agreement were held in eight separate sessions, running from September 9, 1976, through July 23, 1977. In the later sessions of the negotiations, President Jimmy Carter appointed Alan Boyd, a former chairman of the CAB and the first Secretary of

Transportation, as head of the United States delegation, with ambassadorial rank. Mr. Boyd reached agreement with the British, but the agreement was by no means popular in the United States.

The Bermuda 2 Agreement[159] consists of 21 Articles and 5 Annexes, plus an exchange of letters. The most important differences from the Bermuda 1 Agreement are as follows:

Article 3. *Designation and Authorization of Airlines.* Limitations are placed on the number of airlines that may be designated on particular routes.

Article 8. *Commercial Operations.* This is a new article relating to discriminatory practices.

Article 10. *User Charges.* This is a new article and sets up the standards with which user charges should comply.

Article 11. *Fair Competition.* Contains the Bermuda capacity provisions, with a number of radical changes. The Bermuda 1 requirement that the airlines of one contracting party take into consideration the interests of the designated airline or airlines of the other contracting party "so as not to affect unduly that airline's or those airlines' operations on all or part of the same routes" is amplified to require in particular that when a designated airline of one contracting party proposes to inaugurate services on a gateway route segment already served by a designated airline or airlines of the other contracting party, the incumbent airline or airlines shall each refrain from increasing the frequency of their services to the extent and for the time necessary to ensure that the airline inaugurating service may fairly exercise its rights to a fair and equal opportunity to compete.

The rather loose capacity formula of the Bermuda 1 Agreement is made more concrete by the addition of the following paragraph:

> 4 The frequency and capacity of services to be provided by the designated airlines of the contracting parties shall be closely related to the requirements of all categories of public demand for the carriage of passengers and cargo including mail in such a way as to provide adequate service to the public and to permit the reasonable development of routes and viable airline operations. Due regard shall be paid to efficiency of operation so that frequency and capacity are provided at levels appropriate to accommodate the traffic at load factors consistent with tariffs based on the criteria set forth in paragraph (2) of Article 12 (Tariffs).[160]

While this new paragraph does not radically alter the meaning of the Bermuda 1 capacity provisions, it accomplishes a significant change of emphasis in their application. Under the Bermuda 1 formula, the opponents and the proponents of a particular level of capacity could draw roughly equally strong arguments from the language of the agreement. The addition of the quoted paragraph tends to tip the scales in favor of the opponent of a particular level of capacity by placing upon the proponent the burden of satisfying a relatively objective standard to justify the capacity proposed—it must be at "levels appropriate to accommodate the traffic at load factors consistent with tariffs based on the criteria set forth in paragraph (2) of Article 12 (Tariffs)". Moreover, it is apparent that this standard is subject to arbitration under Article 17 of the Bermuda 2 Agreement, whereas capacity has never been arbitrated under the Bermuda 1 Agreement.

It is significant that capacity on the North Atlantic routes, which were considered by both sides the most important routes covered by the agreement, is removed entirely from the Bermuda capacity scheme and is subjected to a system of capacity predetermination whereby each party can hold capacity increases proposed by the other's airlines to an amount determined by a formula based upon traffic forecasts for the route segment in question. This scheme is set forth in Annex 2.

Article 12. *Tariffs* differs essentially from the provisions of the Bermuda 1 Agreement by placing much less emphasis upon the role of the International Air Transport Association and much greater emphasis upon the role of governments in the establishment of airline tariffs. The approval of both governments is required for a particular rate to become effective. In the event of a failure to reach agreement, or of no consultations having been requested, the objecting party may take action to continue in force the existing tariffs beyond the date on which they would otherwise have expired at the levels and under the conditions (including seasonal variations) included therein, and the other party may take similar action. Neither party may, however, require a different tariff for its own carrier between the same points.

Article 13. *Commissions.* This is a new article which authorizes each country to require the other's airlines to file with its authorities the rates of commission that will be paid by it to sales agents for sales made in its territory and provides further that the level of such commissions shall be subject to the laws and regulations of that party.[161]

Article 14. *Charter Air Service* is a new article. It covers charter services in a manner comparable with the manner in which the Bermuda 2 Agreement covers scheduled services, and provides that there shall be no discrimination between the treatment of charter carriers and scheduled carriers with respect to the carriage of charter traffic nor between the charter carriers of one party and those of the other party. With respect to "charter worthiness," the agreement provides for a "country of origin" regime, except as otherwise provided in Annex 4. Annex 4 originally contained a rather elaborate list of charter worthiness requirements and expired by its terms in 1980. When the parties were unable to agree on provisions to replace the passenger charter regime of Annex 4, it was allowed to expire and by exchange of letters they agreed that "each contracting party would thereafter continue to regulate charter traffic in a responsible manner and on a basis of comity and reciprocity."[162]

Article 17. *Settlement of Disputes.* This article provides for settlement of disputes by any person or body as agreed by the parties, or in the absence of agreement by an arbitral tribunal. It remains to be seen whether use will be made of the arbitration provisions of the Bermuda 2 Agreement. In this connection, it is worth noting that under Bermuda 2, capacity matters on the North Atlantic and tariff matters are, at least in part, expressly excepted from the arbitration procedure of Article 17.

Annex 1. *Route Schedules* sharply limits the ability of United States airlines to carry traffic beyond London and opens up a number of internal American cities to service by the airlines of both countries. The notes to the Annex (Section 5) provide for the carriage of "blind sector" traffic to and from intermediate and beyond points not named in the route descriptions. Such traffic may be carried as transit traffic or as on-line connecting traffic. These provisions benefit United States carriers by allowing them to route flights serving London to points beyond London on a "blind sector" basis, without the need to obtain any special permission from the British. On the other hand, the value of such flights is greatly reduced by the loss of the right to serve points beyond London with traffic rights on a number of such routings which the US carriers enjoyed under the Bermuda 1 Agreemnt. Although the British lost the right to serve Cuba, Jamaica, Panama, "a point in Colombia," "a point in Ecuador," Lima and Santiago as "beyond" points on the London–New York route, and got back in the Bermuda 2 Agreement only the right to serve Mexico City as a point on that route plus the right to serve Venezuela, Colombia, Manaus (Brazil) and Peru on the London–Atlanta and Houston route, the British neither gained nor lost a great deal on this exchange with respect to their own services, because they had never been commercially able to sustain service to South America beyond the United States with traffic rights.

The notes to Annex 1 also allow the designated airlines freely to carry "sixth freedom" traffic.[163] This was a rather surprising development when one considers the uproar that went on about the carriage of sixth freedom traffic by KLM in 1975, although it conforms to later United States practice.

Annex 2. *Capacity on the North Atlantic.* This annex excludes the Bermuda 1 capacity "principles" from the North Atlantic routes and substitutes a regime whereby the parties discuss one another's proposed schedules in advance of their effectiveness and, in the event of objections, exchange estimates of the percentage increase to revenue passenger traffic expected on the gateway sector in question. In the event of a failure to agree on the capacity to be operated, the airline is to be allowed to increase its frequencies above those operated during the previous corresponding season (i.e., summer or winter season) by a percentage calculated by averaging the two forecasts of the percentage of revenue traffic increase previously exchanged.[164] This is obviously a system whereby the capacity is predetermined by agreement, or if agreement cannot be reached, by formula. This system is nothing like the Bermuda 1 Agreement, and it has little resemblance to anything that has before or since been put forward as U.S. air policy.

This clause was modified in September 1986 to provide that if there is disagreement between the two governments over proposed capacity increases, there will be

> floor guarantees that permit the addition of 30 flights in summer and 22 flights in winter. Alternatively one country's carriers have the option of providing as a group 150% of the capacity offered on that route by a carrier or carriers of the other country.[165]

This is more liberal than the original agreement, but it is far from what the United States has traditionally sought in a bilateral air transport agreement.

Annex 3. *Tariffs* established a Tariff Working Group composed of government experts to develop procedures for the exchange on a recurrent basis of verified financial and traffic statistics to assist each party in assessing tariff proposals. This seems to be mainly a reflection of United States distrust of IATA.

Annex 4. *Charter Air Service.* This annex is interesting as an example of an attempt at establishing agreed rules under which airlines are to be permitted to operate charters. Since it has expired and the parties have agreed not to renew it, this annex does not appear to have much current importance.

Annex 5. *North Atlantic Cargo Operations* was added to the Bermuda 2 Agreement by exchange of notes in 1980.[166] After a transitional period, ending December 31, 1982, this annex established a separate, more liberal regime for the regulation of all-cargo services on the North Atlantic.

The new Bermuda 2 Agreement was considered by those directly involved in its negotiation as a major step forward in the regulation of international air transport. President Carter said

> The Agreement is one that reflects well on our two great nations. Its quality, its fairness, and its benefits to the consumer and to airlines should make it last as long as the original 1946 Bermuda Agreement. It continues our long and historic relationship with the United Kingdom.[167]

In a joint statement Ambassador Alan Boyd and Member of Parliament Edmund Dell said

> a new era of international travel promising more direct flights and greater route flexibility for airlines to serve public interests began today with the signing in Bermuda of a new Air Services Agreement between Bermuda and the United States.[168]

United States Secretary of Transportation Brock Adams said

> Americans from every section of our country will find air travel cheaper and more convenient as a result of the new "Bermuda Agreement" signed today.[169]

Among those who were not involved in the negotiation, however, the reaction in the United States to the Bermuda 2 Agreement was rather generally unfavorable. Comments made in the hearings in the House of Representatives before the subcommittee on aviation of the Committee on Public Works and Transportation held on September 29 and October 3, 1977,[170] were in the main derogatory.

Alfred Kahn, chairman of the Civil Aeronautics Board (appointed by President Carter after the Bermuda 2 negotiations had concluded), said, "Our concern with Bermuda 2 is that it brings greater, rather than less, government interference in carrier operating decisions that we believe are better left to management discretion."[171] In 1981, Chairman Kahn said in a public speech, "Bermuda 2 included terms that were so contrary to our fundamental competitive principles that many of our airlines were astounded." [172]

In its Annual Report to Congress for the fiscal year 1978, the Civil Aeronautics Board said

> The renegotiated United States–United Kingdom bilateral agreement (known as Bermuda 2, signed July 23, 1977) is the last episode in the history of restrictive markets and triggered a major turning point in US international aviation policy. While the United States has seen to it that interpretation and implementation of the Bermuda 2 Agreement has been done in the most competitive way possible, Bermuda 2 symbolizes the direction we are moving away from. Rather, the United States international policy is now based upon active competitive principles. This procompetitive approach has governed US bilateral aviation negotiations since fall 1977.[173]

Although the "Bermuda era" may be said to have ended with the signature of the Bermuda 2 Agreement, the Bermuda 1 model continues to have its importance. Nevertheless, it seems highly unlikely that the Bermuda 1 formulation will ever again form the cornerstone for United States air policy, even as the pendulum swings back from the extreme of "deregulation" and "procompetitive agreements."

8. DEREGULATION: UNITED STATES POLICY AND LEGISLATION

The original movement for the "deregulation" of the airlines in the United States related to the domestic industry. From the beginning there has been a recognition that different considerations affect the regulation (and the deregulation) of international air transportation. The most obvious of these is that by definition international air transportation involves at least two soverign governments, both of whose agreement, or at least acquiescence, is necessaary for radical changes in the manner of regulating transportation between their respective territories.

The movement to deregulate the United States domestic air transport industry came as a reaction to the scheme of regulation originally imposed by the Civil Aeronautics Act of 1938,[1] later amended and reenacted in the Federal Aviation Act of 1958.[2] Under this legislation the Civil Aeronautics Board was given control over the entry and exit of airlines in the operation of air transport routes,[3] over their fares and rates[4] and over agreements and mergers among them,[5] accompanied by a declaration of policy that among other things called for "competition to the extent necessary to assure the sound development of an air transportation system properly adapted to the needs of the foreign and domestic commerce of the United States, of the Postal Service and of the National Defense."[6]

As early as 1963, President John F. Kennedy was calling for more competition in the airline business.[7] In 1962, in an often-cited study of the regulation of American airlines, Richard E. Caves concluded that the U.S. domestic airline business does not have the characteristics that call for strict economic regulation by the government.[8] A similar view was advanced by various economists writing in later years.[9] Oddly, however, in view of the political impact the movement had, there was not a great deal said on the subject by the public at large. By 1975, the movement had grown to a point where President Gerald Ford supported deregulation of the U.S. domestic airlines and submitted to Congress an aviation bill for that purpose.[10] President Jimmy Carter, shortly after he assumed the presidency, endorsed this bill,[11] although it did not in the end become law. During this period, there were a number of committee hearings in Congress on the subject,[12] and most of the economists who testified in those hearings supported the idea of deregulating the American domestic industry. In October 1978, the Congress passed the Airline Deregulation Act of 1978.[13] This legislation was drafted to exclude international ("Foreign") aviation from most of its provisions.

The Airline Deregulation Act called for the removal of many of the controls on domestic routes contained in the Federal Aviation Act, with respect to operating rights[14] and pricing.[15] It was made a great deal easier for domestic airlines to obtain the right to operate new routes, and to terminate service on existing routes. With respect to pricing, a "Standard Industry Fare Level" was established on the basis of the fares in effect on July 1, 1979, and this level was to be adjusted

> not less than semi-annually by the percentage change from the last previous period in the actual operating cost per available seat mile for interstate and overseas transportation combined.[15]

A "zone of reasonableness" was established whereby airlines could increase their fares up to 5 percent above the standard industry fare level, and decrease them by up to 50 percent below the standard industry fare level without interference by the CAB. The provisions of the Federal Aviation Act remained substantially unchanged with respect to operating rights and pricing for international services.

Although the major effect of the 1978 deregulation act was on interstate and overseas air transportation, it made a number of changes in the Federal Aviation Act of 1958 that affected international airline operations, and formed part of the United States' attempt to "deregulate" international aviation to and from the United States. Among the most significant of these changes is that[17]: (1) that the Deregulation Act abolished the name "supplemental air carriers," and renamed them "charter air carriers." This change applied to both domestic and international operations.[18] The Deregulation Act also provides[19]:

> (2) No rule, regulation or order issued by the Board shall restrict the marketability, accessibility, or variety of charter trips provided under a certificate issued under this section except to the extent required by the public interest, and shall in no event be more restrictive than those regulations regarding charter air transportation in effect on October 1, 1978.

This amendment applies to domestic and international charters. Both it and the renaming of supplemental air carriers represent a considerable victory for the charter airlines. The renaming got away from the second class status implied in the word "supplemental" (which was itself adopted to get away from the invidious connotations that had developed around the term "non-scheduled air carriers"). The requirement that no restriction be more onerous than those in effect on October 1, 1978, meant that the charter carriers could lobby the Civil Aeronautics Board for a lessening of the restrictions that applied to them, but their opponents, the scheduled carriers, could have no hope of success in lobbying for greater restriction.

Section 401 (c) of the Federal Aviation Act was amended to expedite the handling of applications for certificates of convenience and necessity.[20]

Section 401 (d) of the Federal Aviation Act was amended to provide for fill-up rights on domestic segments of the international routes of United States airlines.[21]

Section 401 (j) of the Act was amended to simplify the procedures for suspending or terminating service.[22]

Section 403 (c) was amended to simplify the procedure for giving notice of fare changes.[23]

Section 406 of the Act was amended to phase out all subsidy payments to United States carriers for both domestic and international service by January 1, 1986.[24]

Section 408 was amended with respect to both domestic and international air transportation to provide that normal United States antitrust provisions will govern consolidation, merger and control of American airlines,[25] with a further provision that where the standards of the Sherman and Clayton acts[26] are not met, the transaction may nevertheless be approved if it meets serious transportation needs of the community to be served and if there is no reasonably available less anticompetitive alternative to the merger.

Section 409 of the Federal Aviation Act was amended to narrow the class of persons to which it applies. This section previously prohibited interlocking relationships without CAB approval between air carriers, common carriers or any other person "engaged in a phase of aeronautics." This amendment changes the portion in inverted commas to make it refer to persons "substantially engaged in the business of aeronautics."[27]

Section 414 of the Federal Aviation Act was amended to make it optional with the CAB whether to exempt from the operations of the United States antitrust laws matters that it had approved under sections 408, 409 or 412.[28] Previously such exemption had been automatic.

The amended section provides further that the Board may not grant such an exemption unless it finds that it is in the public interest. This adds one more hurdle to the requirements of Section 408.

The Deregulation Act provided further for the abolition of the Civil Aeronautics Board itself, with effect December 31, 1984.[29] At that time, the

CAB's authority under Sections 406 (b), (3) and (c) of the Federal Aviation Act (compensation for air transportation to small communities) as well as its authority over foreign air transportation was transferred to the Department of Transportation.[30]

With respect to "foreign" (international) air transportation, the authority of the CAB over consolidation, merger and acquisition of control (Federal Aviation Act Section 408) prohibited interests (Section 409), pooling and other agreements (Section 412), as well as its authority over legal restraints (i.e., relief from the operation of the United States antitrust laws) (Section 414) with respect to those sections, was transferred to the Department of Justice, effective January 1, 1985.[31] In October 1984, the Civil Aeronautics Board Sunset Act of 1984[32] was enacted and provided that instead of going to the Department of Justice, this authority of the CAB should go to the Department of Transportation, effective January 1, 1985.[33]

The abolition of the Civil Aeronautics Board on January 1, 1985, and the transfer of most of its functions to the Department of Transportation have had an effect on the regulation of international air transportation that is still developing. The difficulty of assessing its effect was increased by the requirement that upon transfer of the CAB's authority to it, the Department of Transportation "shall exercise such authority in consultation with the Department of State."[34] Although the Department of State has always had a strong influence upon the dealings of the Civil Aeronautics Baord with international air transportation, it has in the past had to assert its influence from outside in the name of the larger interest of the conduct of the foreign affairs of the United States. Under this legislation it appeared that the Department of State should have been in a position to exert a stronger influence on international air transportation when the authority of the CAB passed to the Department of Transportation. No major change in influence appears to have taken place, however.

The amendment of the Airline Deregulation Act of 1978 by the Civil Aeronautics Board Sunset Act of 1984 to reassign from the Department of Justice to the Department of Transportation the CAB's authority under sections 408, 409, 412 and 414 with respect to foreign air transportation avoided a potentially awkward situation. If the Department of Justice had retained this authority it appears almost inevitable that it would never have exercised it so as to alter the normal operation of the antitrust laws, since its function in the government hierarchy is to enforce those laws. As a result, for example, it would very probably have been impossible to convince the Department of Justice to exempt from the operations of the antitrust laws capacity agreements or pricing agreements, however desirable a particular agreement might appear to the Department of Transportation from a commercial point of view and to the Department of State from a foreign policy point of view.

It is significant, however, that pressure is developing in Congress to give antitrust authority with respect to mergers and competitive matters back to the Department of Justice because of frustration with the Department of State's tendency to soften the impact of the antitrust laws on foreign airlines.[35]

Section 801 (a) of the Federal Aviation Act, entitled "The President of the United States," was amended to clarify its operation.[36] Previously Section 801 (a) provided that certificates of convenience and necessity for United States airlines for foreign air transportation or for air transportation between places in the same territory or possession and foreign air carrier permits for foreign airlines, or any CAB orders affecting them, were subject to presidential approval before they could become effective. There had been considerable controversy over this provision because it had been claimed that the president had acted politically, rather than on the basis of foreign policy considerations.[37]

As originally written, Section 801[38] had no limitations on the authority of the president to approve, disapprove or change an order of the CAB affected by this section. Moreover, approvals, disapprovals and affirmative action by the president were not reviewable in court,[39] nor were such cases reviewable before they were submitted for presidential action, because they did not at that time constitute final action by the Civil Aeronautics Board.[40] In 1972 Section 801 was amended [41] to provide that in order to disapprove an order subject to Section 801, the president must find "that disapproval is required for reasons of the national defense or the foreign policy of the United States." Despite this amendment, however, there remained a question whether cases not disapproved by the president were subject to review by the courts. (There was also a question whether the president, when he acted in such cases, was in fact acting for reasons of national defense or the foreign policy of the Untied States, rather than reacting to political pressures.)

In an effort to resolve this problem, President Ford in 1976 issued an executive order[42] instructing the executive departments and agencies of the U.S. government to make recommendations concerning CAB orders transmitted to the White House pursuant to Section 801 only on the basis of defense or foreign policy considerations, and to make their comments on other aspects directly to the CAB. At the same time, the executive office of the president was instructed not to discuss such orders with any interested private party. The executive order went on to provide:

> Orders involving foreign and overseas air transportation certificates of US Carriers that are subject to the approval of the President are not subject to judicial review when the President approves or disapproves an order for reasons of defense or foreign policy. All disapprovals necessarily are based on such a Presidential decision, but approval by the President does not

> necessarily imply the existence of any defense or foreign policy reason. For the purpose of assuring whatever opportunity is available under the law for judicial review of the CAB decisions, all departments and agencies which make recommendations to the President pursuant to Section 801 should indicate separately whether, and why, if the order or any portion thereof is approved, the President cannot state in his approval that no defense or foreign policy reason underlies his decision.[43]

The Amendment to Section 801 (a) effected by the Airline Deregulation Act of 1978 specifically provides that the president's right to disapprove CAB action may be exercised only on the basis of

> foreign relations or national defense considerations which are within the President's jurisdiction, but not on the basis of economic or carrier selection considerations.

The new section goes on to say

> Any such Board Action not disapproved (within stated time limits) shall take effect as Action of the Board, not the President, and as such shall be subject to judicial review as provided in Section 1006 of this Act.

This amendment appears to have finally settled the problems with Section 801, except for the case where the president acts for political reasons, but says that he is acting for reasons of defense or foreign policy. For that, there does not appear to be any solution.

The deregulation of interstate and "overseas" (i.e. between the United States and its overseas possessions) aviation is an interesting subject, and one about which there has been a great deal of controversy.[44] Nevertheless, it is germane to the regulation of international aviation only to the extent that it influenced that area. I propose herein to take a neutral stance concerning the merits of "deregulation" for American domestic aviation and simply to take account of it as a fact. As a fact, the movement to deregulation had a profound effect on the policy of the United States toward international aviation.

As we have seen, the Airline Deregulation Act of 1978 excluded international aviation from the most radical of its changes. The advocates of deregulation, however, appear to have been eager to take on the task of bringing it to the international area.

One of the prime movers in the drive to bring the United States' international aviation business under the regime of deregulation was Alfred Kahn. Kahn had been a professor of economics at Cornell University in New York State and was at the time of his appointment to the CAB serving as chairman of the New York State Public Service Commission. Appearing at the 1975 oversight hearings chaired by Senator Edward Kennedy,[45] Kahn testified in favor of deregulation of the air transport industry, saying that regulation is an imperfect institution, antithetical to competition, a producer of cartelization and inefficiency and, to the extent the industry is competitive, the producer of excessive service and high prices. In the spring of 1977, President Carter appointed Kahn chairman of the Civil Aeronautics Board, evidently with the mandate to deregulate the United States air transport industry. Kahn did not wait for legislation to begin the task, but introduced a number of domestic proceedings before the CAB leading to the grant of route authority to a multiplicity of airlines on a permissive basis, with the idea that market forces would determine which airlines would in the end operate the routes.[46]

Kahn expressed his views concerning the deregulation of international aviation in a paper presented at a symposium March 4, 1978, at Georgetown University in Washington, D.C.[47] This paper describes his rationale for the cluster of policies and actions that have gone under the name of "international deregulation" in the United States and provides a blueprint of what he was doing and proposed to do to make it effective. The article is worth summarizing for the light it sheds on the thinking behind the changes in United States attitudes with respect to the economic regulation of international rates, routes, and commercial practices during this period.[48]

The paper starts out by calling attention to the deregulation of the domestic air transport industry, which Kahn says is already in progress and will pick up momentum with the passage of the then-pending Airline Deregulation Act of 1978. "The central theme of my remarks," he says, "will be that there is every reason to adopt the same goal for the international market as for the domestic."[49] He acknowledges that a complicating factor in the reordering of international air transportation is that one must deal with foreign governments that are sovereign in their own territories and do not necessarily share his ideas, and that in particular, most foreign governments do not share the view that free competition is desirable in international air transport, but on the contrary many of them have asserted that they will not permit it to be given a trial in their territory.

Kahn says the reasons foreign governments protect their airlines from competition are: (1) national defense; (2) noneconomic motives such as national pride, prestige, national unity, and communication with former colonies; and (3) economic motives (Kahn says "or pseudo-economic") such as balance of payments and commercial linkages for the promotion of trade, tourism and capital flows.

To rebut these views, Kahn says that most countries that hold them have, as airlines, chosen instruments that they subsidize on certain routes, in part by sheltering them from competition, in the expectation that they will use the profits from sheltered routes to provide service on other unprofitable routes. He says this produces a vicious circle. Where the airlines are protected from competition, they become inefficient, which requires that they be further subsidized and protected from competition.

Kahn says that prior to his arrival at the CAB the United States was guilty of the same logic, citing as an example that the CAB staff had recommended that the United States refuse to consider granting the Belgians new route rights in the United States because the Belgians were already carrying more than their fair share of United States–Belgian traffic and were also carrying excessive fifth freedom traffic and because they had nothing to offer the United States in return for further route rights.[50]

Kahn observes that the clue to the error of the ways of the American authorities is that they had been viewing the function of air transport negotiations as exchanging landing privileges and trading other privileges on behalf of United States airline companies, rather than on behalf of American travelers and shippers. Thus, he says, they were regarding the exchange of such rights as a "zero sum game," where if foreign airlines are given a new right to pick up traffic in the United States, this is at the expense of American airlines, who are then deprived of the ability to carry the same traffic, whereas the proper view is that developed by Adam Smith and David Ricardo: eliminating barriers to international trade increases the wealth of all nations, and the essence of free trade is that it benefits both parties. Kahn then goes on to state his principles in a parargraph that is worth quoting in full:

> The cornerstone of the altered approach to international aviation that we have been following during the past year—some of the most striking manifestations of which have been our letting Sabena into Atlanta, offering the Dutch access to Los Angeles and their choice of another city, and looking the other way when someone complains about their competitive aggressiveness in picking up fifth and sixth freedom traffic—is our belief that the function of economic policy is to serve consumers rather than protect producers, and that the best way to do that is by promoting competition at home and abroad, rather than by cartelization. The underlying premise is that this is not a zero-sum game; that the public benefits by mutual extension of competitive opportunities; and that once we think of our constituents as travelers and shippers, rather then airlines, there are indeed things that those importunate foreigners have to offer us—most prominently an assured hospitality to competition—multiple designation and low-fare scheduled service, an acceptance of liberal charter rules—as well as the competing services that their own carriers are so anxious to offer us. Our intention is to trade liberalizations for liberalizations, offering foreign governments expanded access to our markets instead of capacity limitations, restrictions on gateways, and prohibitions of price competition. In this way, we think, "we"—properly defined—gain both by what we "give" and by what we receive.[51]

Kahn says that opponents of a competitive regime make three arguments to show why it will not work in the international area: (1) The airline industry has an inherent tendency to be destructive. (2) While competition may work in the rich American market with its long distances and heavy reliance on air travel, it will not work for other countries where hauls are shorter and routes are thinner. And (3) the wide-spread practice of subsidization makes it impossible for competition among international airlines to work. Kahn says that these opponents state that the result of free competition will be that only the inefficient nationally owned carriers will survive and the unsubsidized privately owned companies will go out of business.

His rebuttal of the first claim is that the air transportation business does not have the necessary attributes of a natural monopoly, so it does not require regulation as a public utility.

His answer to the second claim is that it is simply not true that the characteristics of the American market are different from those of the international market.

The third claim he answers by saying that if foreign taxpayers want to subsidize the availability of low-cost air service to American and foreign travelers, he would not necessarily regard that as an unmitigated catastrophe. He also observes that the harm produced by cartelization is far worse than the harm caused by airline subsidies.

Kahn concludes by saying that the United States recognizes that it cannot force its views on other nations, but that it intends to persuade other nations to agree to bilateral agreements that promote competition by offering them valuable route rights to the United States in exchange. He says he believes that as the benefits of a more competitive regime become evident, internal pressure from travelers and shippers will force the countries that have held to restrictive capacity and fare practices to change their ways.

Putting Kahn's expression into a very compressed form: He planned to extend to international aviation the same elements of deregulation that were already being applied to United States domestic aviation. These were in essence low fares, unregulated competition, and freedom of entry and exit into particular markets.[52] This is to be achieved in the face of recognized foreign opposition by using liberal grants of access to U.S. route points to induce selected countries to sign with the Untied States bilateral air transport agreements providing for freedom of pricing by the airlines, freedom from restrictions on competitive behavior, and the right of each government to designate a multiplicity of airlines. Pressure for low fares and competitive service will be increased by promoting charter service through charter bilateral agreements. The geopolitical pressure of such bilateral agreements with strategically placed countries would cause other countries to perceive it to be in their self-interest to sign similarly liberal agreements with the United States, with the result that in the end the United States would have converted the rest of the world to the philosophy of deregulation.

An important part of Kahn's strategic plan is that he considers that it will not cost the United States anything to give away route rights in exchange for promises of liberal treatment for American airlines because granting such rights constitutes an elimination of barriers to free trade, and under the views of Adam Smith and David Ricardo, eliminating these barriers to international trade will benefit the United States as well as the nation that gets the right to operate on the routes.

Although the intellectual underpinnings of Kahn's paper are not nearly so important as the fact that the views expressed decisively influenced United States air transport policy for a considerable period and continue to have an influence, certain comments appear in order. In the first place, he does not meet head on the problem created by the opposition of a very large proportion of foreign governments to the liberalization expressed in the U.S. concept of "deregulation." This opposition goes back to the period in 1945, 1946 and 1947 when the United States was promoting the idea of "freedom of the skies" in the negotiations for a multilateral agreement. The nearest the United States could come at that time to "open skies" was the Bermuda Agreement which, as interpreted by the United States, was not anything like "deregulation" and, as interpreted by many other countries, actually produced a restrictive regime. Moreover, the evolution of foreign opinion since Bermuda had favored the limitation of international competition and the opposition to "open skies" had hardened.

Kahn did not point to any change in the thinking of foreign governments, nor did he propose a program to convince them of the error of their ways. Kahn recognized this opposition, but he confined himself to producing economists' rebuttals to the reasons he says foreign governments assign for their preference for a regulated regime. These arguments may or may not be the final correct answers, but given the nature of economic debate, it was obvious that economists of the opposite persuasion would have a reply to them.

The solidity of such foreign opposition to the whole idea of deregulation or "open skies" is exemplified by the results of the special air transport conference held by the International Civil Aviation Organization in Montreal in April of 1977. This conference was called to consider means to regulate international civil air transportation and the overwhelming consensus was in favor of *a priori* control of airline capacity, with the United States as one of very few objectors.[53]

The nub of Kahn's final position is that the United States is to bring the rest of the world to accept deregulation by inducing certain countries to sign liberal bilateral air transport agreements through extremely liberal route grants with the intention that other countries will be forced to follow suit by internal pressure from their citizens to obtain similar benefits. Apart from the question whether things really would happen this way, this position has a couple of very serious flaws. In the first place, a trade of immediate operating rights for a promise of liberal treatment in the future runs the risk that the opposite party will figure out some way to avoid delivering on the promise of liberal treatment in the future. Such devices could include things in the nature of "non-tariff barriers," such as craftily drafted fuel restrictions and exaggeratedly high user fees. They could also take the form of a direct refusal to allow the liberal treatment that had been promised, or of a twisting of its language to avoid performance.

In the second place, the grant of route rights to foreign airlines is the price the United States must pay to obtain route rights for American airlines in foreign countries, and if they are given away too liberally for other elements or for no consideration at all, the United States will be left with nothing to trade for routes, which are the fundamental reason for the existence of bilateral air transport agreements.

It is unlikely that the United States was, in any case, motivated by doctrinaire economic reasons to adopt international deregulation as a policy. At this stage one can only guess at the true underlying reasons. The following is a list of possible reasons:

1. Whatever political reasons supported the adoption of a policy of deregulation for domestic aviation would also tend to support the application of a similar policy for international.[54]

2. There was a need for a new international air policy in the United States. Bermuda 1, which had formed the basis of United States air policy for 31 years, was discredited by the signature of the Bermuda 2 Agreement. The Bermuda 2 Agreement itself was repudiated throughout the United States government, and in any case was so contrary to the generally liberal tenor of American air policy that it could not serve as the basis for a new policy.

3. The United States was undergoing at the time a reaction to the relatively restrictive policies of the early 1970s, when the airlines were permitted to enter capacity limitation agreements, and the CAB imposed a "route moratorium."

4. Although the concept of "open skies" that the United States had promoted in the multilateral negotiations in the mid 1940s was probably what the American advocates of deregulation really wanted, it was evident that in the late 1970s "open skies" as a slogan was no less a loser than it was in the 1940s. "Deregulation" can be seen as a way of serving up "open skies" in a new suit of clothes, with the further advantage that it permitted a gradual, piecemeal approach that would have been incompatible with the all-or-nothing concept of "open skies."

5. "Deregulation" was not confined to the airline business. It was part of the entire movement to return to the free market that affected

the banks and the financial industry even more than the airlines. The movement had strong academic support.

Having adopted the idea of deregulation as part of its international air policy, the United States took a number of specific actions to produce a greater freedom of competition in commercial air transportation to and from the United States.

The first such step was to attempt to persuade foreign nations to sign with it bilateral air transport agreements reflecting the new "pro-competitive" policies that were clustered under the name of international deregulation. On March 31, 1978, the United States signed a protocol to the U.S.-Netherlands agreement[55] that gave the Dutch greatly improved route rights in exchange for liberalized capacity, fare and charter provisions.[56]

The Dutch protocol was followed by agreements with Israel (1978),[57] Germany (1978),[58] Belgium (1978),[59] Costa Rica (1979),[60] Singapore (1979),[61] Thailand (1979),[62] Netherlands Antilles (1980),[63] Jamaica (1979),[64] Finland (1980),[65] and Jordan (1980).[66] Each of these agreements differs in certain respects from the others. To provide an appreciation of what the United States was seeking to accomplish in this series of agreements it appears useful to review the standard form of bilateral agreement that was developed by the United States as the vehicle to bring deregulation to the rest of the world.

This model agreement was reproduced and commented on by Richard Bogosian, chief of the Aviation Negotiations Division, Office of Aviation, Department of State, in a 1981 article in the *Journal of Air Law and Commerce.*[67] The relevant portions of this model may be summarized as follows:

Article 3. *Designation and Authorization.* This article is similar to the corresponding article in the United States model agreement based on the Bermuda type, except that it is more specific as to the right to designate multiple airlines. This addresses a problem that had arisen under the Bermuda-type agreements where a number of countries had insisted that there was no right to designate more than one airline, despite fairly clear language allowing multiple designation.

Article 8. *Commercial Opportunitites.* This article represents an attempt to preclude interference with the ability of United States airlines to compete abroad by means of restrictions on such things as the establishment of offices, the employment of foreign personnel, ground handling arrangements, the ability to sell transportation directly and through agents, the ability to make sales in local currency or in other freely convertible currency, and the ability to remit abroad money received for sales of air transportation, net of local expenses. All of these devices had been used by foreign governments at one time or another to restrict the activities of

United States airlines. This type of clause is of great value to US airlines in avoiding discrimination. The problem is that there are so many ways in which a government can interfere with an airline's ability to compete that it is impossible to list them all.

Article 9. *Customs Duties and Taxes* is similar to the corresponding article in the United States model based on the Bermuda-type agreements. This type of article is important in a "pro-competitive" bilateral agreement because customs duties and taxes can be used as a way of limiting the ability of foreign airlines to compete in the local market by increasing the cost of operating.

Article 10. *User Charges* represents an attempt to limit user charges (navigation charges, landing fees, ground handling fees, etc.) to

> an equitable portion of the full economic cost to the competent charging authorities of providing the airport, air navigation and aviation security facilities.

To an increasing degree, aviation authorities have used this type of charge to build up funds for unrelated purposes at the expense of foreign airlines through such devices as throwing into the cost pool of an international airport costs related to all domestic airports in the country. Also, the British have included a charge intended to accumulate capital to improve the facility at some future time, and even to build a new airport. Where the national airline is subsidized, excessively high user charges can be used as a means of discouraging competition by foreign airlines even where there is no apparent discrimination. (The full impact of the charge is felt by the foreign airlines. Sums paid by the national airline come right back in the form of subsidy, even though the charge is not ostensibly discriminatory.)

Article 11. *Fair Competition.* This article introduces a number of significant changes in the language of the corresponding clause of the United States model based on the Bermuda-type agreements. The Bermuda Agreement itself reads

> That there shall be a fair and equal opportunity for the carriers of the two nations to operate on any route between their respective territories (as defined in the agreement) covered by the agreement and its annex.[68]

This article changes the language to read (in subparagraph 1)

> Each party shall allow a fair and equal opportunity for the designated airlines of both parties to compete in the international air transportation covered by this agreement.

The change is pretty clearly intended to meet a problem that had arisen when certain nations argued that the Bermuda-type language calls for equality of results, rather than equality of opportunity to compete. The new language would preclude any such interpretation.

Subparagraph 2 requires each party to eliminate discrimination or unfair competitive practices affecting the other's airlines. The problem addressed by this provision is similar to the problem addressed in articles 8, 9 and 10 and the other subparagraphs of this article; namely, the use by governments of indirect means to suppress competition by United States airlines where they had agreed in bilateral agreements not to use direct means.

Subparagraph 3 forbids direct unilateral traffic and capacity restrictions. This is new in a model agreement but the device had been used in other bilateral agreements, primarily in the form of side-agreements.[69]

Subparagraph 4 applies to charters and forbids the imposition of first refusal requirements, uplift ratios or "no-objection fees." All of these are devices that have been used to limit the ability of United States airlines to compete for charter traffic in foreign countries and to limit the ability of charter carriers to compete with scheduled carriers. The United States itself at one time applied uplift ratios to charters. This is a requirement that a given carrier must perform a certain ratio of inbound charters to the number of outbound charters. The object was to limit the foreign airline's ability to compete in the local market. The rationale was that foreign airlines should not be allowed to capture a great deal larger amount of traffic in the U.S. market for carriage abroad than they were able to capture in their own home markets for carriage to the Untied States. The concept is analogous to the concept of "an equitable exchange of economic benefits," although it is not the same. It is, of course, inconsistent with the idea of "deregulation."

Subparagraph 5 forbids the parties to require filing of schedules, programs of charter flights or operational plans for approval, except as may be required under paragraph 3 (i.e., where required for customs, technical, operational or environmental reasons).

This article (Article 11), together with articles 8, 9 and 10, is absolutely essential in a "pro-competitive" bilateral agreement in order to prevent the United States from losing to subterfuge the liberalization it thought it was buying with the agreement. The absence or ineffectuality of such articles is seriously prejudicial to United States airlines, but the problem goes deeper: if the foreign country can avoid the effect of the liberalized bilateral agreement through use of the class of devices prohibited by these articles, then the United States has gone through a futile exercise in negotiating the bilateral agreement, since the very restrictiveness it thought it was abolishing is reintroduced through the back door. A further aspect of the problem is that no matter how carefully clauses like articles 8, 9, 10 and 11 of the model agreement are drafted, they can never cover all possible devices that could be used to profiteer at the expense of foreign airlines, and to restrict their ability to compete with the national airline.

Article 12. *Pricing (Mutual Disapproval).* This article goes about as far in the direction of deregulating airline pricing as it could go, short of abolishing government control entirely. It applies to all pricing, passenger fares, and cargo rates, as well as to scheduled and charter service between the two countries. In order for a price proposed for application between the territories of the two parties to be disapproved, they must both agree that it should be disapproved.

The grounds for disapproval are limited to: (a) prevention of predatory or discriminatory prices or practices; (b) protection of consumers from prices that are unduly high or restrictive because of the abuse of a dominant position; and (c) protection of airlines from prices that are artificially low because of direct or indirect government subsidy or support.

Moreover agreement of both parties is required to disapprove prices proposed by an airline of a third country, as well as those proposed by the airlines of the two countries party to the bilateral agreement. The requirement for mutual agreement in order to disapprove prices applies to transportation between the territories of the two parties and to transportation between the territory of one of them and a third country. Finally, each party is required to allow the other's airlines as well as third country airlines to meet any competitive price charged between their territories or between the territory of one of them and a third country.

Another type of rate article that was being used was a "country of origin" rate article, which placed control of prices in the government of the country where the transportation commenced. (The Dutch Protocol supra [p. 158] contains such a rate clause.) Under the Bermuda 1 Agreement, if either party disapproves the fare, it becomes ineffective ("a single disapproval" type agreement).

Annex 1. Scheduled Air Service. Section 1 covers the routes to be exchanged and Section 2 permits a very high degree of routing flexibility.

Section 3. Permits changes of gauge at any point along the route, provided they form part of a service to or from the territory of the country that designated the airline. The provision declares specifically that there is no limit as to change in type or number of aircraft. This appears to mean that in the outbound direction, for example, an airline could substitute one or more aircraft for onward carriage bearing a total capacity greater than that used on the route from the home country to the point of change. This is a radical departure from previous practice, which typically required the use of smaller aircraft for the onward carriage in the case described, either explicitly as in the Bermuda 1 and Bermuda 2 agreements,[70] which refer specifically to the use of a smaller aircraft, or by implication as in the French agreement,[71] which prohibits changes that would alter the long-range characteristics of the route or would be inconsistent with the Bermuda 1 type capacity provisions.

Annex II. Charter Air Service. Section 1 provides that designated airlines may offer to or via the territory of the other party (a) to or from the territory of the party that designated the airline, or (b) to or from third countries, charter transportation which transits the other party or which has its origin or destination in the other party, provided the traffic has made a stopover of at least two consecutive nights in the territory of the designating party.

Section 2 provides that the laws, regulations and rules of the party in whose territory the traffic originates shall be applicable to such traffic. The most important of such laws and regulations are those that govern what sort of traffic may travel on a charter.

A "capacity clause" is conspicuously absent from the United States model agreement. Subparagraph 3 of Article 11 would prevent unilateral capacity control by one party over the airlines of the other. If one party should wish to complain of allegedly excessive capacity offered by the other's airlines, it could presumably invoke Article 11, subparagraph 1, to claim that its airlines were being denied a "fair and equal opportunity" to compete by the excessive capacity offered by the other's airlines. Such a complaint would probably not prosper unless the other party were well disposed toward it because it is by no means clear that either party is required by the agreement to limit the competitive vigor of its airlines. On the contrary, the preamble to the model agreement says that the parties desire

> to promote an international air transport system based on competition among airlines in the market place with a minimum of governmental interference and regulation.

The agreements that were negotiated during this period were not all exactly like the model agreement. They were however similar in advancing the "pro-competitive" views of the United States' aviation authorities. They also had in common that the United States paid a heavy price in route grants to induce the foreign governments to enter this type of agreement. The following are examples of some of the richer routes. The Israelis got a route that reads:[72]

> Israel via points in Cyprus, Turkey, Greece, Rumania, Italy, Spain, Portugal, Switzerland, Austria, Federal Republic of Germany, France, Luxemburg, Belgium, Netherlands, United Kingdom, Eire and Montreal to New York and four additional points in the United States [only two of these four additional points may be served until August 1, 1979] and beyond (a) one specified US point to Mexico City, and (b) any specified US points to South America and Asia, without traffic rights between Montreal and US points or between US points and points beyond the United States.

The German protocol[73] provides for the following route:

> From the Federal Republic of Germany via intermediate points to Anchorage (1) Atlanta, Boston, Chicago, Dallas/Fort Worth, Los Angeles,

> Miami, New York, Philadelphia, San Francisco, San Juan and one additional point in the United States to be selected by the Federal Republic of Germany (2) and beyond to any points outside, without directional limitation.
>
> [Notes:] 1. Rights beyond Anchorage are limited to Tokyo and Osaka, Japan, notwithstanding the grant of general rights as contained in this route description. Flights serving Anchorage must serve a point in the Federal Republic of Germany and Tokyo and/or Osaka, Japan. Full traffic rights, including stopover rights, are granted at Anchorage on the sector Anchorage–Federal Republic of Germany. Only stopover traffic may be embarked or disembarked at Anchorage on the sector Anchorage Japan.
>
> 2. This additional point shall be available for use effective April 1, 1981 and shall be notified to the United States through diplomatic channels.

The Jamaicans got the following route[74]:

> From Jamaica via points in the Caribbean (1) and the Bahamas (2) to ten points in the United States (3) and beyond (a) Continental U.S. points to three points in Canada (4) and (b) Puerto Rico to one point in Europe (4).
>
> [Notes:] 1. For purposes of this schedule, the term "Caribbean" shall comprise the following: Cayman Islands, Cuba, Haiti, Dominican Republic, St. Maarten, British Virgin Islands, Antigua, St. Kitts, Nevis, Anguilla, Montserrat, Guadeloupe, Dominica, Martinique, St. Lucia, St. Vincent, Grenada, Barbados, Trinidad and Tobago, Aruba and Curaçao.
>
> 2. With traffic rights between the Bahamas and three of the US points, which are to be selected and changed in accordance with the procedures set forth in footnote 3.
>
> 3. These ten US points are to be selected by the Government of Jamaica and notified to the United States Government. Changes in the points selected may be made at intervals of not less than six months with 60 days' notice to the United States Government.
>
> 4. To be selected and changed in accordance with the procedures set forth in footnote 3.

The Costa Ricans got the following route[75]:

> From Costa Rica via intermediate points to San Juan, Miami and three additional points in the United States (1) and beyond to three points in Canada (2).
>
> [Notes:] (1) The three additional US points are to be selected by the Government of Costa Rica with notification to the United States Government. Changes in the points selected may be made at intervals of not less than six months with 60 days' notice to the United States Government.
>
> (2) To be selected and changed in accordance with the procedures set forth in footnote 1.

When viewed in the light of Alfred Kahn's underlying premise that the United States gains by what it gives away in a route trade, as well as by what it receives, these routes are not particularly startling. They are indeed startling, however, when one views them in the light of the uproar that went up over the relatively very modest routes that the United States granted to the Germans in 1957 that were the subject of the Smathers hearings in the Senate.

As the Civil Aeronautics Board began signing its "pro-competitive" bilateral air transport agreements, it undertook to open up international routes to multiple United States carriers, by holding a series of international route cases. These were:

The *U.S.-Zurich/Tel Aviv Show Cause Proceeding*[76] where National Airlines and Trans International Airlines were given certificates of convenience and necessity for routes to Zurich and Tel Aviv under expedited procedures;

The *U.S.-Benelux Low Fares Proceeding*[77] where 13 United States airlines were given "permissive" authority (i.e., authority they were not required to use) between U.S. points and points in Belgium, the Netherlands and Luxembourg;

The *U.S.-Bahamas Proceeding*[78] where 13 American airlines were given permissive authority between 44 U.S. cities and points in the Bahamas Islands;

The *U.S.-Costa Rica Show Cause Proceeding*[79] where 12 American airlines were given permissive authority between various U.S. cities and Costa Rica, under expedited procedures;

The *Central American Show Cause Proceeding*[80] where 13 U.S. airlines were given permissive authority to operate between various United States cities and points in one or more Central American countries under expedited procedures;

The *U.S.-Germany Show Cause Proceeding*[81] where 19 American carriers were given new or additional authority on a permissive basis between any point in the United States and any point in West Germany under expedited procedures;

The *Bermuda Show Cause Proceeding*[82] where 11 American airlines were given permissive authority to operate between nine U.S. gateways and Bermuda under expedited procedures; and,

The *Trans Pacific Low Fare Route Investigation,*[83] where United States airlines were given new or additional authority across the Pacific on a permissive basis.[84]

In August 1978, President Carter issued his *United States Policy for the Conduct of International Air Transport Negotiations.*[85] The accompanying statement by the president says, in part:

> Our policy seeks to encourage vigorous competition, with the goals of permitting lower fares, better service to more cities, and fewer government restrictions on charter travel. Travelers from many coutnries have already benefited from recent agreements which reflect our competitive policy. I hope our formal statement, by making our position clear, will ease the difficult process of negotiating additional air agreements with other countries.

The policy itself is divided into five major headings. The introduction stresses international airline competition and low prices. It observes that bilateral aviation agreements should serve the interests of both parties and implies a faith that foreign countries share the U.S. belief that the economic prosperity of their airlines will be enhanced by a policy of expansion of economic opportunity rather than restriction.

The second section is captioned "Goals of US International Air Transportation Policy." The major goal is said to be to

> Achieve a System of International Air Transportation that places its principal reliance on actual and potential competition to determine the variety, quality, and price of air service.

The third section is captioned "Translating Goals into Negotiating Objectives." This section presents the following specific objectives:

> 1. Creation of new and greater opportunities for innovative and creative pricing that will encourage and permit the use of new price and service options to meet the needs of different travelers and shippers.
> 2. Liberalization of charter rules and elimination of restrictions on charter operations.
> 3. Expansion of scheduled service through elimination of restrictions on capacity, frequency and route operating rights.
> 4. Elimination of discrimination and unfair competitive practices faced by US airlines in international transportation.
> 5. Flexibility to designate multiple US airlines in international air markets.
> 6. Encouragement of maximum traveler and shipper access to international markets by authorizing more cities for nonstop or direct service, and by improving the integration of domestic and international airline services.
> 7. Flexibility to permit the development and facilitation of competitive air cargo services.

The fourth section is captioned "Explanation of Objectives." It expands upon the seven objectives listed above.

The fifth section, captioned "Negotiating Principles," reads as follows:

> The guiding principle of United States negotiating policy will be to trade competitive opportunities, rather than restrictions with our trading partners. We will aggressively pursue our interests in expanded air transportation and reduced prices rather than accept the self-defeating accommodation of protectionism. Our concessions in negotiations will be given in return for progress toward competitive objectives, and these concessions themselves will be of a liberalizing character.
>
> Proposed bilateral agreements which do not meet our minimum competitive objectives will not be signed without presidential approval.

This policy statement makes official the views expressed by Alfred

Kahn in his *Air Law* article. Note that the Carter policy embraces the idea of trading route rights for promises of liberality, when it says

> our concessions in negotiations will be given in return for progress toward competitive objectives, and these concessions themselves will be of a liberalizing character.

The United States' deregulation policy was extended by law to international airline operations in amended form by the International Air Transportation Competition Act of 1979.[86] This legislation is a sort of grab-bag of amendments to the Federal Aviation Act of 1958, most of which fall within the concepts that have been identified as deregulation policy, but a number of which seem to have been thrown in as an afterthought.

Section 17 of the International Air Transportation Competition Act of 1979 (hereinafter sometimes referred to as the "International Competition Act") contains an amendment to Section 1102 of the Federal Aviation Act which includes a list of "goals for International Aviation Policy" that in most cases reflects and deepens the "negotiating objectives" of the Carter policy but alters them in the case of the policy for route trades. The amended Section 1102 provides that the specific goals that are to be included in the formulation of air policy are the following:

> 1. The strengthening of the competitive position of United States air carriers to at least secure equality with foreign air carriers, including the attainment of opportunities for United States air carriers to maintain and increase their profitabilty in foreign air transportation;
> 2. Freedom of air carriers and foreign air carriers to offer fares and rates which correspond to consumer demand;
> 3. The fewest possible restrictions on charter transportation;
> 4. The maximum degree of multiple and permissive international authority for United States air carriers so that they will be able to respond quickly to market demand;
> 5. The elimination of operational and marketing restrictions to the greatest extent possible;
> 6. The integration of domestic and international air transportation;
> 7. An increase in the number of nonstop United States gateway cities;
> 8. Opportunities for carriers of foreign countries to increase their access to the United States points if exchanged for benefits of similar magnitude for United States carriers or the traveling public, with permanent linkage between rights granted and rights given away;
> 9. The elimination of discrimination and unfair competitive practices faced by United States airlines in foreign air transportation, including excessive landing and user fees, unreasonable ground handling requirements, undue restrictions on operations, prohibitions against change of gauge and similar restrictive practices; and,
> 10. The promotion, encouragement and development of civil aeronautics and a viable, privately owned United States air transport industry.

These goals supersede the objectives stated in the Carter policy, and until this law is repealed, they will remain the official statement of United States air policy goals. Their principal difference from the Carter goals is one of emphasis. The Carter goals give very little emphasis to the needs of United States airlines, evidently being based on the view of CAB chairman Kahn that air transport negotiations are conducted for the benefit of travelers and shippers and not for the benefit of producers.

Although the statutory goals do not adopt the view that bilateral air transport agreements are negotiated exclusively for the benefit of airlines, they do recognize the need to keep United States carriers on an equal competitive footing with foreign air carriers and to promote opportunities for them to maintain and increase their profitability (paragraph 1).

In paragraph 8, the statutory goals recognize that the airlines are legitimate beneficiaries of route trades, along with shippers and travelers, and call upon the United States negotiators to obtain benefits of similar magnitude for routes traded away. Note that although this language does not preclude trading routes for promises of liberal treatment, it tends to discourage the practice by stressing that the value of what is received must be commensurate with the value of what is given away. The last sentence of paragraph 8 of the statutory goals, which calls for a "permanent linkage between rights granted and rights given away," is evidently intended to forestall attempts by foreign governments to obtain valuable route rights by promises of liberal treatment for United States airlines and then to avoid delivering on the promise once they have the route rights in hand. To make this effective, the United States will have to require foreign governments to agree in advance that if they should fail to deliver on their end of the bargain, they would have to give up route rights granted them by the United States. It seems to me that it would be very difficult to get a sovereign government to sign such an agreement. To do so would entail at least two unacceptable implications: that the government could not be trusted to live up to its promises, and that the government had sold out its principle for new route rights. It would also be extremely difficult to enforce such a clause.

It appears significant that the model bilateral air transport agreement set out in R.W. Bogosian's 1981 article,[87] although it was the current model well after the promulgation of this law, contains no machinery for establishing such a linkage. So far as I know, no recent United States bilateral air transport agreement contains a provision for the sort of linkage described here.

It appears likely that the underlying motivation for the insistence in this section upon receiving fair value for routes given away and upon maintaining a linkage between what was given away and what was received back in return is to be found in the rather profligate route grants in the early "pro-competitive" bilateral agreements. Once the perspective changed so that granting routes was no longer viewed as a removal of obstacles to international trade, but as a "giving away" of valuable rights, the policy of "an equitable exchange of economic benefits" almost automatically came back into play.

Although the United States continued to sign bilateral air transport agreements with exaggeratedly generous route grants for foreign airlines after the passage of the International Air Transportation Competition Act,[88] this appears to have been a matter of momentum, and the United States has not made a practice of signing agreements with disproportionate route grants since 1980.

The International Air Transportation Competiton Act[89] is of great importance in the development of the United States' international air transport policy and requires a rather detailed summary. Section 2 of the Competition Act includes sweeping changes in Section 102 of the Federal Aviation Act of 1958 which are related to the changes in the "goals for International Aviation Policy" described above.

Section 102 (a) of the Federal Aviation Act is captioned "Declaration of Policy: The Board." As amended by this section, it states that the Civil Aeronautics Board "shall consider the following, among other things, as being in the public interest, and in accordance with the public convenience and necessity." The items listed may be summarized as follows:

1. [Relates to safety of operations.]
2. [Relates to safety of operations.]
3. The availability of adequate, economic, efficient and low price services by air carriers and foreign air carriers without unjust discrimination and undue preferences or advantages or unfair or deceptive practices, the need to improve relations among, and coordinate transportation by, air carriers, and the need to encourage fair wages and equitable working conditions for air carriers.
4. The placement of maximum reliance on competitive market forces and on actual and potential competition (a) to provide the needed air transportation system, and (b) to encourage efficient and well-managed carriers to earn adequate profits and to attract capital, taking account, nevertheless, of material differences, if any, which may exist between interstate and overseas air transportation on the one hand and foreign air transportation on the other.
5. [Calls for the development of a sound regulatory environment] in order to facilitate adaptation of the air transportation system to the present and future needs of the domestic and foreign commerce of the United States the postal service and the national defense.
6. [Calls for the encouragement of air service at major urban areas through secondary or satellite airports.]
7. The prevention of unfair, deceptive, predatory, or anticompetitive practices in air transportation, and the avoidance of: (a) Unreasonable industry concentration, excessive market domination and monopoly power;

and (b) Other conditions that would tend to allow one or more air carriers unreasonably to increase prices, reduce services, or exclude competition in air transportation.

8. [Calls for the maintenance of good service in small communities, with payment of subsidy, if required.]

9. The encouragement, development and maintenance of an air-transport system relying on actual and potential competition to provide efficiency, innovation, and low prices, and to determine the variety, quality, and price of air transportation services.

10. The encouragement of entry into new air transportation markets by new air carriers, the encourgement of entry into additional air transportation markets by existing air carriers, and the continued strengthening of small air carriers so as to assure a more effective, competitive airline industry.

11. The promotion, encouragement and development of civil aeronautics and a viable, privately-owned United States Air Transport Industry.

12. The strengthening of the competitive position of United States air carriers to at least assure equality with foreign air carriers, including the attainment of opportunities for United States Air Carriers to maintain and increase their profitability in foreign air transportation.

The framework into which these amendments to Section 102 of the Federal Aviation Act fits was established by the Airline Deregulation Act of 1978[90] with respect to interstate and overseas air transportation. The amendments introduced by the International Air Transportation Competition Act of 1979 had the principal effect of making the amendments of the 1978 act apply also to "foreign" (i.e., international) air transportation. It is to be noted at the outset, however, that the provisions of the new policy do not call for exactly the same treatment of domestic and international services. Item 4 above, which calls for maximum reliance on market forces, expressly recognized that it is necessary to take account of differences between interstate and overseas air transportation on the one hand and foreign air transportation on the other. Items 1, 2, 3, 5, 7, 8, 9, 10, and 11 make no distinction between domestic and international carriage. Items 6 and 8, by their context, evidently apply only to domestic air transport. Item 12 by its context applies only to international.

The language of the items that apply to both domestic and international transportation appears sufficiently broad so that their application to international transportation should not cause serious problems in most cases. It appears likely, however, that item 7 may be a cause of difficulties between the United States and other nations. This item calls for the Civil Aeronautics Board to take action wherever "unreasonable industry concentration, excessive market domination and monopoly power" become evident, since it declares the prevention of those elements to be in the public interest. This would not cause problems in interstate and overseas air transportation, where only United States airlines are involved, but in foreign air transportation, the signs are already present that foreign governments will object strenuously to the application of the United States' antitrust laws to their national airlines.

Section 7 of the International Competition Act amends Section 402 b of the Federal Aviation Act of 1958 to provide that where there is a bilateral air transport agreement covering the transportation for which a foreign airline is applying, and the applicant is qualified and has been designated by its government to perform the service, the CAB need not make a separate finding that the transportation will be in the public interest. The Civil Aeronautics Board had been troubled for many years about the relation between the implication in the signing of a bilateral air transport agreement that the transportation was in the American public interest, and the need to make a separate finding of public interest in a foreign air carrier permit case. Litigating the public interest where there is a bilateral air transport agreement tends to irritate foreign governments. This amendment allows the CAB to accept the existence of a bilateral agreement as establishing that the proposed service is in the public interest.

Section 9 of the Act adds to Section 402 f of the Federal Aviation Act a new Section 2 which reads as follows:

> (2) Whenever the Board finds that the Government, Aeronautical Authorities, or foreign air carriers of any Foreign country have, over the objections of the Government of the United States, impaired, limited or denied the operating rights of United States Air Carriers, or engaged in unfair, discriminatory or restrictive practices with a substantial adverse competitive effect upon United States Air Carriers, with respect to air transportation services to, from or through the territory of such country, the Board may without hearing, but subject to the approval of the President of the United States, summarily suspend the permits of the foreign air carriers of such country, or alter, modify, amend, condition, or limit operations under such permits if it finds such action to be in the public interest. The Board may also, without hearing, but subject to Presidential approval, to the extent necessary to make the operation of this paragraph effective, restrict operations between such foreign country and the United States by any foreign air carrier of a third country.

The Senate report accompanying this legislation[91] says this section

> will significantly contribute to the Board's ability to protect US Carriers' interests against anticompetitive actions by foreign governments. It is to be anticipated that as the United States moves towards a more competitive international aviation regime there will be occasions when furtherance of the US international aviation policy will require confrontation with foreign nations who are determined to maintain restrictive controls on capacity and rates, with governmentally prescribed divisions of the market between the carriers of the two countries. If such a regime is legal under the existing bilateral, negotiation (not confrontation) will be the course to pursue. But in many cases the imposition of restrictions are [sic] contrary to the bilateral, and it

may be that negotiation, arbitration or other means cannot satisfactorily resolve the matter. However, most foreign governments possess the power to impose by government edict whatever restrictions on operations to their country they choose. If the US Government is unable to move effectively to counter such restrictions, the result is likely to be a tightly governmentally controlled capacity and rate regime with virtually no competition in the market place. To successfully counter the restrictive moves of such governments, it is essential that the US government have available to it the same powers which foreign governments have, and in fact exercise. Too often the United States is faced with an inability to cope with foreign government restrictions because the delays inherent in our procedural processes render US counter action, or threats of counter action, untimely and, therefore, ineffective.[92]

The Senate report also observes that the amendment extends the suspension and amendment powers to the carriers of third countries in order to prevent foreign carriers from avoiding its impact through pools.

Section 10 of the International Air Transportation Competition Act of 1979 amends Section 407 of the Federal Aviation Act of 1958 to empower the Civil Aeronautics Board to require foreign airlines as well as United States airlines to submit traffic, financial or other data or copies of contracts or agreements. The Senate report says of this section:

> If a competitive international environment is to be maintained, the Board should have power to secure information as to potential anti-competitive agreements which could place US carriers at a significant competitive disadvantage.[93]

Section 11 of the International Competition Act amends Section 412 of the Federal Aviation Act (which relates to the filing of agreements with the Civil Aeronautics Board and their approval by the Board) to make optional for both American and foreign airlines the filing with the Civil Aeronautics Board of copies of or requests for authority to discuss

> cooperative working arrangements . . . or any modification or cancellation thereof between such air carrier, or foreign air carrier and any other air carrier, foreign air carrier or other carrier.

Prior to this amendment, United States airlines were required to file a much more detailed class of agreements and there was no provision for foreign airlines to file their agreements nor for them to obtain approval of such agreements.

The Civil Aeronautics Board is required to disapprove any contract filed with it that it finds adverse to the public interest or in violation of Subtitle IV of the Federal Aviation Act and to approve any such contract that it does not so find, except that the Board may not approve any contract which

> substantially reduces or eliminates competition, unless it finds that the contract . . . is necessary to meet a serious transportation need, or to secure important public benefits, including international comity or foreign policy considerations and it does not find that such need can be met or such benefits can be secured by reasonably available alternative means having materially less anticompetitive effects.

There is a further provision that forbids approval of any agreements between an indirect air carrier (freight forwarders, consolidators, tour organizers and the like) and

> a common carrier subject to [the Air Carrier Economic Regulation provisions of the Federal Aviation Act] governing the compensation to be received by such common carrier for transportation services performed by it.

This is evidently intended to preclude discriminatory arrangements for particular freight forwarders, consolidators and tour organizers.

This section also forbids the Board to approve any agreement affecting "interstate or overseas transportation" (i.e., domestic transportation)

> that limits the level of capacity among air carriers in markets in which they compete, or that fixes rates, fares or charges between or among air carriers (except for joint rates or charges).

There is no such prohibition for international transportation.

It is worth noting also at this stage that the Deregulation Act of 1978[94] amended Section 414 of the Federal Aviation Act to provide that in order for the Civil Aeronautics Board to grant immunity to the United States antitrust laws for the parties to an agreement approved by it, the Board must affirmatively declare that it is granting such immunity. Prior to the amendment the approval of the agreement automatically conferred immunity.

Section 13 of the International Competition Act amends Section 416 (b) of the Federal Aviation Act (Classification and Exemption of Carriers) to permit the Civil Aeronautics Board to grant foreign airlines exemptions from the other provisions of the Federal Aviation Act. Prior to this amendment, the Federal Aviation Act provided for the use of the exemption procedure only for United States air carriers. This section also amended Section 416 (b) of the Federal Aviation Act for foreign air lines so as to allow them cabotage traffic between points in the United States for a period of 30 days, where the Secretary of Transportation has found that

> because of an emergency created by unusual circumstances not arising in the normal course of business, traffic in such markets cannot be accommodated by air carriers holding certificates under Section 401 of the [Federal Aviation] Act.

This permission is hedged in by restrictions, including one to require that where a labor dispute is involved, no undue advantage to either side will accrue. This provision is what remained of an attempt by the most zealous of the deregulators to give foreign airlines general permission to carry cabotage traffic in the United States.

Sections 14, 15, 16 and 24 of the International Competition Act relate to pricing. They have the effect of amending Section 1002 of the Federal Aviation Act to provide for a "standard foreign fare level," which is defined as the level of fares in foreign air transportation filed with the Civil Aeronautics Board and permitted by it to go into effect on or after October 1, 1979 (with seasonal adjustments), or the fare level determined by the Board in any case in which the Board determines that the fare level in effect on October 1, 1979, was unjust or unreasonable. The amendment provides further that the Board does not have authority to find a proposed fare unjust or unreasonable on the basis that it is too low or too high if it is not more than 5 percent higher or more than 50 percent lower than the Standard Foreign Fare Level for the sector concerned.

This section is patterned after the similar amendment to Section 1002 in the Airline Deregulation Act of 1978, which provided for much greater flexibility in American domestic air transportation. It is to be noted that in both cases, the flexibility to lower fares is greater than the flexibility to raise fares.

The "standard fare level" for both domestic and international transportation applies only to passenger fares. There is no similar "standard level" for cargo rates.

Section 21 of the International Competition Act amends Section 1117 of the Federal Aviation Act, which provides that government-financed passengers and property must move on United States airlines, not only between the United States and points abroad, but also between two foreign points. The penalty for using foreign airlines where service from a U.S. airline is available is that the Comptroller General of the United States will disallow payment for the transportation from appropriated funds (and thus the passenger will have to absorb the cost himself). This legislation is similar in its general outlines to the legislation of many foreign countries, and was adopted in part in response to the claims of the United States airlines that foreign airlines should be shut out of the market for carrying U.S. government-financed traffic because American carriers were precluded from carrying traffic financed by foreign governments.

The regulation caused some inconvenience and a great deal of anger among United States government employees based abroad, particularly employees of the Department of State, who resented being required to use U.S. airlines when they might have found foreign airlines more convenient. The amendment introduced by this section provides that the transportation of persons or property on foreign airlines is not precluded by the statute if it is provided under the terms of an air transport agreement between the

United States and a foreign government or governments and is consistent with the goals for international aviation policy set forth in the Federal Aviation Act and provides for the exchange of rights or benefits of a similar magnitude.

This legislation evidently contemplates a reciprocal exchange of rights to carry government-financed traffic. Where the exchange is between the United States and another country with a similar presence abroad and a similar international airline network, or between the United States and a country with a much smaller volume of government-financed international traffic and a much smaller network of international airline service, there would not be a reason to question whether the deal constitutes an "exchange of benefits of a similar magnitude." This criterion would not, however, be satisfied with a reciprocal exchange of rights between the United States and a country with relatively little government-financed international traffic and a large network of international airline services.

Section 23 of the act amends the International Air Transportation Fair Competitive Practices Act of 1974[96] to allow the Civil Aeronautics Board, subject to presidential approval, after a finding of discriminatory practices by a foreign nation,

> to take such actions as it deems to be in the public interest to eliminate such practices or restrictions. Such actions may include, but are not limited to the denial, transfer, alteration, modification, amendment, cancellation, limitation or revocation of any foreign air carrier permit or tariff pursuant to the powers of the Board

under the Federal Aviation Act of 1958. The amendment also gives United States airlines as well as any government agency the right to file complaints of discrimination under the new section.[97]

Thus, after the doubts and hesitations that attended the passage of Part 213 of the CAB's economic regulations in 1970, the United States has now come to the position of authorizing the Board to act unilaterally to eliminate discrimination against American airlines by taking "such action as it deems to be in the public interest," including restrictions on foreign air carriers' operating rights or tariffs under the International Air Transportation Fair Competitive Practices Act.

The panoply of weapons the United States now has to impose counter-restrictions in order to protect U.S. airlines from discrimination and restriction abroad includes Part 213 of the CAB's economic regulations, the new Section 2 of Section 402 (f) of the Federal Aviation Act added by the present Act, and the International Air Transportation Fair Competitive Practices Act of 1975 as amended by the present Act. The new goals for International Aviation Policy introduced by the International Air Transportation Competition Act make it clear that the United States is to

> strengthen the competitive position of United States air carriers to at least secure equality with foreign air carriers, including the opportunity for United States air carriers to maintain and increase their profitability in foreign air transportation.[98]

Although this insistence on protecting United States airlines may seem paradoxical in a regime of deregulation, it is a necessary feature of that regime. If the United States is going to relax its own competitive control over foreign airlines in exchange for foreign governments' agreement to relax their competitive control of U.S. airlines, it is essential for it to retain a means to apply pressure on foreign governments through their airlines if they fail to deliver on their part of the bargain, and to act directly against foreign airlines if they damage U.S. airlines by unfair competitive behavior.

Sections 3, 4, 5, 6, 8, 12, 18, 19, 20, 22, 25, 26, 27, 28 and 29 of the International Air Transportation Competition Act of 1979 are not summarized, because they are purely administrative in nature, or because they relate to matters that are not treated herein, or because they were temporary in nature.

9. DEREGULATION: INTERNATIONAL REPERCUSSIONS

While the executive pronouncements and laws that established the setting for the United States' attempt to "deregulate" international aviation were being put into place, there were a number of developments in the relationship of the United States to other nations concerning commercial international aviation that were influenced by and at the same time influenced the formation of U.S. policy.

One such development was Sir Freddie Laker's "Skytrain" service. We have seen how the United States permitted the supplemental carriers to increase their participation in the North Atlantic market at very low fares, hemmed in by restrictions, and how in 1968 the United States Congress permitted the scheduled carriers to match the supplemental airlines in the offering of all inclusive tour packages.

In the early 1970s there was an excess of capacity on the North Atlantic, resulting in part from the introduction of wide-bodied equipment and in part from the competition between scheduled and supplemental carriers.[1] This led the scheduled airlines to engage in extensive rebating despite the provisions of the IATA resolutions and the Federal Aviation Act prohibiting such practices.[2] In August 1972 the CAB ordered an investigation of the North Atlantic passenger market,[3] and in 1974 the Department of Justice called a grand jury to investigate the situation.

In the end, all of the scheduled airlines operating across the North Atlantic, both U.S. and foreign (excluding the carriers from the Iron Curtain countries), agreed to plead *nolo contendere* to a criminal information alleging ten misdemeanor counts, to pay fines totaling $655,000 and to be bound by an injunction against rebating for five years.[4] Although this episode did not violate the terms of any bilateral air transport agreement the United States had with the countries whose airlines were fined, it is likely that it was viewed by the European countries as an instance of high-handedness and willingness to take unilateral action by the United States.

Sir Freddie Laker commenced charter operations in 1970 between the

United Kingdom and the United States, with Laker Airways. As early as 1971, he began to seek permission to operate a service he called "Skytrain" between London and New York. This was to be a low-cost, no-reservations scheduled service with very limited on-board amenities. The fares were to be at or below those charged by the supplemental airlines for charter service. He had problems in both the United Kingdom and in the United States, but finally in June 1977 he obtained a permit from the Civil Aeronautics Board to operate the service.[5] Permission from the British had already been obtained, after initial difficulties.

Laker announced a round-trip fare of $236 between New York and London. The IATA carriers responded with standby and budget fares of $256 and a super apex fare of $229. The CAB approved the standby fares only, and ordered the others investigated.[6] President Carter, by a letter dated September 26, 1977, reversed the Board and ordered all of the fares approved, saying his new aviation policy supported low fares.[7]

Thereafter Laker competed with the scheduled and supplemental carriers for transatlantic traffic until February 5, 1982, when Laker ceased operations and went into liquidation. On November 24, 1982, Laker brought an action in the United States District Court for the District of Columbia under the Sherman Act[8] and the Clayton Act[9] against Pan American, TWA, McDonnell Douglas Corporation, McDonnell Douglas Finance Corporation, British Airways, Lufthansa, Swissair, and British Caledonian. On February 15, 1983, an essentially similar action was brought by Laker in the same court against Sabena and KLM.[10]

According to the opinion of Judge Harold Greene on Laker's motion for a preliminary injunction, the complaints alleged that prior to Laker's Skytrain service the IATA carriers charged fares higher than those which would prevail in a competitive market. The complaints allege further that in response to Laker's low-cost service, the IATA carriers entered a scheme to destroy both Laker's charter service and its Skytrain service, whereby some of them charged below-cost fares on the London–New York route, and eventually in 1981 Pan American, TWA and British Airways decided to match Laker's fares on all its transatlantic routes but retain their own attractive high cost services. The complaint also claims that in the winter of 1981–82, there was an agreement in IATA to inaugurate a new and higher level of fares for the summer of 1982, but to fix the fares of IATA members at Laker's level as long as Laker stayed in business. There was a further allegation that the defendants interfered with Laker's financing by pressuring Laker's lenders to deny it financing to buy new equipment from the McDonnell Douglas aircraft company, which was the final blow that forced Laker into liquidation.

On January 21, 1983, British Airways filed an action for declaratory judgment against Laker in the Queen's Bench Division of the High Court of Justice in England, seeking a declaration of nonliability to Laker and a permanent injunction preventing Laker from continuing with its suit against British Airways in the United States. At the same time British Airways obtained a temporary restraining order against interference with the conduct of the British court proceedings. British Caledonian, Lufthansa and Swissair filed similar petitions in the British court and were granted similar restraining orders against Laker's seeking a counter injunction.

Laker moved in the United States district court for a temporary restraining order and preliminary injunction against the remaining defendants, TWA, Pan American, McDonnell Douglas, McDonnell Douglas Finance, KLM and Sabena, enjoining them from participating in the British law suit and seeking partial summary judgment with respect to the issue of *forum non conveniens,* which had been raised in the British court.

By order dated March 2, 1983, the British court enjoined Laker from taking any steps in the U.S. court in the action against the two British carriers (British Airways and British Caledonian).

Judge Greene in the U.S. district court issued a temporary restraining order immediately and in the present opinion (March 9, 1983) issued the temporary injunction that had been sought by Laker and deferred the question of *forum non conveniens* for later decision.

At that point, Laker was prevented by the British order of March 2, 1983, from going forward in the United States court.

The opinion in the case reveals a high level of indignation in Judge Greene against the interference of the British court and one can infer from the excerpts from the British decisions quoted by Judge Greene that the British courts were equally irritated by the United States' application of its antitrust laws to British airlines in these circumstances. A report in the *Aviation Daily* for December 1, 1983, indicates that Judge Greene had appointed an *amicus curiae* to assist the court in studying ways to go forward with the case, which Judge Greene said he was determined to do. Among the possibilities mentioned by Judge Greene was the appointment of a trustee or receiver to conduct the litigation in Laker's name.[11]

The irritation at the British end of the route was undoubtedly increased by the appointment of a federal grand jury to consider criminal aspects of the case under the United States antitrust laws. An item in the *Baltimore Sun* of May 12, 1984, indicates that the Justice Department had closed its criminal investigation of the allegation that the transatlantic airlines had interfered with Laker's financing to purchase new aircraft, but that a federal grand jury was

> continuing its probe into other aspects of the collapse of Sir Freddie Laker's popular Skytrain, apparently focusing now on whether Sir Freddie's competitors engaged in collusion to cut their fares in order to drive him out of business.[12]

In June 1984, it was reported that on appeal the House of Lords had denied the British Airways request for an injunction against Laker's proceeding in the United States court. On November 20, 1984, it was announced that President Ronald Reagan had ordered the criminal antitrust proceeding terminated "based on foreign policy reasons."[13] This ended the criminal phase of the case, but it apparently did not mollify the British government, which announced on November 21, 1984, that it would maintain a ban on cheaper winter fares across the North Atlantic until agreement was reached resolving the long term problem of antitrust prosecutions.[14] The civil antitrust case continued until October of 1985, when it was finally settled.[15]

There is no need to try to decide who was right in this case, but it does appear appropriate to point out that this is just the sort of controversy that can be expected to arise when there is no meeting of the minds among governments concerning the rules of the game that ought to govern the operation of international air transport.

In June 1978, the Civil Aeronautics Board managed to stir up a hornet's nest by the issuance of its IATA show cause order.[16] The order directed the International Air Transport Association and other interested persons to show cause why the Board should not make final its tentative finding and conclusion that the IATA traffic conference resolutions and related agreements were no longer in the public interest and should therefore no longer be approved. The issuance of this order caused a storm of protest abroad, and the United States Department of State received numerous diplomatic protests from all over the world. The European governments were particularly concerned because it appeared that if the CAB should withdraw its approval of IATA, not only would United States carriers be precluded from participating in its traffic conferences, but foreign carriers would be subject to prosecution under the U.S. antitrust laws if they should act pursuant to the IATA agreements, at least with respect to transportation to and from the United States. Foreign governments also professed to fear that the United States was preparing to unleash a rate war on the world. Fairly early the U.S. authorities seem to have become convinced that carrier agreement on "facilitation functions" is essential, quite apart from their views about fare agreements. "Facilitation functions" have been described as

> agreement on baggaging, airlines ticket acceptability, exchange, and coordination on the multiple functions that are necessary simply to serve as the basis for the foundation from which commercial development could take place.[17]

The European pressure had an effect, particularly in the second ICAO Special Air Transport Conference held in February 1980.[18] (The first and second ICAO Special Air Transport conferences are discussed below.)

In April of 1980, the CAB issued an order saying in effect that they had found that the IATA traffic conference provisions substantially reduce competition, but that they would nevertheless approve them for two years for political reasons, provided that United States airlines might not participate in the IATA rate-making traffic conference[19] for travel across the Atlantic.[20]

Most of the United States airlines took the cue from the Board and either withdrew from IATA entirely or remained in the organization but withdrew from the fare-setting traffic conferences.

Although this attempt by the Civil Aeronautics Board to put IATA out of business entirely ended up in a suspension of the show cause proceeding, the episode further consolidated foreign opposition to the United States movement for international deregulation.

The Board's IATA investigation succeeded in sharply curtailing the Association's activities, at least so far as concerns transportation to and from the United States, even though the investigation was terminated without reaching a formal conclusion. Nevertheless, one can question whether the legalistic and high-handed manner in which this investigation was conducted is the wisest way to deal with an activity such as air transportation that depends on the cooperation and goodwill of sovereign nations at both ends of the line.

Although the International Civil Aviation Organization (ICAO) had traditionally confined its activities primarily to technical matters, that body convened a Special Air Transport Conference in Montreal in April 1977.[21] In this it was very probably motivated by a perception by other nations of the emerging trend toward deregulation in the United States, and in particular by the CAB's IATA show cause order.

The United States generally opposed consideration of commercial, as opposed to technical, items in ICAO because it was concerned that ICAO, which operates by majority vote, would establish regulations contrary to the views of the United States, since the U.S. view was in the minority on many commercial subjects. In this opposition the United States was often joined by most of the countries that operated major airlines, even though they did not agree with the United States on many subjects. Apparently this was because they considered it likely that in ICAO, the "Third World" nations would vote as a bloc to put through regulations that would prejudice the larger worldwide airlines. In the case of the Special Air Transport Conference, however, the other countries with worldwide air transport operations seem to have been sufficiently concerned by the early indications of the United States' "deregulation" policy to go along with the holding of a Special Air Transport Conference. The agenda for the conference covered:

1. *Tariff Enforcement.* The conference recommended that tariff filing be required and that tariff compliance be enforced.[22]

2. *Policy Concerning International Non-Scheduled Air Transport.*

The conference recommended that the ICAO council study further a definition to distinguish non-scheduled from scheduled air transport.[23]

3. *Regulation of Capacity in International Air Transport Services.* The conference recommended that the council undertake studies aimed at

> a) Establishing criteria and using these to formulate alternative methods for regulating capacity on scheduled and non-scheduled international air transport services; and
>
> b) Developing a model clause (or clauses) or guidelines for regulating capacity on the basis of prior determination for consideration, along with other clauses or guidelines by contracting states.[24]

The conference also set out a series of items to be taken into account by the council and recommended that meanwhile states coordinate their policies and regulations and include both scheduled and non-scheduled traffic in their considerations.

The third item apears to have been aimed directly at the United States, which had advocated liberal regulations for airline capacity. This recommendation mentions specifically only a model clause for regulating capacity on the basis of *a priori* determination, and recommends that the scheme of regulation include non-scheduled traffic, which had previously fallen outside the regulations of the bilateral air transport agreements and had permitted the mounting of capacity in excess of that permitted under the bilateral agreements, even though each country had the unilateral ability to prohibit the operation of non-scheduled service to its territory.

4. *Machinery for the Establishment of International Air Transport Fares and Rates.*[25] The conference recommended that IATA should be the fare and rate setting body for the members' airlines. It also said

> Unilateral action by governments which may have a negative effect on carriers efforts toward reaching agreement should be avoided so far as possible.

Although the show cause order was not issued until June 9, 1978, it is pretty clear that this conference item was intended to head off such an action by the CAB, which was evidently in the wind in 1977.

A second air transport conference of ICAO was held in Montreal in February 1980.[26] This conference had on its agenda two items. The first was the "Regulation of International Air Transport Services"[27]:

Distinction between categories of air transport service, scheduled and non-scheduled. The recommendation was that the 1952 definition[28] be left unchanged, but that the notes be amended to provide that states (i.e., nations) have discretion to classify as scheduled, flights that are operated frequently and regularly, even though they are in form charters and are subject to restrictions.

It has been observed[29] that whereas the original definition was multilateral in form, this amendment makes it bilateral because if the parties are going to exercise the discretion to reclassify charters as scheduled services, they will have to negotiate the terms with their partners in bilateral agreements. It seems more likely, however, that the nations that provided the votes to pass this recommendation will apply it unilaterally.

In any case, the amended definition appears to have been intended to curb the United States, which had used charters to force down scheduled fares on the North Atlantic.

Regulation of capacity in international air transport services.[30] The conference recommended a model capacity clause for capacity predetermination. The conference referred back to the panel of experts, Bermuda-1 type capacity clauses and "free determination" type capacity clauses "for analysis of the relationship between these two methods of capacity regulation and the objectives and criteria approved by the conference."

The report adds that

> A number of points were raised by many delegates regarding disadvantages of the free determination method. It was noted that markets were not perfect and therefore had to be regulated to ensure that the public interest was protected and to achieve international cooperation in this field. It was not possible for many nations to pursue a market-oriented, competitive policy even if they wished to, since the same conditions do not apply to all, for instance, access to capital markets, to new technology, and to management skills. It was observed in particular that it was difficult for the airlines of most developing nations to acquire the latest and most cost-efficient equipment, a fact that would place them at a disadvantage in conditions of unreasonable competition, since they could not fairly compete at prices below average costs.
>
> For developing nations, political and other factors were added to purely commercial consideratons, and the public interest was broader in scope than the interest of users alone. As regards the freedom to enter or leave markets, it was the experience of many that smaller communities suffered most. Free determination of capacity and freedom to set fares could result in "capacity dumping" and uneconomic fares, and a small airline could be destroyed before the situation could be remedied. A large majority therefore rejected "[a proposal in a United States document explaining the "free determination" method of capacity regulation—that is, nonregulation]—and proposing that the model clause for this method submitted by the Panel of Experts be recommended as a guideline for states and the conference concluded that it would be premature to make any such recommendation to the Council."

This was a vehement rejection of the United States' "deregulation" policies in a world forum.

Under agenda item two, "International Air Transport Fares and Rates,"[31] the United States tried to persuade the conference to adopt a "dual disapproval" rate clause[32] as a supplement to existing standard rate clauses. This was rejected, as was a U.S. proposal for a "country of origin" rate clause.[33]

The report of the February 1980 ICAO conference goes on to say:

> Following the "Show Cause" action of the United States Civil Aeronautics Board (CAB) in June 1978 with regard to its tentative finding that IATA agreements were no longer in the public interest, the council had adopted a resolution in December 1978 requesting contracting States "to refrain from any unilateral action which would endanger multilateral fare and rate setting systems." Similar concern about this question had been expressed by the African Civil Aviation Commission, the Arab Civil Aviation Council, the European Civil Aviation Conference and the Latin American Civil Aviation Commission. Subsequent to these actions and protests by States and airlines, the CAB in December 1979 had announced its intention to bar participation by United States airlines in IATA tariff coordination activities for traffic between Europe and the United States. IATA tariff coordination activities would continue to be permitted for other airlines and for other routes, subject to certain conditions, and participation in all other IATA activities would be unaffected. After a period of two years the situation regarding both North Atlantic and other routes would be reviewed once more.
>
> Most delegates felt that the proposed action by the United States had implications for the international multilateral tariff-setting machinery as a whole, and deplored such unilateral action. It was noted by those delegates that unilateral actions that disrupted multilateral tariff negotiations were contrary to the spirit of the Chicago Convention, placed international cooperation in peril and, through their destabilizing influence, threatened the economic performance of the international aviation system as a whole.
>
> Most delegates expresssed a desire to reinforce SATC Recommendation 11 [which recommended a multilateral approach to international fare agreement, without specifically mentioning IATA] so as to give unqualified support to a multilateral vehicle in the first instance. On the other hand, some delegates felt that it was inappropriate to expand the scope of the recommendation to this extent, or to make specific reference to IATA ....
>
> The Conference eventually adopted the following recommendation, intended to supersede SATC Recommendation 11. Recommendation 9: The Conference
>
> 1. Recommends that the examination of any system for the multilateral establishment of international tariffs should involve the participation of the entire international aviation community;
>
> 2. Recommends that unilateral action by governments which may have a negative effect on carriers' efforts toward reaching agreement should be avoided;
>
> 3. Recommends that international tariffs should be established multilaterally, and when established at regional level, the world wide multilateral system should be taken into consideration; and
>
> 4. Recommends that the world-wide multilateral machinery of the IATA traffic conferences shall, whenever applicable, be adopted as a first choice when establishing international fares and rates to be submitted for the approval of the States concerned, and that carriers should not be discouraged from participation in the machinery....

Even more important than the probable influence of this action by the air transport conference on the action of the Civil Aeronautics Board in terminating the IATA show cause proceeding is the widespread rejection shown by the conference of the concept of unregulated pricing in international commercial aviation.[34] Whatever may be the philosophical correctness of the position in favor of free price competition among international airlines, this vote confirms that most countries with commercial airlines throughout the world reject it. In fact, it is hard to say as a philosophical matter which side of the argument is right, or even if there is a right side. In the real world, each nation takes the position it feels best suits its national interest, and the position of other nations is one factor that each nation must take into account in assessing where its own national interest lies.

The European governments followed up on their efforts to induce the United States to moderate its position with respect to the regulation of airline fares through individual diplomatic representations and approaches through the European Civil Aviation Conference (ECAC). The Europeans were understandably concerned because the 1980 order terminating the IATA show cause proceeding approved the IATA conferences for only two years and in any case did not permit United States airlines to participate in IATA fare conferences on the North Atlantic.[35] After numerous contacts between the American and European aviation authorities, through ECAC and otherwise, the CAB in January of 1982 postponed the effectiveness of the original CAB order in the IATA show cause proceeding so as to permit U.S. airlines to continue as members of the IATA fare making conferences in the North Atlantic for another three months[36] and this suspension was made indefinite in March 1982.[37]

This easing of the restrictions on the carriers operating on the North Atlantic undoubtedly made it easier for the European and American authorities to reach an accommodation for regulating fares. Informal contacts for that purpose between the United States and ECAC began in early 1981, and were related to the European efforts to deal with the CAB's show cause order. In these preliminary negotiations the United States' position was that all controls on passenger fares should be abolished and the regulation of fares should be left entirely to the forces of competition. The position of the Europeans was that all aspects of airline fares should be subject to government control and that the fares should be fixed initially by the airlines in IATA, subject to government approval. They were in most cases prepared to control fares unilaterally if necessary.[38]

Intensive negotiations, in which concessions were made on both sides, took place between April and June, 1982, in both Europe and the United States between the United States representatives and those of the ECAC nations. A text for a memorandum of understanding for the regulation of North Atlantic fares to which the delegates of Belgium, Germany, Greece,

Ireland, Italy, Netherlands, Portugal, Spain, United Kingdom, United States, and Yugoslavia could agree, subject to concurrence by their governments, was worked out and initialed on May 2, 1982.[39] The delegates of France and Switzerland were on the list of signatories, but did not sign. By July 21, 1982, all of the countries that were on the list of signatories, including France but excluding Switzerland, had signified their agreement to the memorandum of understanding and it entered into force on August 1, 1982. The Scandinavian countries signed on February 9, 1983.

The memorandum of understanding provides that fares between parties to it shall be established as is required in the bilateral agreement between such parties (e.g., double approval, country of origin, or double disapproval pricing articles). It provides further that in applying the terms of the bilateral agreements to specific fare proposals, the parties shall refrain from raising objections to fares that fall within specified pricing zones as agreed by the parties and set out in an annex to the understanding. The understanding contains a further provision that in filing fares either above or below the specified pricing zones, the parties will consider the views of a tariff working group established under its terms to ensure that the fares offered for travel from and to its territory "are consistent with sound commercial considerations and the need for a functioning coherent and stabilized system."[40] There was to be consideration given to a central agency for fare information,[41] the parties were to appoint a working group, which could include representatives of nonparty ECAC nations to review the functioning of the understanding and to draft a permanent agreement.[42] There was to be a tariff working group, composed of representatives of the parties, to examine fares falling outside the specified zone and other questions related to fares arising under the understanding and to report to the parties.[43]

The memorandum of understanding was given a six months' duration.

The annexes to the understanding establish levels of reference fares between the United States and the territory of each other party which constitute the zones within which no objection may be made to fares filed. There is also a scale of percentages that may be applied for discount fares, with a further provision that any party may elect not to apply particular discount fares from and to its territory.

In addition to the mechanical part of the understanding, it contains in Article 2 (1) a provision that reads in part:

> no party shall make participation in multilateral tariff coordination a condition for approval of any fare, nor shall any party prevent or require participation by any carrier in such multilateral tariff coordination. In addition, no discrimination against any carrier shall be permitted on the basis of its participation or non-participation in such multilateral tariff coordination.

This had the effect of forbidding the Europeans to force the U.S. carriers to join the IATA North Atlantic fares conferences and of forbidding the United States to force the European carriers to get out of them. At the same time, it also requires the United States to permit the U.S. carriers to belong to the IATA fare conferences for the North Atlantic although it does not require that they become parties.[44]

In September 1982, the CAB approved an agreement filed by IATA on behalf of its members which established an additional forum for multilateral tariff coordination. This forum is open to all carriers operating U.S.-Europe scheduled passenger service, whether or not they are IATA members or participate in the traditional IATA tariff coordination forum.[45] This approval, which included antitrust immunity for fare discussions, applied only to the discussions themselves. Any agreements resulting from them would require separate approval and exemption. The IATA agreement was to run for the life of the memorandum of understanding.

Before its expiration in February 1983, the memorandum of understanding was renewed from February 1983 through October 31, 1984, with only a few changes in certain reference fares.[46]

Although there is a certain irony in the fact that with this understanding the United States has gone from advocating free and open competition on the North Atlantic to allowing the continued existence of the IATA fare conferences with a further level of intergovernmental fare agreement interposed on top of it, thus getting one step further away from free competition than it was before, the ECAC memorandum of understanding reveals a pragmatic approach on the part of the United States authorities that holds forth a promise that they will be able to achieve at least some of the essential aims of deregulation, while at the same time existing in relative harmony with the rest of the world aviation community. The ECAC understanding is on its face an influence toward harmonious relations with the European aviation community, since it was entered into by the ECAC countries of their own free will. Moreover, with this agreement the ECAC countries retain the IATA fare conference machinery for agreeing to individual fares, and they have the assurance that the United States will not reject fares agreed to in IATA, so long as they fall within the range of fares to which ECAC itself has already agreed. The device of permitting carriers not members of IATA to participate in the fare setting activities of the IATA traffic conferences reduces the likelihood of nonparticipation by U.S. carriers.

Similarly, the United States entered the ECAC understanding of its own free will and should not be offended by actions of the ECAC parties that conform to the agreement. Even though the United States might regard the mere existence of IATA fare fixing machinery as offensively anticompetitive, the fact that it has undertaken to accept only IATA-determined fares that fall within a range to which it has already given its assent should serve to alleviate American concern lest IATA should establish unacceptable fares.

Moreover, the ECAC understanding by its terms precludes the ECAC countries from requiring IATA membership by their own carriers or those of other nations, so there is an automatic control on the ability of the IATA airlines to agree on extremely high fares, even within the agreed range, because of the competitive effect of non-IATA airlines' charging lower fares and the danger that carriers might drop out of the IATA fare making conferences to enjoy such a competitive advantage. Furthermore, to the extent the United States has "pro-competitive" bilateral agreements with liberal rate clauses with the ECAC nations, U.S. and foreign airlines are free to charge fares even lower than those in the agreed range between the United States and the country concerned. (The airlines would also be free, subject to the provisions of the bilateral agreement, to charge higher fares, but it seems likely that they would be precluded from doing so by competition.)

The suggestion of the ECAC agreement that the United States government was becoming more pragmatic in its approach and less insistent upon a doctrinaire approach to international deregulation is borne out by statements by various U.S. officials during the period. In May 1982, Transportation Department officials Judith Connor, assistant secretary for policy and international affairs, and Frank Willis, deputy assistant secretary for planning and policy analysis, were quoted[47] as saying:

> [Connor] We are as dedicated as our predecessors were to developing an open and free competitive market place in international aviation, but it is tougher to do now because many of the countries with the liberal agreements are having second thoughts and those without them did not want them to start with.
>
> [Willis] The economic stakes loom larger right now because so many carriers are losing money and they fight hard and we fight harder, we are not so generous as we used to be.
>
> [Connor] The Carter administration's strategy was a unique one which was to start out by putting a whole package on the table. In addition to the fact that we are confronted with the necessity to come to grips with short term fixes, I am personally less inclined to start out a negotiation by saying "here is a whole house; it is built; now take it or leave it," because I do not think it works.... We are going in the direction of trying to get governments to stand back and let carrier managements take over in as broad a range of decision-making as we can get. However, we are not trying to do that by introducing forced capacity in a market on the theory that it will then topple pricing regimes and bring about low fares.... It isn't that we wouldn't like to see low fares in the market, but I think we would rather see economic fares.

Connor also said that although the United States wants more pricing freedom for its carriers, it is "no longer inclined to give up access to U.S. cities specifically in return for pricing provisions."

In an interview August 12, 1982, Matthew Scocozza, deputy assistant secretary of state for transportation and telecommunications, took issue with what he called Connor's "quick fix" approach[48] but his remarks nevertheless follow the basic line of what she said.[49] He said that the United States should review the whole aviation context between it and a particular country before providing relief on particular problems and that it should give priority to solving problems of discrimination against U.S. carriers and restrictions on doing business, because if they have the result of making a bilateral agreement liberal at the United States end and restrictive at the foreign end, the agreement amounts to just a handout to the foreign carriers. He also said that he considers the health of the United States airline industry to be as important as improving the opportunities of the traveling public.

In August 1982 the Subcommittee on Investigations and Oversight of the House Committee on Public Works and Transportation, chaired by Representative Levitas of Georgia, weighed in with a report[50] reminiscent of the 1956 Smathers Report:

> The Subcommittee recommends that the Executive Branch develop and implement an internal air policy that carries out the original intent of IATCA [International Air Transport Competition Act].[51] Despite the recent improvements noted above, major reforms are necessary in order to provide a fair market environment for our flag carriers. It is clear that a much firmer position needs to be taken in international negotiations to insure that discriminatory practices are eliminated and valuable economic routes are not traded away. Our examination of the issues demonstrates that the agencies must improve the negotiation process through earlier and more intensive involvement of our flag carriers, improved agency technical capability, continuity of personnel and policy over time, and a closer interagency coordination. We reiterate the recommendations of the Congress as set forth in IATCA calling for consultation to the maximum extent possible with airport operators and consumer interest groups. The Administration needs to develop a more encompassing international air policy that reflects broader rational goals. U.S. policy should not place any U.S. air carrier at a disadvantage. While we should negotiate for a liberal policy, we cannot permit continuance of a unilateral policy where the other parties to the agreement cannot be and will not be coerced into changing their policies into free access policies.
>
> The Administration should make it clear to other countries, our flag carriers, and even to our citizens exactly what they should expect from United States international air policy. Specifically:
>
> We will not tolerate discrimination.
>
> We will not trade hard rights for soft rights.
>
> We will not negotiate aviation rights for benefits in other economic sectors.
>
> We will continue to seek flexible air fares within zones of reasonableness.
>
> We will return to active participation in IATA and other international forums.

> We will continue to seek multilateral agreements.
> We will actively seek to identify excess user charges and fees, and insist on their elimination.
> We will develop an information system which identifies both formal and informal carrier complaints about discriminatory/unfair practices and follow up on the disposition of such complaints.
> We will improve our capabilities and policies for negotiations.
> We will follow up on bilateral agreements to insure that the terms are implemented by foreign governments.
> In short, we want to insure that there is a fair and equitable market environment for international air travel that provides for profitability for our flag carriers, reasonable rates and quality service for our consumers, and a constant and firm postion to present to foreign governments and their carriers. This would be a policy of which we could be proud and one this Subcommittee hopes will be well established by the time we return to this arena for an assessment of how these recommendations have been implemented.

This statement had an effect. Although the United States has not, as of 1987 issued a new international air transportation policy, the report of the Levitas subcommittee put an end to the advocacy of trading presently valuable route rights for promises of future liberal treatment of United States airlines ("trading hard rights for soft rights"), and it encouraged the U.S. officials who deal with air transport negotiations to pay more heed to the effect of route trades on the profitability of United States airlines.

In commenting on the House subcommittee report, in a speech to the International Aviation Club, James Burnley, general counsel of the Department of Transportation, said

> we intend to continue our quest for deregulation in international aviation markets, but we will not give away benefits unless we receive comparable benefits in return.... The goals of the US Government have not changed. What has changed may be described as the calculus of concern—the weighing of the different considerations that must be accommodated in any negotiating position.[52]

Deputy Assistant Secretary of State Scocozza, in a speech before the International Aviation Club in October 1982, indicated that he too was responsive to the views of the House subcommittee. This speech was reported in the *Aviation Daily,* under the headline "US Changes Emphasis in Bilateral Negotiations"[53]:

> A top State Department official this week said economic conditions in the airline industry necessitate a change in emphasis in US aviation negotiations with foreign countries. Matthew Scocozza, deputy assistant secretary of state for transportation and telecommunications, said the Administration is still strongly in favor of free competition in international aviation, but "one major objective must be to avoid damage to the system."
> In a speech before the International Aviation Club on Tuesday, Scocozza promised that the Reagan Administration "will be even more vigilant in

> protecting our aviation interests. We are intent in preventing wherever possible our aviation interests from being submerged under broader US interests." Scocozza, who has held his job as one of the top US negotiators for nine months, said the government will be "less willing to give benefits to foreign carriers" because "in the current economy, opportunities for foreign airline are more likely to mean losses for US airlines. That is the truth."[54] The US also will actively pursue our aviation interests and ensure that our airlines are not disadvantaged.
>
> Scocozza favors a more pragmatic approach to aviation negotiations, and the US must learn to say "no" to US carrier requests, he said....
>
> The US should also be willing "to explore ways of accommodating foreign desires to establish a safety net to protect their airlines against the dangers of the current situation" as long as such solutions do not reduce any future opportunities for US carriers. Two such solutions might be fare zones like the European Civil Aviation Conference North Atlantic pricing agreement, and "certain kinds of capacity clauses." If the US is pleased with the results of the six month agreement "we certainly will be entitled to extend it and perhaps to enter into similar agreements with other regions" despite the "risk" in such agreements that some airlines might be prevented from "pursuing their preferred policies." Capacity agreements, such as the one currently being explored with Venezuela, "could theoretically promise something to both those who believe in free competition and those who fear predatory competition from those who have exceptional economic power." Scocozza said a capacity agreement could guarantee minimum participation for a weak national carrier while providing for an expansion in capacity to accommodate growth for an efficient airline in the market.

There were a number of actions by the United States aviation authorities that reflected the shift in policy adumbrated by these government pronouncements.

In December 1983, the United States refused to grant Thailand the right to operate a fifth frequency to the United States.[55]

The United States–Thailand bilateral air transport agreement[56] contains, in the accompanying memorandum of understanding, the following provision:

> 3. The Government of Thailand expresses an intent for its airline to begin services over Route 3 at a level of four round trips a week. In light of the present capacity and fuel problems at Tokyo airports, the Thai Government has agreed that operations over Route 3 in addition to the anticipated four round trips per week will be subject to the concurrence of the United States Government. Such concurrence shall be granted without delay if, in the view of the United States, the capacity and fuel problems have been alleviated to a satisfactory extent or if such increases do not seriously impact on those problems. Consistent with the provisions of Article 11 of the Agreement, consultations may be held to determine this status by April 1981.

Article 11 of the agreement provides in part that neither party shall unilaterally limit the frequency or capacity of the other's airlines, except as may be required for customs, technical, operational or environmental reasons.

According to the report in the *Aviation Daily,* CAB member Schaffer observed that the original agreement was written at a time when the United States was interested in exporting to Thailand. She is reported to have said

> It was a major breakthrough to get flexibility in pricing, but now times have changed. We do not have a carrier servicing Thailand. We are questioning what the future benefits to the US can be from the Thais. They want additional frequencies to the US, but unless we can see some future benefits to our side, it is in our best interest to move very cautiously. So that is what we did. We said no additional frequencies unless you show what you can do for us.

On the face of it, one would think that the negotiations would have turned on whether there had been a sufficient change in the capacity and fuel problems at Tokyo to satisfy the U.S. that the increase "did not seriously impact on these problems." Schaeffer seems to have sought some sort of an extra contribution by the Thais. If that was in fact the position taken by the United States, it comes surprisingly close to the sort of "real and effective reciprocity" advocated by Enrique Ferreira of Argentina.

In January 1984, the Department of Transportation announced a moratorium of two to three months on international aviation talks.[57] Scocozza is reported to have said "It is a time to sit down . . . and reason where we are. Let's look at our progress. . . . I think it is a time when we all have to plan, strategize where we have to go next, where our priorities are."[58] In the same interview Scocozza also emphasized the United States' willingness to "get tough" and repeated that the current United States policy calls for a balance of benefits, saying "people now have to show on the record that what we are getting is equivalent to what we are giving them. If they can't do that, then they don't get it."

The Venezuelan agreement referred to by Scocozza and described on page 134 above was a complete departure from the ideal of "open skies," as was the arrangement with the Japanese whereby United Airlines gained access to Japan. Both agreements constituted a pragmatic means of getting over a particular problem. The agreement between the United States and the People's Republic of China[59] is another example of a restrictive agreement, entered into for practical reasons, since no other kind of agreement would be possible with the Chinese.

It is too early to evaluate just where the new elements of United States policy are going or even exactly what they mean. At this point, the trend appears to lean in the direction of both open skies and a willingness to accede to *a priori* regulation, and even of tight-fisted restrictionism.

Schaffer's statement about Thailand seems to go beyond hard trading into the realm associated with some of the more exotic South American doctrines. It implies that the United States will insist upon "real and effective" reciprocity and can be understood to call for some sort of a contribution "in lieu of reciprocity" along the lines of the charges that were attempted in Ecuador and Peru on airlines serving those countries from countries to which the national airline did not operate.

Similarly, when Scocozza speaks of a "balance of benefits," it is not entirely clear that he means the same thing as was meant by Frank Loy when Loy called for "an equitable exchange of economic benefits, expressed in route rights having approximately equal value." Loy's formulation, which was the basis for United States policy prior to the move to "deregulation," is satisfied by an equitable exchange of traffic rights and clearly does not call for equality of results in the operation of the routes. The phrase "balance of benefits" seems to call for the balancing of something more tangible than is implied in Loy's formulation. There is at least a hint that the new policy calls for something more, when Scocozza says "people now have to show on the record that what we are getting is equivalent to what we are giving them."

On the other hand, the Carter air transport policy has not been officially superseded. The "deregulation" provisions of the Airline Deregulation Act of 1978 and the International Airline Competition Act of 1979 remain in effect, so that at least on paper the United States remains committed to many of the elements of international "deregulation."

A somewhat surprising aspect of U.S. activity during this period is the degree to which the suspension of airline operating and commercial rights has been used as a means of expressing political disapproval. In 1980, the CAB required the Russian airline Aeroflot to suspend part of its service to the United States to express disapproval of the Russian invasion of Afghanistan.[60] In 1983 the CAB prohibited Aeroflot from selling air transportation in the United States and conditioned the certificates of convenience and necessity of United States airlines to restrict commercial relations between U.S. carriers and Aeroflot, to express disapproval of the Russians' shooting down Korean Airlines flight 007.[61] President Reagan also "suspended" the United States–Poland bilateral air transport agreement in 1981 for "political reasons" related to the repressive measures that had been taken in Poland in the fall of that year, and at the request of the Department of State the CAB suspended the foreign air carrier permit of LOT, the Polish airline.[62]

These actions are consistent with the traditional view that the exchange of air transport rights is at bottom a political exercise, but they do not appear fully consistent with the rhetoric of a free market.

The entry of the United States trade representative into the contest for primacy among U.S. government bureaus in dealing with international negotiation with respect to air transport marks a possible source of new developments in this field. In the late 1970s and the early 1980s, the Office of the United States Trade Representative began to focus on trade in services, as well as on the trade in goods which had been the traditional focus of U.S. trade policy.[63] The service industries in which particular interest is expressed are banking, insurance, advertising, construction/engineering, motion pictures, shipping, *aviation,* professional services and other financial services.[64] It is too early to tell how this effort will turn out. In the past, the airlines have tended to resist efforts to throw aviation into the pot when dealing with general trade matters, because of the fear that insufficient attention would be paid to the special requirements of the air transport industry. This assessment could change when service industries in general are singled out for special treatment.

United States airlines achieved a marginal increase in their participation in world airline traffic from 1980 to 1985,[65] but the number of U.S. airlines offering international service has declined slightly from 11 in 1980 to 10 in 1986.[66] During the period from 1980 to 1985, the annual revenue ton kilometers performed by the airlines of the world increased by 26.5 percent, or less than 5 percent a year.[67] All this tends to demonstrate that the gross impact of United States deregulation internationally may not have been very great, although its impact on individual U.S. airlines is undeniable.

As of 1988 the United States movement for deregulation has found an echo in Europe and has produced some of the results foreseen by CAB Chairman Alfred Kahn and the early deregulators.[68] The Dutch, the Belgians and the Luxembourgers continue as supporters of deregulation and have been tentatively joined by the British.[69] Nevertheless, there is still considerable resistance to U.S.-style deregulation in Europe,[70] and there is little enthusiasm for it discernible in the rest of the world.

As we have seen, the United States itself has backed away from some of the extreme positions of the early deregulators and has begun to show a less doctrinaire attitude.

It seems likely that within a few years, a new presidential statement of United States international air transport policy will emerge, in which the unworkable parts of the effort to apply the U.S. domestic deregulation policy to international air transportation are discarded and a new set of policies are developed. It is to be hoped that the new policy will permit the United States to conduct its international air transport relations in reasonable harmony with other nations, while at the same time providing reasonable protection to U.S. commercial and consumer interests.

10. CONCLUSION

A review of the history of United States international air transport policy indicates that there have been certain relatively constant elements which, in the absence of some fundamental change in circumstances, can be taken to constitute the natural matrix of U.S. policy. These are:

1. On balance the United States policy tends to be "liberal." The United States has generally sought to allow both American and foreign airlines the greatest freedom consistent with other objectives to regulate their own capacity and rates and has sought similar freedom for U.S. airlines abroad. It has consistently opposed pooling and restrictive agreements among airlines. Although it has on occasion accepted agreements among airlines to limit capacity and it has for many years accepted IATA as the vehicle for agreeing international prices, the United States has actively opposed restrictions on pricing or capacity when it has encountered them abroad.

2. The United States seeks to provide for U.S. airlines the opportunity to succeed commercially in international service. This goes beyond a simple wish to promote competition and includes a specific desire to promote a level of international operations by American airlines commensurate with other U.S. international activities.

3. The United States has tended to promote the U.S. airline manufacturing industry in dealing with air transport policy. This is probably a reflection of the political power of the manufacturing industry as well as a recognition of its importance to national defense. This consideration leads the United States to promote the American airline industry as a market for U.S.-made aircraft and it also leads the United States to provde competitive opportunities for foreign airlines so they will buy U.S.-made aircraft.

4. The United States has historically had the view that United States airline operations, including international operations, are an aid to national defense. This consideration has not been so much in evidence in recent years, to the extent that the Carter "Policy for the Conduct of International Air Transport Negotiations" of 1978 does not even mention national

defense. Nevertheless, national defense continues to figure in the policy section of the Federal Aviation Act, and the Department of Defense continues to keep the Civil Reserve Air Fleet in being. Moreover, common sense tells one that in the event of a war a large international airline network and the accompanying air transport capacity would inevitably be of service, just as it has been in the past, most recently in the Vietnam war, where most of the air lift between the United States and Vietnam was provided by U.S. commercial airlines under contract to the military.

5. Although the United States has generally shown a preference for a regime of "open skies" and "freedom of the air," where little or no regulation is imposed on airline pricing or capacity, the United States has in fact been fairly pragmatic in reaching agreements with other countries to regulate both pricing and capacity where it has been necessary to do so. From 1946 to 1977, the United States had as the backbone of its air transport policy the Bermuda-1 Agreement, which was essentially a compromise between the United States views and the far more restrictive views of the British.

Although the Bermuda system of capacity regulation was criticized in the United States as being unduly restrictive, it was generally recognized that it provided a degree of stability and liberality that it would have been very difficult, if not impossible, to achieve otherwise. Similarly, as part of the Bermuda bargain, the United States accepted the International Air Transport Association as the vehicle for establishing airline fares and rates, despite serious criticism of IATA in the United States as a "cartel" and an anticompetitive monopoly.

Although the rather doctrinaire approach of the United States authorities during the most enthusiastic period of deregulation led them to attempt to do away with IATA entirely through the IATA show cause proceeding, they did not stay with this approach to the point of causing a complete breakdown in aviation relations with other countries. When the United States authorities observed that they had overstepped the bounds of what the rest of the world would accept, they pulled back and terminated the proceeding so as to permit IATA membership by U.S. airlines, while establishing a special regime for multilateral government agreement on price levels for the North Atlantic routes through agreement with the European Civil Aviation Conference (ECAC).

Moreover, in its dealings with countries with nonmarket economies, such as Russia and the People's Republic of China, as well as with certain South American nations, the United States has accepted air transport agreements based on *a priori* governmental regulation of capacity and pricing. This has made possible the presence of U.S. airline service in areas where it would otherwise have been impossible, at least in the case of the communist countries.

The United States has also agreed to a measure of predetermination of capacity in Bermuda-1 type agreements through "screening agreements" which provide for governmental discussion of proposed capacity increases, with the possibility that they may not become effective.

6. In spite of the generally liberal and pragmatic tenor of its air policy over the years, the United States has shown itself capable of surprising swings toward both doctrinaire free trade positions, as in the recent attempt to impose deregulation on the rest of the world, and toward anticompetitive measures, as in the signature of the Bermuda-2 Agreement, the sanctioning of capacity restriction agreements and the "route moratorium" of the early 1970s.

7. A theme to which the United States tends to return in its analysis of international air transport policy is the "equitable exchange of economic benefits." In 1967, when Frank Loy gave form to the doctrine that in the exchange of traffic rights the United States should obtain an equitable exchange of economic benefits, he said he was describing the rationale for the bargaining process employed by the United States during the previous twenty years (i.e. beginning with the negotiation of the Bermuda-1 Agreement). Although the details provided by Loy in his 1967 McGill University speech were new at the time, the idea of an exchange of economic benefits clearly underlay the Bermuda-1 Agreement, as well as the other agreements entered into by the United States on the Bermuda model.

The phrase "equitable exchange of economic benefits" was cited as a United States objective in the Eisenhower air transport policy in 1954, 13 years before Loy's speech. This concept was part of every presidential policy from the time Loy enunciated it, until it was repudiated in the era of deregulation, and it was an inchoate part of previous policies and of the Smathers report. Moreover, as the pendulum swings back from deregulation, the concept of an equitable exchange of economic benefits has again begun to figure in statements by United States authorities purporting to enunciate U.S. international air transport policy. It appears to be a fair statement that the policy has been that when the United States makes a trade of air transport rights, the U.S. negotiators are expected to get their money's worth, and that historically they have been criticized when they have failed to do so.

8. Although during the period from 1928 through 1944 the United States *de facto* had a "chosen instrument" policy, with Pan American (with its affiliate Panagra) as the sole U.S. airline operating abroad, the subsequent history clearly establishes as a constant element of United States air policy the desire to have a number of American airlines operating abroad, and where possible to have American airlines competing with one another on international routes. There does not appear to be any likelihood of the United States' reverting to a "chosen instrument" policy, even on a regional

basis for the foreseeable future. A further implication of this is that the United States is firmly committed to using privately owned airlines to provide international air transportation and there is no presently existing or foreseeable tendency for the United States to create a government-owned airline to operate commercially on international routes. Further, there is no discernible evidence that the United States will in the future pay subsidy to U.S. airlines for international operations. (If, however, the United States should at some future date change its policy and pay international subsidy, it would be rational for it to protect the subsidized airline from competition by other U.S. airlines.)

9. The strength of the United States market for air transportation, although it is not strictly an element of the country's policy, is a constant element that clearly has an effect on the policy. Most other countries desire to have their airlines serve points in the United States because there are heavy traffic flows to and from the United States. This desire has both a commercial motivation, arising out of the wish to exploit the traffic, and a political motivation, arising out of the desire to have the national flag carrier provide a national presence in an area that has political importance for the government.

This factor provides great bargaining leverage for the United States in dealing with other countries, and has enabled the United States to persuade other countries to accept elements of U.S. policy in bilateral agreements that would otherwise be unacceptable to them. For example, the Bermuda Agreement itself was probably never understood or really accepted by many of the countries that signed Bermuda-type agreements with the United States. The strategy worked out by CAB chairman Alfred Kahn in the late 1970s to induce other countries to sign "pro-competitive" or "open skies" type bilateral air transport agreements was frankly based on the use of the bargaining power of the United States market.

On the other hand, it must be recognized that there are definite limits to what the United States can impose on the rest of the world. Even when the United States induced other coutries to accept U.S.-style air transport agreements, it did not always get what it thought it was getting. For example, novel interpretations of the Bermuda-type agreements turned them into instruments for *a priori* capacity control in a number of countries. The recent complaints about trading "hard rights" for "soft rights" reflect dissatisfaction with the United States authorities' having traded immediately usable route rights for promises of future freedom for American airlines to increase and decrease their fares and capacity at will, which were either not kept or were frustrated by discriminatory practices similar to nontariff barriers in the trade of goods.

It should be noted that the ability of the United States to use the value of the U.S. market as a form of bargaining leverage has been impaired by the rather lavish grants of route authority made to a number of countries to induce them to enter "pro-competitive" bilateral agreements. In many cases the routes already granted are so rich that there is little likelihood that the foreign government would make concessions to the United States to gain further route authority.

10. The vigor and resilience of United States airlines as business entities is another relatively constant element that does not form a part of the nation's air policy, but exercises an influence on it. Although this superior vigor and resilience are in some measure a myth, in the sense that U.S. airlines are no less subject to being damaged by discriminatory and restrictive practices than any other airlines, and they cannot hold out forever in rate wars against government-subsidized airlines, it has certainly been true over the years that United States airlines have been technically equal to if not superior to the very best of the foreign airlines. In addition, they have had good access to capital and credit and they have generally followed good business practices which have enabled them to expand their services and to compete vigorously for international traffic. A belief in the competitive strength of U.S. business undoubtedly underlay the earliest United States advocacy of "freedom of the skies" and confidence in the competitive ability of American airlines must have been a partial motivation for support of liberal air transport policy throughout the years, including the recent trend to deregulation.

11. Another constant that does not form part of United States air transport policy, but exercises an influence on it, is the attitude of other governments. "Freedom of the skies," or even the concepts embodied in the U.S. "pro-competitive" bilateral agreements, are clearly unpalatable to the great majority of other countries that have international airlines. The preference of most such countries, as expressed in ICAO, is for a regime of *a priori* capacity control and of fare and rate fixing through the International Air Transport Association. To be effective, any air policy adopted by the United States must offer a means for handling the regulation of capacity and fares and rates that provides a bridge between the views of the United States and those of the rest of the world. As originally conceived, the Bermuda-1 type agreement did this. The Bermuda-1 formula, however, appears to be too greatly discredited through having been repudiated by the United States itself for the United States to attempt to revive it for general application. Nevertheless, the Bermuda-1 system had in it an element that could serve as a basis for a new United States policy for use with certain countries. This is the concept that the airlines themselves should be allowed initially to fix their own capacity, subject to control by the governments if one of them perceives that its airlines are being prejudiced by the capacity offered by the airlines of the other.

12. There are also certain constants inherent in the business of

running an airline that must be taken into account in the establishment and administration of governmental air transport policy. Among the most important of these is a need for stability and predictability in the regulatory environment. Long lead times are required by commercial airlines to plan their services. Equipment must be ordered as much as several years in advance of commencement of service. Commitments for tours and agency arrangements must be made as much as a year in advance. Promotional efforts must be set up and carried out and tariffs must be published well in advance of the period for which the service is planned.

In order to make these commitments and to obtain the necessary financing, the airline management must have reasonable assurance that it will be able to operate the service as planned. If the operation of a particular schedule pattern is frustrated after money has been raised, equipment has been obtained, commitments made to tour operators and travel agents, and after promotional efforts have been carried out, the effect on the airline is devastating. It is left with idle equipment and personnel, which it canot immediately place in service elsewhere, because of the long lead times. Its credibility with the public, with tour operators and travel agents and most importantly with banks and other lenders and with equity underwriters is damaged to a point where the airline's effectiveness is likely to be reduced for several years into the future, quite apart from the immediate losses arising out of the inability to operate the service.

Moreover the airline management requires the ability to plan further capacity increases well into the future. The management needs to know not merely that a particular increase will be permitted to take place, but it also needs to know that it will be able to exploit a successful performance through further increases, since there would not be much point in spending large amounts of money and effort to promote the growth of a service that could not grow because of governmental restrictions.

Another feature of the business aspect of running an airline that must be taken into account in the establishment of governmental international air transport policy is the extreme vulnerability of airlines to discriminatory and restrictive practices by government regulatory authorities, whether such practices be carried out through direct regulation or through indirect maneuvers after the manner of "nontariff barriers" in the trade of goods. The airline business is characterized by a large flow of cash, which comes in in the form of receipts for the sale of transportation and most of which goes out almost immediately in the form of payments for fuel, food, supplies, salaries and payments under loan agreements and leases (particularly equipment loans and leases). In addition, much of the cash taken in by an airline goes out immediately in the form of payment to other airlines under interline sales agreements.

When there is a serious interruption in the inflow of cash in a particular country through such a device as a refusal to permit United States airlines to convert and remit abroad the proceeds received in the country for the sale of transportation, net of local expenses, the whole financial structure of the airline can be affected. (Obviously the degree of effect on the airline depends on the ratio of the receipts in the particular country to the total receipts of the airline.)

It is reasonable to expect United States airlines to assume their own business and operating risks, but it is not reasonable to expect them to defend themselves without government assistance against the assaults of other sovereign governments bent on using their political power to advance the fortunes of their own airlines and to raise funds by discriminatory and excessive charges against American airlines. Whether or not United States air policy is generally calculated to promote the commercial success of U.S. airlines, it appears essential that it be protective of U.S. airlines in the sense that it should protect them from being restricted by foreign governments for the purpose of improving the fortunes of their own airlines and from having unreasonable or discriminatory charges imposed on them by foreign governments.

* * *

Beyond observing that a future United States international air policy should attempt to reconcile the foregoing elements, or at any rate to recognize that a degree of inconsistency may be necessary in particular cases to achieve the government's overall purposes, I do not propose to attempt to enunciate a new version of what the future U.S. policy should be. Certain observations concerning a future United States policy may nevertheless be helpful:

It is essential that the United States have an international air transport policy and that such a policy be administered in a rational and consistent manner.

Careful thought should be given to how much of the United States' international air policy should be made public. In general it appears desirable to publish as much of the policy as possible because it is difficult for governmental authorities to operate from an undisclosed agenda in American society. On the other hand, to publish a policy in too much detail could give an unwarranted advantage to other countries in negotiation with the United States and could expose the U.S. government to exploitation of real or invented inconsistencies in U.S. policy by other governments.

Even more important than the content of the policy itself are the skill, knowledge and consistency of the poeple who are called upon to administer it. It is important that the government personnel dealing with international air transport matters should be carefully selected and given long enough tours of duty so that they can learn to understand the commercial realities behind the various elements of government policy and to build up a fund of experience on which to draw in dealing with air transport problems.

The United States government bureau having primary responsibility for dealing with matters of international air transport policy should be provided with some means of insulating the field from other branches of the government who approach it from the point of view of a single issue.

Since the amendment of the Deregulation Act of 1978 by the Sunset Act of 1984 to put the administration of sections 408, 409, 412 and 414 of the Federal Aviation Act under the Department of Transportation, rather than under the Department of Justice, this is not a serious current problem. Nevertheless, the fact that it was possible to provide in the Deregulation Act of 1978 that the Department of Justice, which is charged with enforcement of the antitrust laws, should also have sole charge of providing relief from those laws in cases where it is required by special air transportation needs indicates that the national policy should explicitly call attention to the need for a certain sensitivity on this topic.

Since the United States' views on the subject of regulating international commercial air transport are distinctly in the minority, the country should avoid multilateral forums for agreeing on commercial air transport matters and should try to stick to bilateral negotiations where it can deal with one nation at a time. The experience of the two ICAO air transport conferences demonstrates that when the United States attempts to deal with air transport matters on a multilateral basis, the rest of the world tends to gang up against it.

United States international air transport policy should take into account that it necessarily involves other countries. However ideal a policy may be from the sole point of view of the United States, it will be useless unless it can obtain a degree of acceptance from other countries. American policy should have as its primary purpose to promote the interests of the United States, but it must be so constituted as to have a reasonable degree of acceptance abroad. In particular, there is no chance that a policy of "open skies," or unlimited mutiple designation of U.S airlines, will receive more than a very limited acceptance by other nations. Experience has shown that even where completely unlimited capacity provisions and rights of unlimited designation are achieved on paper, the countries that agree to them often contrive to avoid actually putting them into effect. Rather than insisting on unworkable provisions to achieve a theoretical ideal of free market conditions, the United States would be better advised to seek a more limited agreement that would actually produce conditions under which a limited number of United States airlines could operate successfully.

Paradoxically, *a priori* agreement on a level of capacity, accompanied by a schedule of increases over a period of years, can produce the level of predictability and room for expansion required by United States airlines as effectively as a regime of unfettered managerial discretion. Sometimes it is possible to agree on a specific level of service that satisfies the needs of United States airlines well into the future although it is impossible to achieve agreement on a set of principles to govern capacity levels.

The United States is called upon to walk a very fine line in dealing with *a priori* capacity agreements. It is clear that an *a priori* agreement that gives the United States the level of capacity it requires over a reasonably lengthy period is *prima facie* preferable to suffering unilateral capacity restrictions through a refusal to make such an agreement because of some notion that there is a serious point of principle involved that would be prejudiced by making the agreement. On the other hand, the United States would indeed suffer if the word should get out generally that the way to induce the United States to make restrictive capacity deals is to impose harsh restrictions on U.S. airlines by unilateral action. The United States seems to have dealt with the problem adequately thus far by reserving *a priori* capacity agreements for use in dealing with countries with nonmarket economies, such as China and Russia, and with certain South American countries (such as Argentina) that are known to have unique aviation doctrines, while taking retaliatory measures against countries that attempt to impose restrictions unilaterally on United States airlines.

The foregoing paragraphs are not intended to add up to a new United States international air policy nor even to a basis for one. They are intended primarily to call attention to certain elements that have recurred over the years in the formulation and administration of U.S. international air policy and to suggest ways of dealing with certain of them.

At the most fundamental level, the main issue to be considered in formulating United States international air transport policy is whether or not it does in fact serve the long-term interest of the nation. Decisions on air transport policy should not be motivated by doctrinaire social theories, particularly when they cannot be enforced, as has been the case with the recent efforts to "deregulate" the international air transport industry.

If the United States is to have a healthy international air transport industry, and if the needs of the American public for international air transport are to be well served, the United States government must focus carefully on the development of U.S. international air transport policy and it must recognize as its primary goals a healthy U.S. industry and an air transport system that serves the needs of the public. Although it may sound somewhat simple-minded to state goals thus starkly, I believe that by doing so, the United States will be assisted in focusing on the goals it really wants and in avoiding blind alleys of policy that have from time to time in the past diverted the efforts of the United States aeronautical authorities.

APPENDIX: THE "BERMUDA AGREEMENT," FINAL ACT

Chairman: L.J. Dunnett (United Kingdom).

Delegates.	*Delegate.*
John D. Hickerson.	N.J.A. Cheetham.
Stokeley W. Morgan.	

The Final Plenary Session was held on the 11th February, 1946.

As a result of the deliberations of the Conference there was formulated an Agreement between the Government of the United Kingdom and the Government of the United States relating to air services between their respective territories, and Annex thereto [not printed here].

The following resolution was adopted:

Whereas representatives of the two Governments have met together in Bermuda to discuss Civil Aviation matters outstanding between them and have reached agreement thereon,

Whereas the two Governments have to-day concluded an Agreement relating to air services between their respective territories (hereinafter called "the Agreement"),

And whereas the two Governments have reached agreement on the procedure to be followed in the settlement of other matters in the field of Civil Aviation,

Now therefore the representatives of the two Governments in Conference resolve and agree as follows:

(1) That the two Governments desire to foster and encourage the widest possible distribution of the benefits of air travel for the general good of mankind at the cheapest rates consistent with sound economic principles; and to stimulate international air travel as a means of promoting friendly understanding and good will among peoples and ensuring as well the many indirect benefits of this new form of transportation to the common welfare of both countries.

(2) That the two Governments reaffirm their adherence to the prin-

ciples and purposes set out in the preamble to the Convention on International Civil Aviation signed at Chicago on the 7th December, 1944.

(3) That the air transport facilities available to the travelling public should bear a close relationship to the requirements of the public for such transport.

(4) That there shall be a fair and equal opportunity for the carriers of the two nations to operate on any route between their respective territories (as defined in the Agreement) covered by the Agreement and its Annex.

(5) That, in the operation by the air carriers of either Government of the trunk services described in the Annex to the Agreement, the interest of the air carriers of the other Government shall be taken into consideration so as not to affect unduly the services which the latter provides on all or part of the same routes.

(6) That it is the understanding of both Governments that services provided by a designated air carrier under the Agreement and its Annex shall retain as their primary objective the provision of capacity adequate to the traffic demands between the country of which such air carrier is a national and the country of ultimate destination of the traffic. The right to embark or disembark on such services international traffic destined for and coming from third countries at a point or points on the routes specified in the Annex to the Agreement shall be applied in accordance with the general principles of orderly development to which both Governments subscribe and shall be subject to the general principle that capacity should be related:

(a) To traffic requirements between the country of origin and the countries of destination;

(b) to the requirements of through airline operation; and

(c) to the traffic requirements of the area through which the airline passes after taking account of local and regional services.

(7) That, in so far as the air carrier or carriers of one Government may be temporarily prevented through difficulties arising from the War from taking immediate advantage of the opportunity referred to in paragraph (4) above, the situation shall be reviewed between the Governments with the object of facilitating the necessary development, as soon as the air carrier or carriers of the first Government is or are in a position increasingly to make their proper contribution to the service.

(8) That duly authorised United States civil air carriers will enjoy non-discriminatory "Two Freedom" privileges and the exercise (in accordance with the Agreement or any continuing or subsequent agreement) of commercial traffic rights at airports located in territory of the United Kingdom which have been constructed in whole or in part with United States funds and are designated for use by international civil air carriers.

(9) That it is the intention of both Governments that there should be regular and frequent consultation between their respective aeronautical

authorities (as defined in the Agreement) and that there should thereby be close collaboration in the observance of the principles and the implementation of the provisions outlined herein and in the Agreement and its Annex.

In witness whereof the following Delegates sign the present Final Act.

Done at Bermuda the eleventh day of February, 1946.

This Final Act shall be deposited in the Archives of the Government of the United Kingdom and a certified copy shall be transmitted by that Government to the Government of the United States of America.

United States of America.	*United Kingdom.*
George P. Baker.	A.H. Self.
Harllee Branch.	Wm. P. Hildred.
Stokeley W. Morgan.	W.J. Bigg.
George C. Neal.	L.J. Dunnett.
Garrison Norton.	Peter G. Masefield.
L. Welch Pogue.	
Oswald Ryan.	
John Sherman.	

REFERENCES

1. INTRODUCTION

1. See Matte, *Treatise on Air-Aeronautical Law* (1981), p. 251.
2. Bin Cheng, *The Law of International Air Transport* (1962), p. 174.
3. Bin Cheng, *op. cit.,* p. 174.
4. See Bin Cheng, *op. cit.,* p. 121; Johnson, *Rights in Air Space* (1965), p. 60; Craig, *National Sovereignty at High Altitudes* 24 JALC 379 (1957); Cooper, *The Russian Satellite* 24 JALC 349 (1957).
5. Hazeltine, *The Law of the Air* (1911), p. 9.
6. *Op. cit.,* p. 48.
7. See Wagner, *International Air Transportation as Affected by State Sovereignty* (1979), p. 35; Bin Cheng, *op. cit.,* p. 3-7.
8. *Le Domain Aerien et le Régime Juridique des Aerostats* (1901) 8 Rev. Gen. Droit Int. Pub. 44; *La Circulation Aerienne et les Droits des États en Temps de Paix* (1910) 17 Rev. Gen Droit Int. Pub. 55. Wagner, *International Air Transportation as Affected by State Sovereignty,* p. 13-38 gives a review of the various theories of state sovereignty over the airspace above the national territory.
9. *Revue Juridique Internationale de la Locomotion Aerienne,* Vol. 1 (1910), p. 101: "Pour sauvegarder leur droit de conservation les états peuvent fermer a la circulation certaines régions de l'atmosphere. Ils ont notamment le droit d'interdire la navegation au dessus, ou aux alentours des ouvrages fortifiés." See also Johnson, *op. cit.,* p. 12-21; Bin Cheng, *op. cit.,* p. 120, footnote 46; Wagner, *op. cit.,* p. 19.
10. Bin Cheng, *op. cit.,* p. 120; Wagner, *op, cit.,* p. 13-31; Matte, *op, cit.,* p. 69-156, Johnson, *op, cit.,* p. 12-21.
11. Cooper, *The Right to Fly* (1947), p. 16.
12. See *ibid.,* p. 291, for a text of the Paris Convention of 1919.
13. In an article published in 1952, "The International Aviation Conference, Paris 1910," 19 JALC 127 (1952), John Cobb Cooper argues that general agreement was reached among the nations of Europe as early as 1910 that states have full sovereignty over the airspace above their territory.
14. Cooper, *United States Participation in Drafting the Paris Convention,* 1919. 18 J of Air L 266 (1951).
15. See Billyou, *Air Law* (1964), p. 16-39.
16. 44 Stat. 568 (1926).
17. *Ibid.,* Section 6, currently reflected in Article 1108a of the Federal Aviation Act of 1958 (72 STAT 778, 1958).
18. Convention on International Civil Aviation, April 4, 1947 (Chicago Conven-

tion), 61 stat 1180, 1947. See also *Proceedings of the International Civil Aviation Conference, Chicago, Illinois, November 1-December 7, 1944.*

19. Cooper, *op. cit.,* p. 35; Bin Cheng, *op. cit.,* p. 120; Matte, *op. cit.,* p. 136–137; Wagner, *op. cit.,* p. 53 and p. 95.
20. See e.g. Matte, *op. cit.,* p. 69–89; Wagner, *op. cit.,* p. 174.
21. See Lissitzyn, *World Air Transport and National Policy* (1942), p. 2.
22. See Bin Cheng, *op. cit.,* p. 8–9: "For obvious reasons states desirous of fostering their respective Civil Aviation industries, therefore, do all in their power to protect their own airlines and to resist the freedom of foreign airlines to fly over territories subject to their jurisdiction."
23. ICAO DOC 2187. Proceedings of the International Civil Aviation Conference, Final Act, Convention on International Civil Aviation, Appendix IV (1948).
24. Although the "Five Freedoms Agreement" considered the determinative element to be the nationality of the aircraft, subsequent practice under the Bilateral Air Transport Agreements has made the nationality of the designated airline the determinant element for purposes of economic regulation. Although in most cases, airlines will operate aircraft registered in the state of which they are national, this is not necessarily the case. The airline might be operating with an aircraft leased from a foreign airline, or it might be operating a joint service after the manner of the Scandinavian Airlines System (SAS), which operates aircraft registered in one or the other of all three component nationalities, Swedish, Norwegian or Danish. See Gazdik, *Nationality of Aircraft and Nationality of Airlines as means of Control in International Air Transportation* 24 JALC 1 (1957).
25. For an elaborate exposition on this subject, see Bin Cheng, *op. cit.,* p. 9–17.
26. See Gazdik, *Rate Making and the* IATA *Traffic Conferences* 16 JALC 298 (1949).
27. Hazeltine, *op. cit.,* p. 48; Cooper, *The Right to Fly* (1947), p. 16.
28. See Wagner, *op. cit.,* p. 64 et seq.; Slotemaker, *Freedom of Passage in International Air Services* (1932); Bin Cheng Loc Cit N 22 supra, H.J. Wasenbergh, *Postwar International Aviation Policy and the Law of the Air* (1957), p. 26, 27, 38 and 105.
29. For example, the *Encyclopaedia Britannica* (11th ed., 1957, Vol. 18, 744F), under the heading "Public Utility," says; "The following have been treated as and classified into groups of public utilities: (1) Services of transportation (common carriers); (2) Services incidental to transportation; (3)...."
30. A pamphlet entitled *Rationale of Federal Transportation Policy,* by Ernest W. Williams, Jr., and David W. Bluestone, issued by the United States Department of Commerce in April 1930, describes "The General Objectives of Controls of Entry in Transport" as follows (page 11): "Controls of entry are justified as being in the public interest to assure adequate, efficient and safer transportation by carriers serving the general public. Entry controls can accomplish these broad objectives in several ways. First, essential common carrier services can be required of carriers given franchises. Second the monopoly or limited competition resulting from closed entry and operating authority restrictions are said to encourage adequate investment and modernization in essential transport by ensuring profitable return and by lessening market risks. Third, standards of service can be improved by encouragement of able and responsible carriers. Fourth, transportation can be more efficient because duplicating fixed investment can be avoided and excess capacity can be reduced. Fifth, economy in transport can be gained through coordination between agencies of transport. Finally, closed entry facilitates the collec-

tion of information about the companies performing the service, information very useful, both in peace and in war."

31. Cf. Transcript, inter-governmental consultations on the United States Civil Aeronautics Board's "IATA Show Cause Order," Bogotá, July 23, 1979, wherein Dr. Gaviria, the Colombian Delegate, cites as one reason for the need to provide commercial protection for the international operations of the national airline, the dependence of the Colombian public upon its domestic service for transportation in the mountainous terrain of Colombia, which might be jeopardized if its international operations should become unprofitable.
32. *Ibid.* p. 67–71 and 88–89.
33. Taneja, *U.S. International Aviation Policy* (1980), p. 70.
34. Lissitzyn: *International Air Transport and National Policy* (1942), p. 93; see also Cooper, *The Right to Fly* (1947).
35. Lissitzyn, *op. cit.,* p. 38 et. seq.
36. See e.g. Thornton: *International Airlines and Politics:* Ann Arbor (1970), p. 80–86.
37. See Straszheim, *The International Airline Industry* (1969), p. 16.
38. Straszheim, *op. cit.,* p. 9.
39. *Ibid.*
40. See Matte, *op. cit.,* p. 249.
41. Cooper, *op. cit.,* p. 138; Matte, *op. cit.,* p. 159; Wagner, *op. cit.,* p. 53; Lissitzin, *op. cit.,* p. 371.
42. See Cooper, *op. cit.,* p. 163.
43. Air Service Agreement between the Government of the United States of America and the Government of the United Kingdom of Great Britain and Northern Ireland, including amendments through 1980, U.S. Department of Transportation, Washington (1980). (Agreement signed July 23, 1977.)
44. See Lowenfeld: "A New Takeoff for International Air Transport," *Foreign Affairs,* Vol. 54, No. 1 (Oct. 1975), p. 36, where the author proposes the abolition of IATA as a rate making body and its reconstitution as a body for airline agreements on capacity. The author appears to have had his tongue at least part way in his cheek.
45. For example: U.K.-Argentina Agreement 17 March 1946; Portugal-Argentina Agreement 7 May 1947; Spain-Argentina Agreement 1 March 1947; Chile-Argentina Agreement 14 December 1948. All of the foregoing are published in pamphlet form by the Secretaría de Aeronáutica of the Argentine Government. Also Bin Cheng cites the UK-Netherlands Agreement as having a similar provision. Bin Cheng, *op. cit.,* p. 424–425.
46. Revenue pooling has been very common in liner conferences in the maritime industry for many years. See FMC Docket No. 70-30, agreements Nos. 9847 and 9848 Revenue Pools, U.S. Brazil trade, Nov. 18, 1970; FMC Docket No. 71-71, agreement No. 9932, Equal Access to Government Controlled Cargo and interim cooperative working arrangement, Agreement No. 9939—Pooling Sailing and Equal Access to Government Controlled Cargo Agreement, March 22, 1973; FMC Docket No. 68-10 Inter-American Freight Conference-Cargo Pooling Agreements Nos. 9682, 9683 and 9684, Sept. 14, 1970; FMC Docket No. 1212, Mediterranean Pools Investigation, Jan. 19, 1966. In the shipping industry, pools appear to be regarded by the United States as a necessary evil, rather than things to be desired.
47. Bin Cheng, *op. cit.,* p. 280–281.
48. Wheatcroft, *The Economics of European Air Transportation* (1956), p. 261–268.

In a later publication, *Air Transport Policy* (1964), Wheatcroft indicated that he had modified his view to the extent that he felt at that time that where aircraft size had increased much faster than traffic growth, with the use of IATA aircraft pooling could serve as a way to build excess capacity (p. 102).

49. National Aero Commercial Transport Policy Law No. 19030 modified by Law No. 19, 534 (B.O. 22. 392 29 Mar. 1972) Article 28 (Argentina).
50. The United States relented and allowed foreign-owned DC-8 and 707 aircraft to continue to serve the United States for a considerable period after the original deadline. Joint Resolution of Senate and House based on Senate Resolution No. 99, as amended by the House. (Congressional Record—(House) Page H 11893, Oct. 10, 1984) on its face required the airline to produce evidence of a signed contract with an approved provider to perform the required modification of the aircraft prior to December 31, 1985, with an irrevocable deposit of $75,000, in order to continue operating beyond January 1, 1985, without the required modification.
51. Under GATT, Part II, signatories have contracted that there will be no new non-tariff barriers, although older ones (i.e., enacted before October 30, 1947), may continue. It is not clear to what extent this provision will be applied to air transport.

2. EUROPEAN AIR TRANSPORT POLICY, 1919–1944

1. Hazeltine, *The Law of the Air* (1911). See also Cooper, *The International Air Navigation Conference, Paris, 1910,* 19 Journal of Air Law and Commerce 127 (1952).
2. *The Aero* Incorporating *Flying* (established 1902) and *The Aership,* Vol. IV, No. 88 (Jan. 25, 1911), (London) p. 71, *Aeroplanes in War* by Von Hesser.
3. See Cooper, *The Right to Fly* (1947), p. 291 for a text of the Paris convention.
4. Semphill, *The Air and the Plain Man* (1931), p. 11.
5. *World Airline Record* (1965), p. 177; Corbett, *Politics and the Airlines* (1965), p. 26.
6. See *World Airline Record* (1965), p. 245.
7. Simond and Emeny, *The Great Powers in World Politics* (1939).
8. Marchand: *Un Paradoxe Économique; La Renaissance du Mercantilisme a l'Epoque Contemporaine* (1937).
9. Cooper, *op. cit.*
10. See Matte, *Treatise on Aero-Aeronautical Law* (1981), p. 251.
11. Such agreements are Denmark-Norway, (13 CINA Bulletin 4); Sweden-Norway, (13 idem 12); Poland-Austria, (14 idem 4); Poland-Czechoslovakia, (16 idem 20).
12. Commission Internationale pour la Navegation Aerierenne, in French. This was the primarily technical executive body established under the Paris Convention of 1919. The Official Bulletin of CINA consists of 28 volumes, covering material from 1919 through 1939, the last year of civil air operations in Europe prior to World War II. The first volume is dated November, 1922, and the last volume (No. 28) is dated December, 1945. Publication was interrupted by World War II at Volume 27, and Volume 28 was issued after the war to cover the latter

portion of 1939. With the establishment of the International Civil Aviation Organization in 1945, the International Commission for Air Navigation ceased to exist, and its functions were taken over by that body.

13. Poland-Austria, (14 CINA Bulletin 4); Poland-Czechoslovakia, (17 idem 20); Czechoslovakia-Austria, (17 idem 8); Italy-Spain, (17 idem 10); Italy-Austria, (17 idem 12); Austria-Yugoslavia, (19 idem 9); Persia-U.S.S.R., (19 idem 15); Spain-France, (19 idem 16); France-Poland, (19 idem 18); Greece-Poland, (20 idem 19); Czechoslovakia-Germany, (21 idem 17); Italy-Czechoslovakia, (21 idem 27); Germany-Poland, (22 idem 37); Italy-Germany, (24 idem 28); Poland-Romania, (25 idem 22); Bulgaria-Poland, (25 idem 28); Italy-Netherlands, (25 idem 33); Greece-Yugoslavia, (26 idem 23); Belgium-Czechoslovakia, (26 idem 30); Bulgaria-Romania, (26 idem 33); Italy-Romania-Yugoslavia, (27 idem 27); Greece-Romania, (26 idem 20).
14. Denmark-Norway, (13 CINA Bulletin 4); Sweden-Norway, (13 idem 12); Poland-Austria, (14 idem 4); Italy-Spain, (17 idem 10); Italy-Austria, (17 idem 12); Austria-Yugoslavia, (19 idem 9); Persia-U.S.S.R., (19 idem 15); Italy-Czechoslovakia, (21 idem 27); Germany-Poland, (22 idem 37); Poland-Romania, (25 idem 25); Italy-Netherlands, (25 idem 33); Greece-Romania, (26 idem 20); Greece-Yugoslavia, (26 idem 23).
15. Poland-Czechoslovakia, (17 CINA Bulletin 20); Czechoslovakia-Austria, (17 idem 8); Spain-France, (19 idem 16); France-Poland, (19 idem 18); Greece-Poland, (20 idem 19); France-Greece, (21 idem 21); Italy-Germany, (24 idem 28); Bulgaria-Poland, (25 idem 25); Belgium-Spain, (25 idem 28); Greece-Italy, (24 idem 28); Belgium-Czechoslovakia, (26 idem 30); Bulgaria-Romania, (26 idem 33); Italy-Romania-Yugoslavia (3-way agreement), (27 idem 27); Italy-Germany, (27 idem 34).
16. These are Italy-France, (17 CINA Bulletin 14); France-Belgium, (20 idem 9); Great Britain-Greece, (20 idem 13); Great Britain-Italy, (21 idem 9); Great Britain-Austria, (22 idem 36); Spain-Germany (Both the aeroplane agreement and the air ship agreement), (23 idem 27).
17. Poland-Austria, (14 CINA Bulletin 4); Poland-Czechoslovakia, (16 idem 20); Czechoslovakia-Austria, (17 idem 8); Italy-Spain, (17 idem 10); Italy-Austria, (17 idem 12); Austria-Yugoslavia, (19 idem 9); Persia-U.S.S.R., (19 idem 15); France-Poland, (19 idem 18); France-Belgium, (20 idem 9); Greece-Poland, (20 idem 19); Czechoslovakia-Germany, (21 idem 17); France-Greece, (21 idem 21); Italy-Czechoslovakia, (21 idem 27); Germany-Poland, (22 idem 27); Spain-Germany, (23 idem 27); France-Italy (the 1929 agreement), (17 idem 14) does not make clear whether multiple designation is allowed. The 1936 agreement (24 idem 20) establishes clearly that only one airline may be designated by each party); Italy-Germany, (24 idem 28); Poland-Romania, (25 idem 22); Bulgaria-Poland, (25 idem 25); Belgium-Spain, (25 idem 28); Italy-Netherlands, (25 idem 33); Greece-Romania, (26 idem 20); Greece-Yugoslavia, (26 idem 23); Greece-Italy, (26 idem 27); Belgium-Czechoslovakia, (26 idem 30); Bulgaria-Romania, (26 idem 33); Italy-Romania-Yugoslavia, (27 idem 27).
18. Italy-Spain, (17 CINA Bulletin 10); Italy-France, (17 idem 14); Great Britain-Greece, (20 idem 13); Great Britain-Italy, (21 idem 20); France-Greece, (21 idem 21); Great Britain-Austria, (22 idem 36); Belgium-Spain, (25 idem 28); Italy-Netherlands, (25 idem 33); Greece-Italy, (26 idem 33).
19. Denmark-Norway, (13 CINA Bulletin 4); Sweden-Norway, (13 idem 12); Poland-Czechoslovakia, (16 idem 20); Czechoslovakia-Austria, (17 idem 8); Persia-U.S.S.R., (19 idem 15); France-Poland, (19 idem 18); Czechoslovakia-Germany,

(21 idem 17); Poland-Romania, (25 idem 22); Bulgaria-Poland, (25 idem 25); Bulgaria-Romania, (26 idem 33); Greece-Poland, (20 idem 19); Greece-Romania, (26 idem 20).

20. Poland-Austria, (14 CINA Bulletin 4); Italy-Austria, (17 idem 12); France-Belgium, (20 idem 9); Italy-Czechoslovakia, (21 idem 27).
21. Spain-Germany, (23 CINA Bulletin 27).
22. Germany-Poland, (22 CINA Bulletin 37); Italy-Germany, (24 idem 28); Italy-Netherlands, (25 idem 33); Greece-Yugoslavia, (26 idem 23); Belgium-Yugoslavia, (26 idem 20 & 23); Belgium-Czechoslovakia, (26 idem 30); Italy-Romania-Yugoslavia, (27 idem 27).
23. Italy-France, (17 CINA Bulletin 14); Great Britain-Greece, (20 idem 13); Great Britain-Italy, (21 idem 20); Great Britain-Austria, (22 idem 36); France-Greece, (21 idem 21); Greece-Italy, (26 idem 27).
24. Spain-Germany, (23 CINA Bulletin 35).
25. Italy-Spain, (17 CINA bulletin 10); France-Belgium, (20 idem 9); Germany-Poland, (22 idem 37); Italy-Germany, (24 idem 28); Greece-Yugoslavia, (26 idem 23).
26. Italy-Austria, (17 CINA Bulletin 12).
27. Italy-Czechoslovakia, (21 CINA Bulletin 27).
28. Belgium-Czechoslovakia, (26 CINA Bulletin 30); Italy-Romania-Yugoslavia, (27 idem 27).
29. Wagner, *International Air Transportation as Affected by State Sovereignty* (1970), p. 64.
30. Cooper, *The Right to Fly* (1947), p. 2 and 94.
31. Wagner, *op. cit.,* p. 65.
32. Wagner cites as authority for this information, Slotemaker, *Freedom of Passage in International Air Routes* (1932). The same episode is referred to by David Corbett in *Politics and the Airlines* (1965), p. 29. Corbett also mentions (p. 30) an instance where the Greeks refused the British the use of the "strategically placed Navarino air base." Corbett observes, "The British Government was continually involved in bargaining with dozens of states to keep the air routes open."
33. The foregoing description of British airlines is derived from *World Airline Record,* 6th ed. (1965), p. 245.
34. *Ibid.,* p. 177.
35. Lissitzyn, *International Air Transport and National Policy* (1942), p. 60.
36. *World Airline Record,* supra note 33, p. 245.
37. See Tombs, *International Organization in European Air Transport* (1936), p. 14. See also Wheatcroft, *The Economics of European Air Transport* (1956), p. 204 and Slotemaker, *The Internationalization of Civil Aviation,* 3 Journal of Air Law and Commerce 648 (1932).
38. See Van Zandt, *Civil Aviation and Peace,* Washington D.C., (1944), p. 41–43.
39. Sheehan, "Air Cabotage and the Chicago Convention," *Harvard Law Review,* Vol. 63, No. 7 (1950), p. 1157, at 1159.
40. See P 172 Infra.
41. Lissitzyn, *op. cit.,* N. 35 supra at p. 395.
42. Tombs, *op. cit.,* N. 37 supra, at p. 35.
43. See Gazdik, "Rate Making and the IATA Traffic Conferences," 16 JALC 298 (1949).
44. International Air Transport Association, *IATA, The First Three Decades,* Montreal (1949), p. 15.

45. *Ibid.*, p. 24.
46. *Ibid.*
47. *Ibid.*, p. 68.
48. *Ibid.*, p. 30.
49. *Ibid.*, p. 64.
50. P 65–70 infra.
51. See Cooper, *The Right to Fly* (1947), p. 153ff.
52. House of Commons Debates, 5th Series, Vol. 1. 387, Col. 995, March 11, 1943.
53. House of Lords Debates, 5th Series, Vol. 129, Col. 214 et seq., Oct. 20, 1943.

3. AMERICAN INTERNATIONAL COMMERCIAL AIR TRANSPORT POLICY, 1919–1944

1. But see Lissitzyn, *International Air Transport and National Policy* (1942), p. 3, where he mentions service between Seattle and Victoria, B.C., which started on March 3, 1919, and lines connecting Florida with Cuba and the Bahamas that were started soon afterward. Davies, in *Airlines of the United States since 1944* (1972), p. 5–10, reports that Florida West Indies Airways, Inc., later known as Aeromarine Airways, operated services at various times between 1919 and 1923 from Key West, Fla., to Havana; from Miami to Bimini and from Miami to Nassau. This airline had a contract for the carriage of U.S. mail between Key West and Havana. The company went out of business in 1923. All of these services went out of business soon after they were started and appear to be of no importance to a study of U.S. policy, except as confirmation that commercial air operations at that time were impossible without subsidy.
2. Westwood and Bennett, "A Footnote to the Legislative History of the Civil Aeronautics Act of 1938 and Afterword," *Notre Dame Lawyer,* Vol. 3, No.3 (1967), p. 310.
3. 43 Stat 805 (1925).
4. Lissitzyn, *op. cit.*, N1, p. 142.
5. 45 Stat 594 (1928).
6. *World Airline Record* (1965), p. 420.
7. Daley, *An American Saga* (1980), p. 17.
8. *Ibid.*, p. 18.
9. Trippe was already president of Aviation Corporation of the Americas and on October 11 he was elected president of Atlantic, Gulf and European Airways. All of this was leading up to a merger of the three companies. Daley, *op. cit.*, p. 33.
10. The foregoing account folows the account in Daley, *op. cit.*, p. 5–68. The story is also related in Bender and Altschul, *The Chosen Instrument* (1982). The Bender-Altschul account differs in certain details, but the broad outline is similar.
11. International Convention for Aerial Navigation, 1919. League of Nations Treaty Series XI 173; Cooper, *The Right to Fly,* p. 359. Generally cited as "Paris Convention of 1919."
12. Cooper, *The Right to Fly* (1947), p. 138.
13. See Lissitzyn, *op. cit.*, p. 370–373.
14. 44 Stat 568 (1926).
15. *Ibid.*, Section 6.
16. *Ibid.*, Section 26.

17. Lissitzyn, *op. cit.,* p. 370–373.
18. Act of June 8, 1872, Ch 335. §§ 243–44, 249. 17 STAT 288, 313 (1875), requiring advertising for all airmail contracts.
19. 45 Stat 248 (1928); Amended 45 Stat 1449 (1929).
20. 46 Stat 259 (1930).
21. See Westwood and Bennett, *op. cit.,* p. 311.
22. Westwood and Bennett, *op. cit.,* p. 312; see Pacific Air Transport v United States, 98 CT of claims 649 at 695.
23. Daley, *op. cit.,* p. 29.
24. The foregoing account follows Daley, *op. cit.,* p. 56–68 and 80–86. See also Bender and Altscuhul, *op. cit.,* p. 116–122 and 166–176.
25. Lissitzyn, *op. cit.,* p. 242, citing letter to Captain Thomas B. Doe, Eastern Air Transport, Inc., quoted in *Hearings Pursuant to S. Res. 349, Before a Special Committee on Investigation of Air Mail Contracts,* 73rd Congress 2nd Session, 1934 pt. 6, 2459.
26. The Special Committee on Investigation of Air Mail and Ocean Mail Contracts, under the chairmanship of Senator Black, created pursuant to S. Res. No. 349, 72nd Congress, 2nd Session; 76 Cong. Rec. 5008 (1933).
27. See Westwood and Bennett, *op. cit.,* p. 312. The air force lost 12 pilots in the three months following the takeover.
28. Investigation of Air Mail and Ocean Mail Contracts, letter from the Post Master General ... transmitting Individual Reports and accompanying exhibits on Foreign Ocean and Air Mail Contracts, 718 Senate Committee Print, 74th Congress 1st Session, 1935. See Westwood and Bennett, *op. cit.,* p. 315 N 42; Lissitzyn, *op. cit.,* p. 340.
29. Lissitzyn, *op. cit.,* p. 242, Citing Hearings on HR 7370 before a subcommittee of the House Committee on the Post Office and Post Roads, 75th Congress, 1st Session (1937), 67–68, 72.
30. Lissitzyn, *op. cit.,* p. 384.
31. *Ibid.*
32. International services operated by South and Central American Airlines prior to World War II were as follows: CíaMexicana de Aviación (Mexico), Mexico–Los Angeles, 1935; Panair do Brasil (Brazil) 1931–34 Rio–Buenos Aires; Cruzero do Sul (Brazil) 1934 Porto Alegre–Buenos Aires, 1935 extended to Santiago, Chile. Of these, Cía Mexicana de Aviación and Panair do Brasil were wholly owned subsidiaries of Pan American. In addition, commencing in 1932, the countries of Central America except Guatemala were linked by a network provided by a holding company with various national subsidiaries named Transportes Aéreos Centro-Americanos (TACA). The holding company was named TACA de Honduras. The operating subsidiaries were named TACA of the particular country where they were organized. Lissitzyn, *op. cit.,* p. 312.
33. Faucett Airlines manufactured a version of the Stinson monoplane in its workshops in Peru for its own use during the prewar period, but this was a very small operation. W.A.M. Burden, *The Struggle for Airways in Latin America* (1943), p. 29ff.
34. For example, in Chile a military airline was established in 1929, which became Línea Aérea Nacional (LAN) in 1934 (Government owned). In Venezuela, the government-owned airline, Línea Aeropostal Venezolana, took over the internal Venezuelan routes previously operated by the French company Aeropostale in 1933. In 1928, the Peruvian Military established Línea Aérea Nacional del Peru. In 1929, the only private airline in South America at the time, Faucett Airways,

was established in Peru. The Brazilian airline C.A.M. was started in 1931 for the carriage of mail. See Burden, *op. cit.*

35. These were Sociedad Colombo Alemán de Transporte Aéreo ("SCADTA"; later to become Avianca) in Colombia, established 1920. Sindicato Condor, established in Brazil in 1927; Lloyd Aéreo Boliviano "LAB" established in Bolivia 1925; Sociedad Ecuatoreana de Transporte Aéreo ("SEDTA"), established in Ecuador 1937.
36. In 1929, Pan American bought the Mexican Company C[ía]Mexicana de Aviación; in 1931, it bought 84.42% of the Colombian Airline SCADTA, renaming it Avianca; in 1932, it bought 100% of the Cuban airline C[ía]Cubana de Aviación; in 1930 it acquired 100% of a Brazilian company called NYRBA do Brasil, when it bought NYRBA, and named it Panair do Brasil. See Burden, *op. cit.*, p. 24, and Lissitzyn, *op. cit.*, p. 332.
37. In Argentina, Bolivia, Ecuador, Paraguay and Peru, there were no restrictions on the carriage of cabotage traffic. In Colombia, companies engaged in cabotage were required to be 51% Colombian owned. In Venezuela, Pan American was allowed limited cabotage along the coast, but all other cabotage traffic was the monopoly of the government-owned company. In Mexico, companies engaged in cabotage were required to be nationally incorporated. In Brazil, Pan American was allowed limited cabotage rights along the coast. All other companies were required to be nationally incorporated (Burden, *op. cit.*, p. 51). In Brazil, Pan American was faced with an unusual requirement. Brazil insisted that the international operations of foreign airlines within Brazilian air space be carried out by Brazilian companies. For that reason, until 1935, when it obtained an operating permit in its own name, all of Pan American's services in Brazil were carried out in the name of its Brazilian subsidiary Panair do Brasil (see Burden, *op. cit.*, p. 27). This doctrine bears a certain resemblance to the position sustained in the 1940s and 1950s by the U.S. domestic airlines that the routes of foreign airlines to the United States should terminate at the U.S. coastal cities, with onward transportation to inland cities being performed by the American domestic airlines.
38. Daley, *op. cit.*, p. 487.
39. The foregoing account follows Daley, p. 135–168. See also Bender and Altschul, *op. cit.*, p. 227–257.
40. Exchange of notes, Feb. 23, 1929. Lissitzyn, *op. cit.*, p. 388, N. 7 says that this agreement is recorded in a Department of State press release of February 23, 1929, but is otherwise without official publication in the United States. The agreement was terminated upon entry into force of the air transport agreement between the United States and Colombia, signed October 24, 1956, with provisional entry into force January 1, 1957 (TIAS 5338).
41. Daley, *op. cit.*, p. 181, 182, 494. Bender and Altschul, *op. cit.*, p. 255–256.
42. Daley, *op. cit.*, p. 205–213; Bender and Altschul, *op. cit.*, p. 258–266; Lissitzyn, *op. cit.*, p. 244.
43. Lissitzyn, *op. cit.*, p. 401.
44. 52 Stat 1014 (1938).
45. Lissitzyn, *op. cit.*, p. 401.
46. Daley, *op. cit*, p. 244, *World Airline Record,* p. 248.
47. 92 Stat 1705 (1979).
48. 94 Stat 35 (1980).
49. The Civil Aeronautics Act originally provided for a single agency, the Civil Aeronautics Authority, to supervise both the technical and the economic aspects

of civil aviation. By the president's Reorganizaiton Plan 12 of 1940, Section 7 (a) 54 Section 7 (a). 54 Stat, 1235, the Civil Aeronuatics Authority was renamed the Civil Aeronautics Board and its functions were confined to the regulation of economic matters. The regulation of technical and safety matters was turned over to an administrator of civil aeronautics, whose staff was called the Civil Aeronautics Administration. See Westwood and Bennett, "A Footnote to the Legislative History of the Civil Aeronautics Act of 1938 and Afterword," *Notre Dame Lawyer,* Vol. 42, No. 3 (Feb. 1967), p. 309. To avoid confusion, the body dealing with economic regulation of air transport is referred to herein as the Civil Aeronautics Board throughout.

50. Section 401.
51. Section 406.
52. Daley, *op. cit.,* p. 218.
53. See Bender & Altschul, *op. cit.,* p. 291, 293. Daley, *op. cit.,* p. 222 refers to a 1938 deal whereby Pan American offered American Export a bloc of Pan American stock to get out of the airline business, a deal which he says the CAB blocked. This is the only reference to such a deal I have seen and I suspect it is the same deal described herein, as I have seen no other references to it.
54. CAB Dockets 373 and 497, Sept. 1, 1941; Lissitzyn, *op. cit.,* p. 243; Daley, *op. cit,* p. 260–268.
55. CAA Order No. 581. Approved by President July 15, 1940.
56. *Pan American Airways Corp v Civil Aeronautics Board et al* 121 Fed. 2nd 810 (1941).
57. Daley, *op. cit.,* p. 277; Lissitzyn, *op. cit,* p. 249. Daley implies that the operative reason for the decision, at least in the Senate, was that Pan American demonstrated that if the mail pay were appropriated for American Export Airlines, the cost in subsidy to the U.S. government would be $21,000 per flight, whereas Pan American could add extra flights to perform the same service at a cost in subsidy of $9,000 per flight.
58. Thayer, *Air Transport Policy and National Security* (1965), p. 4–8. Thayer goes further and sees in this episode and in the Black investigation (supra note 28) a reason for general hostility by "liberal democrats" to the entire U.S. scheduled airline industry.
59. Quoted in Lissitzyn, *op. cit.,* p. 385, citing CAB Docket No. 238, Exhibits 19, 34.
60. Lissitzyn, *op. cit,* p. 386–389 cites as likely reasons for this decision: (1) Many European states insisted upon government-to-government negotiations; (2) U.S. companies are not in a position to offer reciprocal landing rights in the United States; (3) U.S. companies negotiating on their own might obtain monopolies. Moreover, it could be embarrassing to the United States to have two or more American companies vying for favors from foreign governments. Such rivalry might enable the latter to drive hard bargains and impose terms harmful to American interests as a whole.
61. Quoted at 13 *Journal of Air Law and Commerce* 86 (1942).
62. See Daley, *op. cit.,* p. 335.
63. Burden, *The Struggle for Airways in Latin American* (1943). See also Bender and Altschul, *op. cit.,* p. 329–341.
64. Cleveland, *Air Transport at War* (1946).
65. Daley, *op. cit.,* p. 344.
66. *Aviation Daily,* Vol. 28, No. 12 (July 15, 1943), p. 16, "16 Airlines Adopt International Air Policy, Will Seek New Routes." An interesting sidelight on the

possible genesis of this declaration, and indeed on the entire policy adopted by the United States at the Chicago Conference in 1944 is provided by Daley at pages 345–6, where he says that the organizing force behind the domestic airlines was General H.H. Arnold, chief of staff of the Air Force, who was motivated by jealousy of Juan Trippe, and resentment of having lost, in 1928, the airline that developed into Pan American World Airways.

67. S. 1950 "Mid 1944" "McCarren Bill."
68. Daley, *op. cit.,* Note 8 supra, p. 349–357; Davies, *op. cit,* Note 1 supra, p. 26; Bender and Altschul, *op. cit.,* Note 11 supra, p. 399–414.

4. THE CHICAGO CONFERENCE

1. See e.g. *New York Times,* Dec. 7, 1944, p. 17, Col. 1; Dec. 9, 1944, p. 14, Col. 2.
2. *International Civil Aviation 1945–1948 Report of the United States of America to the International Civil Aviation Organization* (1948).
3. *Proceedings of the International Civil Aviation Conference, Chicago, Illinois, November 1-December 7, 1944* (1948), p. 11. (Hereinafter cited as "Proceedings.")
4. *Ibid.,* p. 13.
5. Oswald Ryan, a member of the Civil Aeronautics Board and of the U.S. delegation at Chicago, writing in 1946 (Ryan, "Recent Developments in United States Air Transportation Policy," *Air Affairs,* Vol. 1, No. 1 (Sept. 1946), p. 45), described the United States attitude in approaching the Chicago Conferences as follows: "Firmly set against the restrictive view of air transport development, the United States delegation carried to Chicago a philosophy of liberal expansion. Experience during the war had persuaded the most skeptical among us that air transportation had come of age and that only a vigorous development of the potential market was necessary to inaugurate a new era of world travel. We were persuaded that air transportation was not operating in a closed market; that on the contrary, the market for air services was much greater than the market for surface transportation, at least in the passenger field, by reason of the great savings of time which opened opportunities for passenger travel to millions; and that all that was needed to assure the realization of that potential demand was to translate progressive reduction in costs into progressive reduction in rates. If the rest of the world was dubious of the future of international aviation, we were prepared, given the opportunity to demonstate that the expanding market for air services would afford ample opportunities for the competitive development of most of the world's air routes, and that our carriers, and the carriers of other nations could find in this expanding market opportunities which would never appear if restrictive policies were to be permitted to obstruct reductions in costs and rates. Where some might assert that reductions in costs should logically precede reductions in rates, we knew from our experience in domestic air transportation and in other public utilities and private enterprises that reduction in rates to develop the market is commonly the most effective way to attain the volume operations that will permit costs to be reduced to a remunerative relationship with the promotional rates."
6. *Proceedings* (1948), p. 1268.
7. *Ibid.,* p. 375–531.
8. *Ibid.,* p. 446.
9. Bin Cheng, *The Law of International Air Transport* (1962), p. 18–24.

10. *Proceedings* (1948), p. 566. (Text of White Paper [CMD 6561] presented by the secretary of state for air to Parliament, Oct., 1944.)
11. *Ibid.,* p. 1–11.
12. *Ibid.*
13. *Ibid.,* p. 539.
14. See Thornton, *International Airlines and Politics* (1970), p. 28.
15. See Masefield, "Anglo American Civil Aviation," *Air Affairs,* Vol. 1, No. 3 (March 1947), p. 310. In describing the British attitude at Bermuda and at Chicago, Masefield says (p. 318), "The British point of view was that unrestricted competition in international air transport would result in extravagant operations, high subsidies and international ill will by driving smaller nations out of business. . . ."
16. Thornton, *International Airlines and Politics* (1970), p. 25.
17. *Proceedings* (1948), p. 515.
18. See Bin Cheng, *op. cit.,* p. 27.
19. See Robinson, *Changing Concepts of Cabotage* 34 JALC 553 (1968).
20. Bin Cheng, *op. cit.,* p. 315.
21. *Proceedings* (1948), p. 61. See also Robinson, "Changing Concepts of Cabotage," 4 JALC 558 (1968).
22. Thornton, *International Airlines and Politics* (1970), p. 119.
23. *Proceedings* (1948), p. 608.
24. *Proceedings* (1948), p. 25.
25. *Proceedings* (1948), p. 127.
26. *Proceedings* (1948), p. 512.
27. *Proceedings* (1948), p. 55.
28. *Proceedings* (1948), p. 64.
29. *Proceedings* (1948), p. 519.
30. Masefield, "Anglo American Civil Aviation," *Air Affairs,* Vol. 1, No. 3, 1947.
31. An attempt was actually made by the British and the United States to adapt the Bermuda capacity language for use in a multilateral air transport agreement, but the results proved unacceptable. "Report of the First Interim Assembly of PICAO May 21–June 8, 1946," *PICAO Journal* (Montreal), Vol. 1, No. 6 (Aug.–June 1946), (1946).
32. Bin Cheng, *op. cit.,* p. 23 Note 50c, citing Cribbett, "The Influence of Bilateral Agreements, Tariffs and Subsidies on International Air Transport," 3 *J.Ac. S. India* (1951), ¶1 at p. 4–5.
33. See for example the speech of Mayor Fiorello La Guardia, *Proceedings* (1948), p. 493–498.

5. THE BERMUDA AGREEMENT AND POST-WAR AMERICAN COMMERCIAL AIR POLICY

1. *International Air Transport Policy Report by the Attorney General, 1945.* February 28, 1945.
2. *Aviation Daily,* Vol. 42, No. 21 (Nov. 27, 1945), p. 121ff.
3. Presumably, this was the view expressed at Chicago. See *Proceedings* (1948), p. 566.
4. See Lissitzyn, *International Air Transport and National Policy* (1942), p. 401.
5. *Aviation Daily,* Vol. 42, No. 33 (Dec. 11, 1945), p. 193.

6. Bin Cheng, *The Law of International Air Transport* (1962), p. 18.

7. "Recent Developments in United States International Air Transportation Policy," by Oswald Ryan, *Air Affairs,* Vol. 1, No. 1 (Sept. 1946), p. 45; "Anglo American Civil Aviation," by Peter G. Masefield, *Air Affairs,* Vol. 1, No. 3 (March 1947), p. 310.

8. Agreement between the United States of America and the United Kingdom of Great Britain and Northern Ireland, Feb. 11, 1946, TIAS 1507.

9. TIAS 8641 (1977).

10. "International Air Transport Policy: Joint Statement by U.S. and British Governments," *Department of State Bulletin,* Vol. XV, No. 378 (1946), p. 577.

11. Bermuda-type agreements (not all of which are currently in effect) were signed with:

Australia
Austria
Belgium
Bolivia
Brazil
Burma
Canada
Chile
Colombia
Cuba
Czechoslovakia
Denmark
Dominican Republic
Ecuador
Egypt
Finland
France
W. Germany
Greece
Hungary
India
Indonesia
Iran
Italy
Japan
Lebanon
Liberia
Malaysia
Mexico
Morocco
Netherlands
New Zealand
Nigeria
Norway
Pakistan
Panama
Paraguay
Peru
Poland
Portugal
Romania
Senegal
Singapore
R. of South Africa
Spain
Sweden
Switzerland
Syria
Thailand
United Kingdom
Uruguay
Venezuela
Zaire

12. *International Air Transport: Law, Organization and Policies of the Future: Proceedings of the Institute of Air and Space Law,* Nov. 17–19, 1976, p. 3. *Politiques Aeriennes Internationales Vues par la France,* by Claude Abraham; see also Bin Cheng, *op. cit.,* p. 239.

13. PICAO Journal, August–June 1946, Vol. 1, No. 6, Montreal (1946), p. 17.

14. *Proceedings of the First Session of the Assembly* 6 May–27 May 1947 International Civil Aviation Organization, Montreal (1952), p. 264. Reso. Al–38.

15. *Records of the Commission on Multilateral Agreement on Commercial Rights in International Civil Air Transport* (session held at Geneva, Nov. 4–27, 1947), International Civil Aviation Organization, Montreal (1948).

16. Sir Frederick Tymms, "Let's Clear the Record on Chicago's 'Freedoms'," *Air Transport World,* Vol. 3, No. 5 (May 1966), p. 17: "It [Bermuda] was a gentlemen's agreement, depending on discussion and adjustments between the parties when difficulties arose in the application of its principles. Such was possible between two parties. Between fifty or a hundred, an agreement must be more definitive."

17. Convention on International Civil Aviation 61 Stat 1180 (1947).

18. "Change of gauge" refers to the practice of terminating a flight with a large aircraft at a point short of the terminus of the route and of continuing the onward

carriage of the passengers to their destination in a smaller aircraft. See Bin Cheng, *op. cit.,* p. 434–440.

19. Taneja, *U.S. International Aviation Policy* (1980), p. 13; Wheatcroft, *The Economics of European Air Transport* (1956), p. 220; Strassheim, *The International Airline Industry* (1969), p. 33; Thornton, *International Airlines and Politics* (1970), p. 34–38; Billyou, *Air Law* (1964), p. 268.
20. Bin Cheng, *op. cit.* p. 99–100, 458–461. Bin Cheng says that advisory reports are in all but name arbitral awards, citing *British Claims in The Spanish Zones of Morocco* (1924–25), (2 UNRIAA, p. 615) and *The I'm Alone* (1935) 3 UNRIAA 1609. Nevertheless, given the weakness of the ICAO council as a tribunal and the reluctance of the parties to seek arbitration on this subject (the United States has never sought arbitration of a capacity matter under a Bermuda-type capacity clause), the importance of arbitration or advisory opinions to the resolutions of problems under the Bermuda Agreements' capacity "principles" can be discounted.
21. Cf. Wassenbergh, *Postwar International Civil Aviation and the Law of the Air* (1957), p. 53-61.
22. Diamond, *The Bermuda Agreement Revisited: A Look at the Past, Present and Future of Bilateral Agreements* (1975), 41 JALC 419.
23. *Ibid.,* p. 450. Cf. the view of Sir Frederick Tymms, note 16 supra, that the Bermuda Agreement was a gentlemen's agreement, depending on discussions and adjustments between the parties when difficulties arose in the application of its principles.
24. TIAS 1587.
25. "Otra Vez el Entreguismo," *Marka* (Lima), 7 Dec. 1978, p. 12.
26. Proceedings of the Institute of Air and Space Law, 25th Conference Nov. 17–19, 1976, "Politiques Aeriennes Internationales Vues par la France," by Claude Abraham.
27. Civil Air Transport Agreement between the United States of America and Japan, August 11, 1952 (TIAS 2854).
28. Agreement between the United States of America and the Netherlands, TIAS 4782.
29. Exchange of notes accompanying Air Transport Agreement between the United States and India, Feb. 3, 1956. TIAS 3504.
30. Although it is not typical of most of these side agreements the Indian Agreement has a further provision (paragraph 8) to the effect that despite the Bermuda-type capacity provisions, which say that capacity is to be justified by the traffic requirements between the country of origin and the countries of ultimate destination of the traffic, "any increase in frequency for a United States airline will be required to be justified primarily for the provision of capacity needed on account of the increase in the amount of the traffic originating in the United States and destined for India and vice versa which is carried by that airline or which that airline can reasonably establish as its anticipated needs for the carriage of the traffic originating in the United States and destined for India and vice versa."
31. The details of these "screening agreements" are not given here because of their "unpublished" status, and because their relevance to U.S. air transport policy is sufficiently established through a general reference to them.
32. Department of State Press Release No. 359, July 8, 1975.
33. Exchange of diplomatic notes between the United States of America and Peru dated July 7, 1975.

34. U.S.-Argentine memorandum agreements, Sept. 22, 1977, TIAS 8978; Amendments, March 11, 1981, TIAS 10440; August 13, 1982, TIAS ____.
35. China, TIAS ____ (1980).
36. U.S.S.R., TIAS 8996 (1966).
37. See Gidwitz, *The Politics of International Air Transport* (1980), p. 23.
38. "Amendment of United States-Colombia Air Transport Agreement," Department of State Press Release No. 245, Oct. 24, 1968.
39. Unpublished exchange of notes, 1966.
40. Unpublished exchange of notes, June 5, 1967.
41. Unpublished exchange of notes, Dec. 15, 1977.
42. Bilateral Agreement, TIAS 1905 (1948). "Capacity Understanding" with Chile, Department of State Press Release No. 242, Oct. 14, 1966.
43. TIAS 1727 (1946).
44. TIAS 4021 (1957).
45. TIAS 3285 (1947).
46. TIAS 1607 (1947).
47. TIAS 2854 (1952).
48. TIAS 3078 (1947). This agreement was signed between the United States and India Nov. 14, 1946 (TIAS 1586); it was made extensive as to Pakistan June 16, 1948 (TIAS 3078). The Indian Agreement was superseded by a new agreement Feb. 3, 1956 (TIAS 3504), but the Pakistan agreement continued in effect.
49. Japan, Article 12; Pakistan Article III.
50. Section VIII of the Resolutions and Recommendations attached to the Final Act of the Chicago Conference, Dec. 7, 1944, ICAO Doc. 2187; 1 Proceedings of the International Civil Aviation Conference, Chicago, Nov. 1-Dec. 7, 1944 (Publ. No. 2820), U.S. Dept. of State, Washington, D.C. (1948), p. 113.
51. This provision is also reflected in Article 33 of the Chicago Convention, with the further proviso that the requirements under which such certificates or licenses were issued are equal to or above those of the Chicago Convention.
52. See for example *Air Jamaica Limited, Foreign Air Carrier Permit* 44 CAB 169 (1966)—Permit granted despite finding that ownership and control were effectively in British West Indian Airways and British Overseas Airways. The Bermuda Agreement was in effect between the United States and Jamaica, which became a party to the agreement in its own right upon independence from the United Kingdom; *Air Jamaica (1968) Ltd. Foreign Permit* 50 CAB 392 (1969)—Permit granted despite indications that Air Canada actually exercised ownership and control. The permit was, however, conditional to prevent Air Jamaica from holding out that the service was being provided by Air Canada.
53. This is particularly evident in the "capacity principles" (Final Act, paragraphs 3-6), which establish elements that can be invoked by both parties to a dispute about whether a given capacity is excessive. It would be quite unlikely that the United States would have agreed to a change in these articles that would assist the proponent to restricitng capacity and equally unlikely that the British would agree to changes favoring capacity increases.
54. Bin Cheng, *op. cit.,* p. 460.
55. e.g. Colombia, TIAS 5338 (1956) Chile; TIAS 1905 (1948). In Peru, the agreement, TIAS 1587 (1946) provides that it will come into effect upon signature, but it has been argued by Peruvian lawyers that it required ratification pursuant to the Peruvian constitution, and that in the absence of ratification the agreement lacked legal force. At the time this argument was made both parties had been treating the agreement as effective for over 20 years, and both and been

receiving benefits under it throughout that period, so the argument was not pressed hard on the Peruvian side. Ultimately the Peruvians denounced the agreement.

Currently, most U.S. agreements are signed "ad referendum," with formal signature later, after review by the U.S. executive branch (primarily directed by the Department of State and its legal section). So far as the United States is concerned the agreement can become definitively effective at that time. In order to avoid the delay caused by the requirement in many countries that the agreement must be ratified by the legislative branch, or by some other body in its absence, U.S. Bilateral Air Transport Agreements often provide that they will become effective "provisionally" upon signature.

56. This power was not conferred on the Civil Aeronautics Board until 1972 (86 Stat 95; 49 USC 1374).
57. See Gazdik, "Rate Making and the IATA Traffic Conferences," 16 JALC 298 (1949); Koffler, "IATA, Its Legal Structure; A Critical Review," 32 JALC 222 (1966).
58. See Cohen, "Confessions of a Former IATA Man," 34 JALC 610, 1968.
59. See Pillai, *The Air Net, The Case Against the World Aviation Cartel* (1960).
60. *Agreement CAB No. 493 IATA Traffic Conference Resolutions,* 6 CAB 639, (1946).
61. Now Federal Aviation Act. The relevant section read: "Sec. 412 Every air carrier shall file with the Baord a true copy of every contract or agreement ... relating to the establishment of transportation rates fares, charges or classification...."
62. Bermuda Agreement, Annex, Section II (f).
63. e.g. France TIAS 1679 (1946); Belgium TIAS 1515 (1946); Japan, TIAS 5244 (1962).
64. e.g. Lacking a rate clause: Bolivia TIAS 5507 (1948); Ecuador TIAS 1606 (1947); Thailand TIAS 1607 (1947); Paraguay TIAS 1753 (1947). Lacking requirement for consultation: Peru TIAS 1587 (1946); Mexico TIAS 4675 (1960); Uruguay, TIAS 5692 (1946): A number of these agreements have since been amended to include rate clauses.
65. *Aviation Daily,* Vol. 42, No. 33 (Dec. 11, 1945), p. 193.
66. Bermuda Agreement. Annex, Section II, paragraph (f).
67. For a useful evaluation of the IATA Traffic Conferences see Taneja, *International Aviation Policy* (1980), p. 77–104.
68. Air Services Agreement between the United States and the United Kingdom, TIAS 8641 (1977), Annex I, Section 5, paragraph 6. Also, Paragraph 6 (a) appears to prohibit the use of two aircraft when it says "operations beyond the point of change of gauge shall be performed by an aircraft having capacity less, for outbound services, or more, for inbound services, than that of the arriving aircraft." The reference to "an aircraft" appears to preclude the use of more than one aircraft.
69. See Second U.S.-France Arbitration, 54 *Intl. Law Rep.* 304 (1979).
70. See Bin Cheng, *op. cit.,* p. 439.

6. UNITED STATES POLICY STATEMENTS IN THE BERMUDA ERA

1. July 23, 1977; curiously, although the Bermuda 2 Agreement is more restrictive than the Bermuda 1 Agreement, the 1977 change in U.S. policy was toward a policy of "deregulation."
2. 52 Stat 973 (1938).
3. For an exposition of the legislative history of this aspect of the Civil Aeronautics Act, see Westwood and Bennett, "A Footnote to the Legislative History of the Civil Aeronautics Act of 1938, and Afterword," *Notre Dame Lawyer,* Vol. 42 (1967), p. 309.
4. President Truman: "Survival in the Air Age; A Report by the President's Air Policy Commission," Jan. 1948. Reprinted 15 *JALC* 69 (1948).
5. President Eisenhower: "Civil Air Policy; A Report by the Air Coordinating Committee, by Direction of the President," May 1954, Washington, U.S. Gov. Printing Office.
6. President Kennedy: "Statement on International Air Transport Policy," White House Press Release, April 24, 1963.
7. President Nixon: "Statement of International Transportation Policy," June 30, 1970; 63 *Department of State Bulletin* 86.
8. President Ford: *International Air Transport Policy of the United States,* Sept. 1976.
9. Examples are: "Rationale of Federal Transportation Policy," by Ernest W. Williams, Jr., and David W. Bluestone, U.S. Department of Commerce, April 1960, "A Statement of National Transportation Policy," by the Secretary of Transportation, September 17, 1975, Washington, D.C. (Press release); Department of State Press Release No. 582, Nov. 14, 1956, "Remarks by the Hon. Herbert Hoover, Jr., Acting Secretary of State," at Government-Industry Aviation Meeting, Department of State, Nov. 14, 1956.
10. Federal Aviation Act § 402 (72 Stat 754).
11. *Ibid.,* § 401 (72 Stat 757).
12. *Ibid.,* § 801 (72 Stat 782). See p. 151 infra.
13. 14 *JALC* 364 (1947). The members of the Commission were: Thomas K. Finletter, New York, chairman; George K. Baker, Cambridge, Mass., vice chariman; Palmer Hoyt, Denver; Henry Ford II, Detroit; Arthur Whiteside, New York.
14. 15 *JALC* 69 (1948).
15. *Ibid.,* p. 69.
16. *Ibid.,* p. 71.
17. *Ibid.,* p. 72.
18. *Ibid.,* p. 73.
19. *Ibid.,* p. 75.
20. *Ibid.*
21. Records of the Commission on Multilateral Agreement on Commercial Rights in International Civil Air Transport, Vol. II, Part 1, p. 69, ICAO Doc. 5230, A2-EC/10, April 1948.
22. For example: Austria, TIAS 1659 (1947); Ecuador TIAS 1606 (1947); Italy TIAS 1902 (1948); Paraguay TIAS 1656 (1947); Syria TIAS 3285 (1947); Thailand TIAS 1607 (1947); South Africa TIAS 1639 (1947).
23. 15 *JALC* 81 (1948).
24. *Ibid.,* p. 82.

25. U.S. Gov. Printing Office, Washington, D.C., May 1954. Hereinafter referred to as "Eisenhower Policy."
26. *Ibid.*, p. 35.
27. *Ibid.*
28. *Ibid.*, p. 36.
29. *Ibid.*
30. *Ibid.*
31. *International Conference on the Freedom of the Air.* Proceedings of the Institute of Air and Space Law, Nov. 3-4, 1967, McGill University, Montreal, Canada.
32. *International Air Transport, Law, Organization and Policies for the Future:* Proceedings of the Institute of Air and Space Law, 25th Anniversary Conference, Nov. 17-19, 1976, McGill University, Montreal, Canada.
33. Eisenhower Policy, p. 8.
34. *Ibid.*, p. 15.
35. *Ibid.*, p. 8.
36. *Ibid.*, p. 36.
37. *Ibid.*, p. 37.
38. *Ibid.*, p. 38.
39. *Ibid.*, p. 39.
40. *Ibid.*, p. 16.
41. See p. 173-74 infra.
42. Eisenhower Policy, p. 17.
43. P. 70 supra.
44. Eisenhower Policy, p. 19.
45. *Ibid.*, p. 20.
46. *Ibid.*, p. 22.
47. See "Civil Air Policy—Hearings before a subcommittee of the Committee on Interstate and Foreign Commerce, House of Representatives 84th Congress on HR 4648 and HR 4677, Bills to Amend the Civil Aeronautics Act of 1938 and HR 8902 and HR 8903, Bills to Amend Subsection 406 (b) of the Civil Aeronautics Act of 1938, as amended. March 18 and July 22, 1955 (Before entire committee); Jan. 17, 18, 19, 20, Feb. 9, 10, 28, 29, March 2, April 18 and 20, 1956 (Before subcommtitee on Transportation and Communications)," U.S. Gov. Printing Office, 1956; p. 191-201, 374-439.
48. Eisenhower Policy, p. 23.
49. *Ibid.*, p. 49.
50. *Ibid.*, p. 60.
51. *Ibid.*, p. 68.
52. The U.S. airlines operating internationally would leave a similar interest to that of the manufacturers, because they would be exposed to pressure by the foreign governments if spare parts were to be available to U.S. airlines, but not to foreign airlines.
53. Eisenhower Policy, p. 71.
54. *International Air Agreements, Report of the Committee on Interstate and Foreign Commerce, United States Senate, 84th Congress, 2nd Session, Report No. 1875,* U.S. Gov. Printing Office, 1956; p. 1. Hereinafter cited as "Smathers Report."
55. *Agreement and Exchange of Notes Between the United States of America and the Federal Republic of Germany,* at Washington, D.C., July 7, 1955. TIAS 3536 (1955). The U.S. routes were: (1). From the United States of America via inter-

mediate points to Hamburg and beyond to points in Europe north and east of the Federal Republic of Germany; (2) From the United States via intermediate points to Düsseldorf-Cologne/Bonn, Frankfurt, Stuttgart and Munich and beyond to points in Europe east and southeast of West Germany and beyond; and (3) From the United States via intermediate points to Frankfurt and beyond to points in Europe south and southeast of the Federal Republic of Germany and beyond to North Africa, the Near East and beyond. The West German routes were: (1) From the Federal Republic of Germany via intermediate points to Boston, New York and Philadelphia and beyond to points in the Caribbean and beyond to South America; (2) From West Germany via intermediate points to Chicago; and (3) From West Germany via intermediate points to San Francisco or Los Angeles (selection of the terminal point in the United States to be determined by West Germany at a later date).

56. See for example, Smathers Report, p. 3–5, 10–12, 25 on the matter of consultation, and p. 15–19, 22–24 on the disparity of the route values. As a matter of interest, the author was employed by Pan American-Grace Airways at the time, and we refrained from participation in these hearings in the belief that the exchange of routes and the manner of the negotiation were so far outside the norms usually observed in such matters that it was probable that the agreement reflected a determination at a very high level in the United States government for overriding strategic and political reasons to allow the Germans extraordinary concessions.
57. *Ibid.*, p. 25, 26.
58. The foreign air carrier permit issued by the United States to Lufthansa to operate beyond the United States to South America pursuant to the Bilateral Air Transport Agreement, *Lufthansa, Foreign Permit,* 43 CAB 301 (1965) required Lufthansa to report the third, fourth and fifth freedom traffic carried on the leg beyond New York to and from South America twice each year. These figures were available in the CAB docket section, and do not reveal an extraordinary element of fifth freedom traffic. It is possible that Lufthansa purposely avoided carrying too much fifth freedom traffic because of the reporting requirement.
59. See *Sociedad Aeronáutica Medellín S.A. Foreign Air Carrier Permit* 26 CAB 53 (1957); *British Overseas Airways Corp., Foreign Air Carrier Permit,* 31 CAB 583 (1959); *Líneas Aéreas Costarricences S.A., Foreign Air Carrier Permit* 26 CAB 429 (1958); *Varig, Foreign Permit* 40 CAB 351 (1964); *Aeronaves de Mexico, Foreign Permit Amendment,* 44 CAB 289 (1966); *Trans Mediterranean Airways S.A.C. Foreign Permit,* 57 CAB 18 (1971).
60. See Kalijarvi, "The Paradox of Foreign Economic Policy," 36 *Department of State Bulletin* 1009 (1957).
61. As one who was on the scene at the time, the writer can assert through personal observation that after this report the position of the airlines improved. In addition it is clear that the Department of State personnel involved in the episode were considerably shaken up by it. See Kalijarvi, Note 60 supra.
62. Smathers Report: Letter, April 3, 1956, from Ross Rizley, chairman, Civil Aeronautics Board to Senator Smathers.
63. The general format for carrier consultation described above has continued in effect to the present time. Over the years new elements have come on the scene. When the charter airlines organized their trade association, The National Air Carrier Association, "NACA," they were permitted to have a representative in negotiations. After 1977, when the U.S. government was caught up in "deregulation," a representative of the Aviation Consumer's Action Project, "ACAP,"

became a member of the U.S. delegations. At about the same time a member of the Airline Pilots Association, International, "ALPA," the pilots union, also became a member of U.S. delegations. To regulate the traffic, the U.S. government representatives announced that these observers were members of "Advisory Committees" and were regulated by Executive Order 11671 of June 5, 1972 (37FR11307). On the government side, the Department of Commerce added its representative to those of the CAB and Department of State. In 1966, the Department of Transportation's representative joined the group, and in 1985, the CAB representative dropped out pursuant to the Civil Aeronautics Board Sunset Act of 1984.

64. *Civil Aeronautics Act* of 1938, Section 102 (a).
65. By letter dated June 22, 1963, the president formally assigned to the Department of State primary responsibility for carrying out international air policy.
66. S. 2647, 83rd Congress, Second Session (1954). S 2647 was an omnibus aviation bill sponsored by Senator McCarran to supplant the Civil Aeronautics Act of 1938. The legislation that finally did supplant the Civil Aeronautics Act was the Federal Aviation Act of 1958, 72 Stat 731. The changes made in the Civil Aeronautics Act of 1938 by the Federal Aviation Act of 1958 had little or no effect on the international commercial air policy of the United States, since that Act had as its main purpose the creation of the Federal Aviation Agency to unite in one body the responsibility for regulating the technical aspects of air transport theretofore shared by the Civil Aeronautics Board and the Civil Aeronautics Administration. (See Senate Report No. 1811, Federal Aviation Act of 1958: Report of Committee on Interstate and Foreign Commerce, to accompany S. 3880, July 9, 1958.)
67. United States Constitution, Article II, Section II.
68. Aviation Study, Section VII, presented by John W. Bricker, Chairman, Interstate and Foreign Commerce, 83rd Congress, Senate Dec. 163, 83rd Congress, 2nd Session (Released Jan. 11, 1955).
69. *Report of the Task Force on National Aviation Goals, Project Horizon,* Washington, D.C., U.S. Gov. Printing Office, 1961.
70. *Ibid.,* p. 116–117.
71. *Ibid.,* p. 122–123.
72. *Ibid.,* p. 128.
73. Statement on International Air Transport Policy. White House Press Release, April 23, 1963; 30 *JALC* 76 (1964).
74. Federal Aviation Act § 102(a); 72 Stat 740 (1958).
75. This episode is described in detail in Hearings on International Air Transportation Rates and S. 1539 and S. 1540 before the Senate Committee on Commerce, 88th Congress, 1st Session (1963).
76. 80 Stat 931 (1966).
77. Department of Transportation Act, Section 2 (b) (1), 80 Stat 931 (1966).
78. *Ibid.,* Sec. 3 (e) (2).
79. *Ibid.,* Sec. 4 (a).
80. Federal Aviation Act of 1958, Sec. 102, 72 Stat 740 (1958).
81. Department of Transportation Act of 1966, Sec. 4 (b) (1).
82. White House Press Release. 63 Department of State Bulletin, 86 (1970).
83. Pan American and TWA.
84. *Foreign Air Carrier Permit Terms Investigation* 54 CAB 175 (1970).
85. Federal Aviation Act, Section 402(d), 72 Stat 757 (1958).
86. CAB Order E 16278, January 18, 1961.

87. Reported in *Foreign Air Carrier Permit Terms Investigation* 54 CAB 175 (1970) at p. 176–177.
88. Presidential approval is required by Section 801 of the Federal Aviation Act, 72 Stat 782 (1958), because the proceedings involved amending foreign air carrier permits.
89. Civil Aeronautics Board, Economic Regulations Part 213—Terms, Conditions and Limitations of Foreign Air Carrier Permits. ER 624 June 4, 1970; 14 CFR Section 213.
90. CAB Reg. E.R. 870, Amendment 4, adding 14 CFR, Section 213.3 (c) (2), adopted by the CAB July 12, 1974, approved by the president, Aug. 21, 1974. Fed. Reg. 30842 (Aug. 26, 1974). This amendment related to the U.S. problems with the Dutch airline KLM.
91. Economic Regulations Part 213, Sec. 213 (3) (d).
92. See e.g., Lowenfeld, "CAB v KLM, Bermuda at Bay," *Air Law* (Netherlands), Vol. 1, No. 1 (1975), p. 2.
93. 86 Stat 95 (March 22, 1972), adding new section 1002J to the Federal Aviation Act, and amending Sections 404 and 801.
94. International Air Transportation Policy of the United States, Sept., 1976. White House Press Release Sept. 8, 1976 (policy published in pamphlet form).
95. Federal Aviation Act of 1958, Section 102 (d) 72 Stat 740, 49 USC 1302 (1958).
96. That is, that the rules of the country where the charter traffic originates should be used to determine whether the charter may be performed.
97. Originally, it was the custom of the Civil Aeronautics Board to permit scheduled carriers to have unlimited charter authority between the points for which they held a U.S. certificate of convenience and necessity or a foreign air carrier permit, and to require them to obtain authority for "off-route" charters pursuant to the Board's economic regulations. See Keyes, "The Charter Policy of the U.S.A.," 39 *JALC* 215 (1973).
98. Clayton Act 15 USC 15; Sherman Act 15 USC 1 and 2.
99. The only time a real pooling agreement was presented to the Board was in 1961, when Pan American presented for approval an agreement with VIASA, the Venezuelan National Airline (*Agreement CAB No. 15385, Pan American–Venezuelan Traffic Arrangements* 34 CAB 800 [1961]). The CAB disapproved it as being inconsistent with U.S. international aviation policy, undesirable as a precedent, and contrary to Section 102 of the Federal Aviation Act. That no other cases have been presented for approval is probably due to the fact that the carriers have generally considered it prudent to have CAB approval to discuss such things as pooling agreements in advance of the discussions to prevent the application of the U.S. antitrust laws (possible under Section 414 of the Federal Aviation Act of 1958) and it has been evident that it would be useless to request such approval.
100. The source for most of this section is the writer's own recollection of positions taken at the time. So far as I am aware, there are no published sources. For further details concerning the Pan American arrangement with Aeroflot, see p. 123 infra.
101. Typically a blocked space agreement is one where one airline leases a block of seats or of cargo capacity on a particular flight to another airline serving the same route to sell as its own. Typically the risk of profit or loss falls exclusively on the lessee, and the lessor gets its rent, whether the space is occupied or not. Governments have generally been willing to regard this arrangement as a lease

of transport capacity, rather than as a pooling arrangement. Nevertheless, the United States requires that both lessor and lessee have U.S. operating authority for the sectors involved. Cases where the U.S. authorities have approved blocked space arrangements are: *Seaboard Blocked Space Agreements* 39 CAB 833 (1963) (involving lease of blocked space on cargo aircraft by Seaboard to Lufthansa, Swissair and British Overseas Airways Corp.). *Air Afrique, Foreign Permit* 40 CAB 759 (1964) (Pan American leased 35 seats to Air Afrique on its flights to Dakar, Robertsfield, Abidjan, Cotonou, Douala and Brazzaville. This agreement has certain aspects of a pool, and the CAB said it would normally disapprove it, but the Department of State said it should be approved "on broader national interest grounds"); renewed 57 CAB 363 (1971). *WAAC (Nigeria) Ltd. Foreign Permit* 41 CAB 111 (1964) (lease of 25 seats by Pan American to WAAC). The CAB has disapproved blocked space agreements where it found an adverse impact on another U.S airline—see *Pan American/Japan Airlines Agreement* 39 CAB 832 (1963).

102. *Braniff et al., Concorde Interchange Agreements.* 79 CAB 752 (1978).
103. The Civil Aeronautics Board (now Department of Transportation) acts to approve the agreements under Section 412 of the Federal Aviation Act of 1958 (49 USC 1382 [1970]), and then, if the Board specifically finds it is in the public interest, it may exempt the parties to it from the operation of the U.S. "antitrust laws." Originally this exemption was automatic [72 Stat 770 (1958), 498 USC 1384]; it was amended to require a finding of public interest and affirmative action by the CAB as part of the Airline Deregulation Act of 1978, 92 Stat 1731 [1978], 49 USC 1384.
104. *Scheduling Committee Agreements* 49 CAB 893 (1968). For a review of the early history and rationale of the U.S. domestic capacity agreements, see Jordan, "Airline Capacity Agreements, Correcting a Regulatory Imperfection," 39 *JALC* 179 (1973).
105. *Discussions Re Flight Schedule Adjustments* 53 CAB 890 (1970).
106. *Midway Airport, Expanded Services* 54 CAB 841 (1970), 60 CAB 920 (1972).
107. *PAA et al., Joint Discussions* 56 CAB 615 (1971).
108. *Schedule Adjustments within Hawaii* 55 CAB 983 (1970).
109. *Limitation of Capacity Agreement* 57 CAB 641 (1971); 59 CAB 822 (1972); 61 CAB 822 (1973); 62 CAB 958, (1973); 63 CAB 707 (1973); 63 CAB 710 (1973).
110. *San Juan Capacity Reductions* 60 CAB 923 (1972).
111. For an interested carrier's-eye view of international airline capacity agreements, see Friedman, *A New Air Transport Policy for the North Atlantic—Saving An Endangered System,* New York, Atheneum, 1976. This work was sponsored jointly by British Airways and Pan American Airways and had as its avowed aim to persuade the U.S. government to adopt a system of capacity controls on the North Atlantic, based upon reciprocal capacity agreements among airlines (p. 39). This proposal was not greeted with any enthusiasm at all by other U.S. airlines that aspired to attain transatlantic routes, since the capacity agreements would effectively lock out all possibility of new competition.
112. CAB Order 74-2-93 (Feb. 22, 1974); CAB Order 74-10-6 (Oct. 2, 1974); CAB Order 74-11-34 (Nov. 7, 1974).
113. CAB Order 74-11-52 (Nov. 12, 1974).
114. CAB Order 74-11-54 (Nov. 13, 1974).
115. CAB Order 74-12-1 (Dec. 2, 1974).
116. CAB Order 75-3-67 (March 21, 1975).
117. CAB Order 75-7-27 (July 3, 1975).

118. CAB Order 77-1-7 (Nov. 16, 1976), 77 CAB 1 (1977) approved by President Ford Dec. 31, 1976.
119. See Lowenfeld, "A New Takeoff for International Air Transport," 54 *Foreign Affairs* (Oct. 1975). See also Lowenfeld, *Aviation Law,* New York, Matthew Bender, 1981; Ch. 5, Sec. 2.
120. 88 Stat 2102 (1975).
121. The Civil Reserve Air Fleet is an arrangement whereby participating airlines agreed to modify their fleets of aircraft and to make them available to the U.S. military for use in the event of a mobilization. It was formulated in the 1950s and has been in existence with varying degrees of participation ever since.
122. International Airline Fair Competitive Practices Act of 1974. Act of January 3, 1975, 88 Stat 2102 (1975).
123. The source for this is the writer's recollection. The matter was dealt with informally through the U.S. Embassy in Seoul, and the outcome was the withdrawal of the order.
124. In the writer's personal recollection, the use of discriminatory exchange rates has occurred in Ecuador, Peru, Chile and Argentina. It took its most vicious form in Chile during the administration of the communist regime of Dr. Salvador Allende when Braniff Airways lost approximately a million dollars to it in one year.
125. In the writer's personal recollection, the United States has alleged that landing fees were too high in Argentina, Bolivia, Colombia, Chile, Ecuador, and Peru, as well as in the United Kingdom. The problem is much wider spread, however.
126. In the writer's personal recollection, this situation has existed in Bolivia, Colombia, and Peru.
127. In the writer's personal recollection, this situation has existed in Bolivia, Peru and Chile.
128. International Air Transportation Fair Competitive Practices Act of 1974, Section 2; 88 Stat 2102, 49 USC 1159 (1975).
129. *Ibid.,* Section 3.

7. INTERNATIONAL AMERICAN NEGOTIATIONS IN THE BERMUDA ERA

1. Finland TIAS 1945 (1949); Sweden TIAS 3013 (1954); Denmark TIAS 3014 (1954); Norway TIAS 3015 (1954); Germany TIAS 3536 (1955); United Kingdom TIAS 1507 (1946); France TIAS 1679 (1947); Portugal TIAS 1656 (1947); Italy TIAS 1902 (1948); Netherlands TIAS 4782 (1957) (Spain did not sign a Bermuda-type agreement with the United States until 1973). The agreements with Finland, Germany, United Kingdom and the Netherlands have been superseded, the U.K. agreement by the Bermuda 2 Agreement, TIAS 8641 (1977) and the others by "pro-competitive" amendments.
2. See p. 90 supra.
3. "Charter services" is a term with a rather flexible meaning. In 1962, it was defined by Representative Oren Harris as follows: "the law is well established that, in air transportation, charter means essentially the lease of the entire capacity of an aircraft for a period of time or a particular trip, for the transportation of cargo or persons and baggage, on a basis which does not include solicitation of the

general public, or any device where individually ticketed services would be offered or performed under guise of charter" (108 Congressional Record 12322, June 29, 1962). As it later developed, in the United States, "charter" meant what the Civil Aeronautics Board said it meant. See p. 109 infra. "Contract service" is carriage pursuant to a contract with an individual shipper or passenger, where the carrier does not hold himself out to serve the general public. (See statement of S.G. Tipton, Hearings before a Subcommittee of the Committee on Interstate and Foreign Commerce, House of Representatives 84th Congress, March 18 and July 22, 1955 and January 17, 18, 19, 20, February 9, 10, 28, 29, March 2, April 18 and 20, 1956; on H.R. 4698, H.R. 4677, H.R. 8902 and H.R. 8903 ¶190, for a consideration of "contract carriage" and a description from the point of view of the scheduled airlines of the problems up to that time with the non-scheduled carriers in domestic operations in the United States. The testimony of James Fischgrund at Page 374 of the same document is a counterattack from the point of view of the nonscheduled carriers).

4. The Project Horizon Report issued in 1961 as a preliminary to the Kennedy Policy statement urges that the Civil Aeronautics Board be given power to issue certificates of convenience and necessity for the "large irregular carriers." *Report of the Task Force on National Aviation Goals, Project Horizon,* Washington, D.C., U.S. Gov. Printing Office.
5. For a detailed presentation of the relevant documents, see Lowenfeld and Burger, *Aviation Law,* New York, Matthew Bender 1981; p. 3-32 to 3-107. See also Lowenfeld and Mendelsohn, "Economics, Politics and the Law: Recent Developments in the World of International Air Charters," 44 *JALC* 479 (1979); Keyes, "The Transatlantic Charter Policy of the United States," 39 *JALC* 215 (1973).
6. PL 87-528 (1962).
7. *Ibid.,* Section 101 (33).
8. *Transatlantic Charter Investigation* 40 CAB 233 (1963, approved 1964).
9. *Ibid.*
10. *American Airlines, Inc. v Civil Aeronautics Board* (USCA, DC) 348 F. 2d 349 (1965).
11. See Lowenfeld and Burger, *Air Law* (1981), p. 3-57–3-108. An "Inclusive Tour Charter": the price of the charter is prorated among the members of a group, who are all engaged in the same all-expense tour. Regulatory details can vary.
12. P.L. 90-514, 82 Stat 867 (Sept. 26, 1968).
13. CAB Reg. SPR-149, enacting 14 CFR § 380, 43 Fed. Reg. 36604 (August 18, 1978). (Civil Aeronautics Board's Economic Regulations Part 380).
14. See Lowenfeld and Burger, *Air Law* (1981), p. 3-1–3-122 for a detailed description of the moves in the game.
15. CAB Order 77-6-68 (1977).
16. See for example, *IATA Agreements Related to Transatlantic Fares,* 53 CAB 266 (1970); *IATA Regulation and Conduct of Traffic Conferences* 55 CAB 912 (1970); *IATA Conduct of Traffic Conferences* 60 CAB 244 (1972).
17. *Agreements Adopted by the International Air Transport Association Relating to the Traffic Conferences,* Docket 32851, Agreement CAB 1175, as amended: Order to Show Cause: CAB Order 78-6-78, June 9, 1978.
18. For a detailed description of the European Civil Aviation Conference, See Bin Cheng, *The Law of International Air Transport,* p. 56–62.
19. ICAO, *ECAC First Session Report* DOC 7676 ECAC/1 (1956), p. 5–6. Cited in Bin Cheng, *loc. cit.*

20. *Ibid.*
21. *Ibid.*
22. Examples of matters considered are: A multilateral agreement on nonscheduled air transport in Europe; standard clauses for use in bilateral agreements; a draft multilateral agreement on certificates of air worthiness, and a draft convention relating to carriage by a person other than the contracting carrier.
23. For a description of the formation and activities of CRAC and of its successor body CLAC, see Bogolasky, "The Expanding Role of the Latin American Civil Aviation Commission," 44 *JALC* 75 (1978).
24. The writer was present at the second and third meetings of CRAC. I believe the following is a fair summation of what was behind CRAC and what took place. Although the ostensible purpose of the first meeting in Rio was to deal with Western Hemisphere fares, CRAC was viewed by many of its members as a means for the South American airlines to present a united front to capture traffic from the European and United States carriers coming into the area. The resolution requiring that 80% of regional traffic must move on the airlines of the two countries concerned was based on the theories of the Argentine law professor Enrique Ferreira. The United States played a rather passive role at the first and second meetings of CRAC (Rio in 1959 and Montevideo in 1961), and merely registered its negative votes against the recommendations which discriminated against its airlines and expressed its opposition to them in the record. By the time of the third meeting of CRAC in Bogotá in 1962, it had become evident that U.S. airlines were being prejudiced by the adoption of the discriminatory CRAC recommendations, and the United States took a more active role in this meeting. The U.S. delegation was headed by Alan Boyd, then chairman of the Civil Aeronautics Board, and later the first to hold the cabinet post of Secretary of Transportation. In addition to being a highly competent lawyer and government official, Boyd has a commanding presence and is able to express himself in Spanish. By careful preparation and vigorous legwork, the United States delegation was able to get the third CRAC meeting to pass a recommendation to the effect that requirements for discrimination against the airlines of particular countries are undesirable and any national legislation based on them should be rescinded. When the other members of CRAC saw that the United States was turning CRAC to its own purposes, they lost interest in it and no further CRAC meetings were called. When LACAC was organized, the United States was not invited to be a member. The resolutions of the first, second and third meetings of CRAC are reprinted in Hooper, *El Derecho Aeronáutico en el Perú.* (1964), First conference, p. 216; Second conference, p. 226; Third conference, p. 246.
25. For example a letter dated December 5, 1980, from LACAC to the U.S. Civil Aeronautics Board objected to a proposal by the Civil Aeronautics Board in CAB Docket 38746 that all fares be filed as maxima, rather than as precise amounts. (The CAB replied that the proposal did not apply to international fares.)
26. See Lowenfeld and Burger, *Aviation Law* (1981), for an interesting exposition of all three cases.
27. *Decision of the Arbitral Tribunal Established Pursuant to the Arbitration Agreement Signed at Paris on January 22, 1963, Between the United States and France. Decided at Geneva on Dec. 22, 1963.* See Lowenfeld and Burger, *op. cit.,* p. 2-16–2-43, and Paul B. Larsen, *Arbitration of the United States–France Air Traffic Rights Dispute* 30 *JALC* 231 (1964) for a discussion of this case.
28. *Agreement Between the Government of the United States of America and the*

Government of the French Republic Relating to Air Services Between Their Respective Territories. TIAS 1679 (1946).
29. *Agreement Between the United States of America and France Amending the Agreement of March 27, 1946, as Amended.* TIAS 5135 (1960).
30. The writer received the backwash of this decision when, in 1980, he tried to persuade Claude Abraham, the French director general of aviation, to allow Braniff Airways to operate on a blind sector basis between Paris and Frankfurt, giving as justification that to do so would help Braniff, without in anyway interfering with an interest of the French, while at the same time putting the French in a position to seek a similar concession from the United States in case of need. The reply came back from Abraham that prior to the 1963 arbitration the argument might have had some weight, but that since that time, he deals with the United States on a strictly cash basis. Abraham also reminded me that when Air France sought blind sector rights between Montreal and New York, using similar arguments, the United States had refused to grant the right, pointing out that such rights had a value for which France should give the United States something in return. (Air France, Foreign Permit, 30 CAB 981 [1960]).
31. *United States of America/France Arbitral Tribunal established by the compromis of July 11, 1978. Case concerning the Services Agreement of March 27, 1946.* Arbitral Award of December 1978.
32. The right to serve Paris via London from the U.S. West Coast without London–Paris traffic rights was added by the Agreement between the United States of America and France Amending the Agreement of March 27, 1946, as Amended, effected by Exchange of Notes. Dated at Paris, April 5, 1960. TIAS 5135 (1960).
33. Although "transshipment" is the term used in the English version of the U.S. Bilateral Agreement with France, it is entirely clear that what was meant was what is generally called in U.S. bilateral air transport agreements a "change of gauge." The term used in the French language version is "rupture de charge."
34. *Annex to the U.S.-France Bilateral Air Transport Agreement* TIAS 1679 (1946), Secton VI. Section IV of the Annex, to which reference is made is the clause which contains the Bermuda Capacity Provisions.
35. CAB Order 78-5-45 (May 9, 1978). 76 CAB 1122 (1978).
36. CAB Order 78-6-82 (May 31, 1978).
37. CAB Order 78-7-33 (July 11, 1978).
38. *Advisory Opinion of the Arbitral Tribunal Constituted in Virtue of the Compromis Signed at Rome on June 30, 1964 by the Governments of the United States of America and of the Italian Republic, and Dissenting Opinion of Mr. Ricardo Monaco.* See: Larsen, "The United States-Italy Air Transport Arbitration: Problems of Treaty Interpretation and Enforcement," *American Journal of International Law,* Vol. 61, No. 2 (April 1967), p. 496.
39. Agreement and Protocol between the United States of America and Italy, Article 2. TIAS 1902 (1948).
40. For an analysis of the arbitral decision and the context in which it arose, see Lowenfeld, *Aviation Law* (1981), p. 2-61–2-91.
41. I have chosen to describe under this heading certain negotiations that took place after 1977, when I have considered the "Bermuda era" to have ended with the superseding of the Bermuda 1 Agreement by the Bermuda 2 Agreement and the emergence of the policy of "deregulation" in the United States, in particular in describing the negotiations with the Soviet Union and China. This was done because in these cases, there was no break in the relation between the parties

occasioned by the adoption by the United States of "deregulation" as a guiding policy. Similarly, despite Bermuda-type agreements in both cases, relations between the United States and Japan and Australia were seldom conducted under the "Bermuda principles" during the Bermuda era, nor were they conducted under the principles of deregulation during the period while that was the U.S. policy.

42. Lowenfeld and Burger, *Aviation Law* (1981), p. 2–62.
43. *Ibid.*
44. As part of the compromis of arbitration, it was agreed that commencing July 11, Pan American could operate approximately half the flights it had intended to operate in the period May 3–December 10, 1978, pending decision by the arbitral tribunal. In fact Pan American never operated the service at all, on the grounds that the late start up made it uneconomical, and in the end terminated service to Paris entirely.
45. *Aviation Week and Space Technology,* Vol. 119, No. 3 (July 18, 1983), p. 35, reports that the French government had denied to the U.S. Department of State that it had instructed French travel agents to sell only French airlines to help the national economy and that the Department of State had accepted this statement. The statement is not, however, inconsistent with the French government's having given instructions to keep the traffic shares of French and U.S. airlines approximately equal.
46. Lowenfeld, *Aviation Law* (1981), p. 2–68.
47. Civil Aeronautics Board Annual Report, FY 1966. Washington, D.C., U.S. Gov. Printing Office, 1966.
48. Civil Aeronautics Board Annual Report, FY 1970. Washington, D.C., U.S. Gov. Printing Office.
49. For evidence of the existence of such an agreement with Italy see CAB Annual Report, FY 1979, p. 79.
50. Civil Aeronautics Board Annual Reports FY's 1975, 1976, 1977, 1978 and 1979. The 1980 Report shows no U.S.-Italy consultations.
51. The foregoing is based upon the author's general recollection, reading of correspondence and conversations with informed individuals. There is no published source for such information of which I am aware.
52. Cf. Wassenbergh, *Postwar International Civil Aviation and the Law of the Air* (1957), wherein it is argued that "fifth freedom" traffic is a combination of fourth and third freedom traffic unless "the service were to be operated as a whole under an agreement or agreements in accordance with a route scheduled therein to points beyond the airline's own country, [in which case it would] . . . be possible to equate 6th freedom traffic on such route with 5th freedom traffic" (p. 71).
53. *Agreement between the United States of America and The Netherlands,* TIAS 4782 (1957), as amended by exchange of notes dated Nov. 25, 1969. Department of State Press Release No. 357, Nov. 25, 1969.
54. *Ibid.,* Article 10.
55. Annual Report of the Civil Aeronautics Board. Fiscal Year 1973, p. 36. U.S. Gov. Printing Office.
56. Annual Report of the Civil Aeronautics Board, Fiscal Year 1975, p. 20. U.S. Gov. Printing Office.
57. Civil Aeronautics Board Economic Regulations, Part 213.3 (c) (2) N. 89, supra.
58. CAB Order 74-11-83, Nov. 19, 1974,
59. *Aviation Daily,* Vol. 219, No. 3 (May 7, 1975), p. 36.

60. See Taneja, *U.S. International Aviation Policy* (1980), p. 65, Note (d); Lowenfeld, "CAB v KLM, Bermuda at Bay," 1 *Air Law Review* (Netherlands) 2 (1975).
61. "KLM Capacity Order Surfaces, White House Never Acted," *Aviation Daily,* Vol. 226 (July 26, 1976), p. 131. "A 1975 CAB decision ordering KLM to reduce capacity to the U.S. was released Friday as a result of a Freedom of Information request. The order was sent to President Ford in March 1975, but was never acted on by the administration. There has been speculation the order was shelved because the Dutch were considering and have since decided to purchase U.S. manufactured F-16 fighter aircraft. The Board's Order set forth specific schedules to be operated by KLM."
62. See e.g. Lowenfeld, *Aviation Law.*
63. Where, as in France and Germany, large travel agents which dominate the local market are government-controlled, they give the government extraordinary power to regulate the flow of traffic to particular airlines.
64. *Civil Air Transport Agreement Between the Government of the United States of America and the Government of the Union of Soviet Socialist Republics,* Signed Nov. 4, 1966, effective Nov. 4, 1966. TIAS 6135 (1966).
65. *Ibid.,* Article 3, subparagraph 1.
66. *Ibid.,* Article 3, subparagraph 3.
67. *Ibid.,* Article 3, subparagraph 14 (3).
68. CAB Annual Report, 1977, p. 175.
69. *Aviation Daily,* Vol. 241 (Jan. 8, 1979), p. 98.
70. The U.S.S.R. became a party to the Chicago Convention, and a member of the International Civil Aviation Organization (ICAO), on Oct. 15, 1970.
71. CAB Order 79-10-210 (Oct. 31, 1979).
72. CAB Order 80-1-43 (Jan. 7, 1980).
73. Civil Aeronautics Board, Annual Report, Fiscal Year 1980, p. 59–60.
74. *Aviation Daily,* Vol. 269, p. 42.
75. *Aviation Daily,* Vol. 283 (Feb. 18, 1986), p.259.
76. CAB Annual Report, Fiscal Year 1978, p. 81.
77. CAB Annual Report, Fiscal Year 1980, p. 59.
78. CAB Annual Report, Fiscal Years 1981–1982, p. 80.
79. *Aviation Daily,* Vol. 272 (April 2, 1984), p. 182.
80. *Aviation Daily,* Vol. 278 (April 18, 1985), p. 276.
81. This agreement, being a "private contract," does not appear in the compilation of U.S. treaties.
82. United States Department of State, Bureau of Public Affairs. Selected Public Documents No. 18: U.S.-China Agreements, Sept. 17, 1980. TIAS 10326, amended Aug. 19, 1972 TIAS 510405.
83. *Ibid.,* Article 12. The last paragraph of this article reads as follows: "(6) If at any time either Party is of the view that traffic is not reasonably balanced, that party may request consultations with the other Party for the purpose of remedying the unbalanced situation in a spirit of friendly cooperation and equality and mutual benefit."
84. *Ibid.,* Annex V, paragraph 1. The relevant language is as follows: "For the purposes of this Agreement a frequency is: one (1) round-trip flight of an aircraft having a maximum certificated take-off gross weight not less than 710,000 pounds, but not more than 800,000 pounds; one and one-half ($1\frac{1}{2}$) round-trip flights of an aircraft having a maximum certificated take-off gross weight equal to or greater than 430,000 pounds but less than 710,000 pounds; and two (2) round-trip flights of an aircraft having a maximum certificated take-off gross

weight less than 430,000 pounds. If a designated airline uses only aircraft having a maximum certificated take-off gross weight of less than 710,000 pounds, it shall be entitled to one additional round-trip flight of an all-freight configured aircraft having a maximum certificated take-off gross weight of less than 430,000 pounds for every two frequencies. All unused frequencies may be accumulated by a designated airline and used at its discretion at any time." In rough terms, this means that each designated airline may operate two wide-bodied frequencies per week, or if it uses narrow-bodied aircraft, it may make a corresponding increase in the number of frequencies.

85. In this account, where no specific citation is given, the account is based upon the writer's personal recollection and contemporary notes, as well as conversations with other participants in the events recorded. In general, official sources are unavailable.
86. Ferreira, *Doctrina Argentina en Derecho Internacional Aéreo* (1947). A copy of this publication is not currently available to the writer. The description of Ferriera's views is based on notes made upon reading his book some years ago.
87. See Folchi, *Politica Aeronautica Argentina* (1966).
88. Republica Argentina. Política Nacional de Transporte Aéreo Comercial. Ley No. 19030, modificada por Ley No. 19534 (B.O. 22392, 29-Mar.-1972).
89. That is, that seats be "roped off."
90. This is a free translation by the author.
91. TIAS 1507. Final Act, Section 4.
92. Gen. Assembly Res. 3281 UN Doc A/RES/3281 (XXIX) (1975). Quoted in J.W. Salacuse: "The Little Prince and the Business Man—Conflicts and Tensions in Public International Air Law," 45 *JALC* 807, at 836 (1980).
93. For example, in the General Assembly Resolution referred to in Note 92 supra, as well as in the "real and effective reciprocity" legislation in Peru and Ecuador.
94. This difference in scheduling was not the result of pure caprice on Braniff's part. Pan American operated between Buenos Aires and the United States via the east coast of South America, where there were two major traffic centers, equal in size to Buenos Aires itself, namely Rio de Janeiro and São Paulo, Brazil. Buenos Aires, Caracas and the Brazilian points could each support one- or two-stop service economically. Braniff, on the other hand served a number of smaller cities on the west coast of South America that could not support a large volume of non-stop and one-stop service: Panama City (Panama); Bogotá and Cali (Colombia); Quito and Guayaquil (Ecuador); Lima (Peru); La Paz (Bolivia); Asunción (Paraguay); and Santiago (Chile). The only way Braniff could maintain an acceptable level of service to these points was to serve them as part of its trunk-route service between the United States and Argentina. Nevertheless, because this type of scheduling resulted in a higher level of fifth freedom carriage in Argentina, Braniff was cast as the sacrificial victim in the U.S.-Argentine negotiations.
95. CAB Order 72-10-19 (October 10, 1972) 60 CAB 931 (1972).
96. CAB Orders 77-3-59 (March 11, 1977), and 77-3-60 (March 11, 1977).
97. Agreement Sept. 22, 1977, TIAS 8978; superseded by agreement Oct. 22, 1985, TIAS.
98. The formula is: One B-747 equals two B-707's/DC-8's; one B-747SP/DC-10/L-1011 equals 1½ B-707's/DC8's.
99. *Aviation Daily,* Vol. 279 (May 6, 1985), p. 29.
100. *Aviation Daily,* Vol. 287 (March 9, 1987), p. 347.
101. *Aviation Daily,* Vol. 287 (March 11, 1987), p. 365.
102. Agreement Between the United States of America and Peru and accompany-

ing notes, signed Lima, Dec. 27, 1946. Entered into Force Dec. 27, 1946. TIAS 1587. Agreement between the United States and Ecuador, signed at Quito, Jan. 8, 1947. Entered into Force April 24, 1947.

103. Agreement signed Dec. 31, 1975.

104. This account is based primarily on the writer's personal recollection. In 1979, the concept of the counterpayment of benefits was modified to apply only to the airlines of countries which the Ecuadorian Airline did not serve. The regulation is published in the Ecuadorian Official Register No. 869, July 6, 1979 at page 4, under the title "Acuerdo No. 075." In order to give an understanding of the concepts underlying this scheme, translations of relevant portions of the decree follow: "Title 1, Article 1: The Regime of Counterpayment of Benefits is the system and the measure which is considered compensatory for the benefit which a foreign airline operator obtains through the unilateral exercise of commercial air rights from and to Ecuador." "Title II, Article 5: The monetary amount of the Regime of Counterpayment of Benefits will be determined on the basis of the receipts arising out of fifth freedom traffic." "Article 6: The receipts mentioned in the previous article are the product of the fifth freedom traffic that has entered or departed from Ecuador, times the normal tariff for economy class then in effect, less ten percent." "Article 7: The basis for the calculation of the monetary amount of the Counterpayment will be 15% of the receipts which the foreign airline operator obtains, calculated in the manner described in the previous paragraph."

The idea behind this concept goes back to the doctrines of the Argentine theorist Enrique Ferreira. The traffic belongs jointly to the two countries between which it moves. When the traffic is carried exclusively by the airline of one of the countries, the other country is owed something for the right of reciprocity in the carriage of the traffic which it has not exercised. Similar charges have been attempted in Bolivia and Peru.

105. TIAS 1587. Dec. 27, 1946.

106. The story of APSA is worthy of treatment in a picaresque novel. For a history of this airline, see *Transportes Aéreos Nacionales S.A., Foreign Air Carrier Permit* 31 CAB 246 (1960), and in particular the Examiner's Report included therein. See Schleit, *Shelton's Barefoot Airlines* (1982).

107. The charge was imposed in 1972 by administrative fiat of the Peruvian aeronautical authorities, who were forcing foreign airlines to sign agreements to pay the charge in order to renew their operating permits or to receive approval for new schedules. In order to make sure that they caught all of the foreign airlines, the Peruvian government issued Supreme Decree 006/74, dated April 3, 1974, which cancelled all operating permits of foreign airlines that had a duration of greater than three years.

108. *Aviation Daily,* Vol. 219 (May 28, 1975), p. 145, and (May 29, 1975), p. 154.

109. *Aviation Daily,* Vol. 220 (July 1, 1975), p. 2; (July 7, 1975), p. 25; (July 10, 1975), p. 54.

110. In the course of the negotiations with the Peruvians, they advanced an interesting reversal of the usual interpretation of the Bermuda capacity language. The Peruvian legal advisor, Alejandro León de Vivero claimed that far from requiring the governments to allow capacity increases proposed by the airlines to become effective, and then expressing their objections to them in *a posteriori* consultations on the basis of the Bermuda capacity "principles," the true meaning of the Bermuda capacity clause authorized each government to regulate unilaterally

the capacity of the other's airline, with the only recourse of the government of the affected airline being to request consultation to try to reach agreement on a withdrawal of the restriction on the basis of the Bermuda capacity languge. Although the context of the original Bermuda agreement, the conduct of the parties and virtually all writings on the subject confirm that it was the intention of the Bermuda language to prohibit unilateral action and to require *a posteriori* consultation, it is difficult to prove conclusively just what the Bermuda language means on the basis of the text itself, and León de Vivero held tenaciously to his interpretation.

111. *Aviation Daily,* Vol. 239 (Dec. 19, 1978), p. 253.
112. *Aviation Daily,* Vol. 242 (April 16, 1979), p. 257.
113. CAB Orders 83-11-49 (Nov. 10, 1983) and 83-11-56 (Nov. 15, 1983). The authority to operate was to run until Jan. 31, 1984, and was continued until April 30, 1984 by CAB Order 84-1-134 (Jan. 30, 1984).
114. CAB Order 84-4-108, (April 30, 1984).
115. "U.S.-Peru Flights Hurt in Dispute," *New York Times,* May 23, 1984, p. A4.
116. *Aviation Daily,* Vol. 286 (Dec. 16, 1986), p. 402.
117. *Ibid.*
118. *Agreement with Annex and Exchange of Notes Between the United States of America and Venezuela.* Signed at Caracas Aug. 14, 1953. Entered into Force, Aug. 22, 1953, TIAS 2183.
119. "U.S. Reaches Capacity Agreement with Venezuela," *Aviation Daily,* Vol. 266 (Oct. 25, 1982), p. 290.
120. "U.S. Reaches Agreement with Venezuelans," *Aviation Daily,* Vol. 266 (April 20, 1982), p. 293.
121. *Agreement Between the United States and Brazil, Signed at Rio de Janeiro, Sept. 6, 1946.* Entered into Force Oct. 6, 1946. TIAS 1900.
122. *United States Treaties in Force,* Jan. 1, 1983.
123. *Agreement Between the United States of America and Colombia, signed at Bogotá, Oct. 24, 1956.* Entered into Force provisionally Jan. 1, 1957, with Exchange of Notes. TIAS 5338.
124. Agreed Minute. Exchange of Notes dated Bogotá, Oct. 23, 1968. Similar side agreements exist with Ecuador, Peru, Panama and Chile, but in the case of Ecuador and Peru they were not always honored.
125. A responsible official of Avianca once told this writer that he regarded the Bermuda-type agreement between Colombia and the United States as nonsense, but that so long as Avianca was able to operate successfully under it, he saw no reason for the government to denounce it. Avianca is a well-managed airline and gives good service. It also has a considerable advantage over U.S. airlines serving Colombia because it has a virtual monopoly over domestic carriage in Colombia, so it has first chance at all international traffic originating at Colombian points not served by U.S. airlines. Presumably, if Avianca should find itself losing out competitively to U.S. airlines, it would induce the government to denounce the agreement.
126. Hamilton, *Manual de Derecho Aeronáutico,* (1960), p. 68.
127. *Agreement and Accompanying Exchange of Notes Between the United States of America and Chile.* Signed at Santiago, May 10, 1947. Entered into Force Dec. 30, 1948. TIAS 1905.
128. This is explicitly recognized in the Ford air transport policy which provides

at Page 8: "Services to Canada, Mexico and the Caribbean should be extensions of the domestic route system."

129. TIAS 5972, Jan. 17, 1966; Amended, TIAS 7824, May 8, 1974.

130. According to the government publication *United States Treaties in Force,* as of Jan. 1, 1987, the status of the U.S. air transport agreements with Mexico was as follows: Air Transport Agreement Aug. 15, 1960 TIAS 4675 Amendment July 31, 1970 TIAS 7167; Dec. 29–30, 1986. TIAS ____ ¶Agreement Relating to Reduced Fares and Charter Services Jan. 20, 1978 TIAS 10115. Extended Dec. 29–30, 1986 TIAS ____.

The 1978 agreement, although it is described as "relating to Reduced Fares and Charter Services," also contained a new route annex which was to remain in force until Dec. 31, 1982.

131. This "screening agreement" was unpublished. It was originally contained in letters bearing dates of Sept. 19 and 20, 1967, Dec. 20, 1966, and August 4, 1965, which are described in an article by Healy, "Revisions to the Mexico–United States Air Transport Agreement, 1965–1970," 32 *JALC* 167 (1966).

132. Canadian Agreement, Jan. 17, 1966. TIAS 5972.

133. Exchange of Notes, May 8, 1974. Dept. of State Press Release #177, May 8, 1974. TIAS 7824.

134. TIAS 10115 (1978).

135. *Nonscheduled Air Service Agreement Between the Government of the United States of America and the Government of Canada.* May 8, 1974. Dept. of State Press Release #177, May 8, 1974. TIAS 7824.

136. *Ibid.,* Annex B.

137. For Mexico, See Healy, "Revisions to the Mexico-U.S. Air Transport Agreement," 32 *JALC* 167 (1966). For Canada, see the position taken in the multilateral discussions described on page 47.

138. TIAS 2854.

139. *Transpacific Route Case* 32 CAB 928 (1961).

140. *Ibid.*

141. "Japanese, U.S. Aviation Officials Bring Hefty Shopping Lists to Next Week's Parley," *Wall Street Journal,* April 6, 1981.

142. "U.S.-Japan Talks End Without Agreement," *Aviation Daily,* Vol. 254, p. 234.

143. 88 Stat 2102 (1975).

144. "CAB Reopens Transpacific Low-Fare Route Case, Orders Further Hearings Before an Administrative Law Judge," CAB Press Release CAB 81-132 Sept. 9, 1981.

145. CAB Orders 81-12-91, Dec. 14, 1981, 93 CAB 707 (1981) and 81-12-93, Dec. 14, 1981, 93 CAB 732 (1981).

146. "CAB Orders Sanctions Against Japan Airlines, Cites Violations of U.S.-Japan Bilateral Agreement," CAB Press Release CAB 81-175, Dec. 14, 1981.

147. "U.S.-Japan Air Dispute Escalates," *Journal of Commerce,* Dec. 29, 1981; "CAB Stays Sanctions Against Japan Airline Pending Further Talks March 8," CAB Press Release, CAB 82-15, Jan. 29, 1982.

148. TIAS 10434 June 4, 1982. The agreement is also reported in "U.S. Japan Interim Agreement signed June 4, 1982," *Aviation Daily,* Vol. 261, p. 203A, 203B and 203C.

149. TIAS 6787, Nov. 12, 1969.

150. "U.S., Japan Settle Air Micronesia Dispute," *Aviation Daily,* Vol. 251, p. 123.

151. *Aviation Daily,* Vol. 282 (Dec. 18, 1985), p. 243.
152. See ¶82–86 supra for the Smathers committee.
153. Agreement Between the United States of America and Australia. Signed at Washington, Dec. 2, 1946. Effective Dec. 3, 1946. TIAS 1574.
154. *Aviation Week,* Vol. 92 (March 30, 1970), p. 29.
155. Docket 23347 *Qantas Airways Schedules.* Order 71-4-192, 4/29/71, 56 CAB 729 (1971); Order 71-7-42, July 8, 1971, 57 CAB 599 (1971). The proceeding involved an attempt by American Airlines to increase its frequency of flights between Australia and the United States, which the Australians refused to permit. The United States in retaliation refused to allow a schedule increase proposed by Qantas.
156. CAB Press Release 78-247, Dec. 14, 1978.
157. UK Notice of Denunciation, 22 June 1976, quoted in Paul B. Larsen, "Status Report on the Renegotiation of the U.S.-U.K. Bilateral Air Transport Agreement [Bermuda Agreement]," *Air Law* (Netherlands), Vol. 2, No. 2 (1977), ¶82 at p. 83.
158. Larsen, Note 157 supra.
159. Agreement Concerning Air Services, with Annexes and Exchange of Letters signed July 23, 1977, effective July 23, 1977. TIAS 8641.
160. The criteria set forth in Article 12, paragraph 2, are a high standard of safety and an adequate return to efficient airlines, cost of service, rates of competitive charter and scheduled services, the prevention of unjust discrimination and undue preferences or advantages. There is a further provision, "To further the reasonable interests of users of air transport services, and to further encourage civil aviaton, individual airlines should be encouraged to initiate innovative cost-based tariffs."
161. The original version of Article 14 and Annex 4 of the Bermuda 2 Agreement were amended by Exchange of Notes dated April 25, 1978 (TIAS 8965). The comments herein refer to the amended version.
162. Exchange of Letters dated Dec. 12, 1980. TIAS 10059.
163. Annex 1, Section 5, paragraph (5) "A designated airline may serve points behind any homeland gateway point shown in Column A, with or without change of aircraft or flight number and may hold out and advertise such services to the public as through services."
164. Annex 2 has very elaborate qualifications and exceptions to the central proposition, but the application of the average of the two forecast percentages to the previous year's capacity is the core of it.
165. *Aviation Daily,* Vol. 285 (Sept. 12, 1986), p. 411.
166. Exchange of Notes, Dec. 4, 1980. TIAS 10059.
167. U.S. Department of Transportation pamphlet: *Air Services Agreement Between the Government of the United States of America and the Government of the United Kingdom of Great Britain and Northern Ireland,* as amended April 25, 1978. Frontispiece: Letter on White House letterhead, dated July 23, 1977, signed "Jimmy Carter."
168. *Ibid.,* p. 72.
169. *Ibid.,* p. 26.
170. *United States International Aviation Negotiations: Hearings before the subcommittee on Public Works and Transportation, House of Representatives, 95th Congress, First Session,* Sept. 29 and Oct. 3, 1977.
171. *Ibid.,* p. 95.
172. Speech, "U.S. International Air Transport Policy: Reflections and Ob-

jectives," before the International Aviation Club, Washington, D.C. Jan. 16, 1981, cited in R.W. Bogosian, "Aviation Negotiations and the U.S. Model Agreement," 46 *JALC* 1004 at 1011 (1981).
173. *CAB Reports to Congress* Fiscal Year 1978, p. 60–61.

8. DEREGULATION: UNITED STATES POLICY AND LEGISLATION

1. 52 Stat 973 (1938).
2. (Act of Aug. 23, 1958), 72 Stat 731 (1958).
3. Federal Aviation Act Sec. 401.
4. *Ibid.,* Sec. 404.
5. *Ibid.,* Secs. 408, 409, 412.
6. *Ibid.,* Sec. 102 (d).
7. White House Press Release, April 23, 1963. *Statement on Air Transport Policy,* p. 2.
8. Caves, *Air Transport and Its Regulators* (1962).
9. For example, Phillips, *The Economics of Regulation* (1969), p. 553: "Economic efficiency can best be promoted in the author's opinion, by substantially reducing government regulation of the transportation industries"; Kieler, "Airline Regulation and Market Performance," 3 *Bell Journal of Economics and Management* 399 (1972), p. 423: "Given that airline regulation on high density routes extracts high social costs and confers very few benefits on anyone, the case against it is strong indeed."
10. Aviation Act of 1975, § 2551, 94th Congress, 1st Session (1975).
11. *Washington Star,* Feb. 3, 1977, at A 6, Col. 3; *Washington Post,* Feb. 24, 1977 at C 13, Col. 2.
12. *Oversight of Civil Aeronautics Board Practices and Procedures:* Hearings Before the Subcommittee on Administrative Practices and Procedures of the Committee on the Judiciary, United States Senate. 94th Congress, First Session (1975). *Regulatory Reform in Air Transportation:* Hearings Before the Subcommittee on Aviation of the Senate Committee on Commerce, 94th Congress, Second Session (1976). *Reform of Economics of Air Carriers:* Hearings before the Subcommittee on Aviation of the House Committee on Public Works and Transportation, 94th Congress, Second Session (1976). *Hearings on S 292 and S 689:* Before the Subcommittee on Aviation of the Senate Committee on Commerce, 95th Congress, First Session (1977). *Aviation Regulatory Reform:* Hearings on H.R. 9297 and H.R. 11, 145 Before the House Committee on Public Works and Transportation, 95th Congress, Second Session (1978).
13. Airline Deregulation Act of 1978, PL 95-504; 49 USC 1301. 92 Stat 1705, Oct. 24, 1978.
14. *Ibid.,* sections 6–21 and 40.
15. *Ibid.,* Sec. 22–25, 37.
16. *Ibid.,* Sec. 37.
17. This summary of the Airline Deregulation Act of 1978 makes no pretense of being exhaustive. I have selected for comment those sections that appear significant or interesting from the viewpoint of international operations.
18. *Ibid.,* sections 8, 15, 20.
19. *Ibid.,* Sec. 20.
20. *Ibid.,* Sec. 7.

21. *Ibid.,* Sec. 11.
22. *Ibid.,* Sec. 19.
23. *Ibid.,* Sec. 22.
24. *Ibid.,* Sec. 24. At the time this legislation was passed, the United States was paying subsidy only to certain of the "local service class" airlines in domestic air transportation. Subsidy had not been paid to domestic trunk lines nor to international lines for many years, and there was no likelihood that it ever would be paid to either class of carriers, with or without this legislation, in the absence of some radical change in circumstances.
25. *Ibid.,* Sec. 26. See also Joint Explanatory Statement of the Committee of Conference of the Hosue and Senate on S 2493, H.R. Rep. No. 1779, 95th Congress, Second Session, p. 72–73 (1978).
26. Clayton Act: 15 USC § 15; Sherman Act: 15 USC §§ 1 & 2.
27. Airline Deregulation Act of 1978, Sec. 27, Supra N 13.
28. *Ibid.,* Sec. 30. Note that this amendment applies to agreements affecting both international and domestic air transportation.
29. *Ibid.,* Sec. 40.
30. *Ibid.*
31. *Ibid.,* With respect to interstate and overseas air transportation the same section of the Airline Deregulation Act of 1978 transferred to the Department of Justice the CAB 's authority under sections 408, 409, 412 and 414 as it relates to those sections, effective Jan. 1, 1983.
32. Civil Aeronautics Board Sunset Act of 1984 PL 98-443, 98 Stat 1703, Oct. 4, 1984.
33. *Ibid.,* Sec. 3a. With respect to interstate and overseas air transportation, the changes made by the Airline Deregulation Act of 1978 in sections 408, 409, and 414, were declared without effect, effective Jan. 1, 1989 by Sction 3(c) of the Civil Aeronautics Board Sunset Act of 1984. With respect to interstate and overseas air transportation and to foreign air transportation, the Sunset Act provides in Section 6(a) that the secretary of transportation shall recommend to the appropriate Committees of Congress not later than July 1, 1987 whether the authority under sections 408, 409, 412 and 414 of the Federal Aviation Act should be retained or repealed.
34. Airline Deregulation Act of 1978 Sec. 40, Supra N13.
35. *Aviation Daily,* April 8, 1986, p. 47.
36. *Ibid.,* Sec. 34.
37. See Lowenfeld, *Aviation Law* (1981), Section 3-120, "International Aviation and the Role of the President."
38. 72 Stat 782 (1958).
39. *Chicago and Southern Airlines v Waterman Steamship Co.* 333 US 103 (1948).
40. *Ibid.;* Cf. *American Airlines Inc. v CAB* 348 F 2d 349 (USCA DC 1965).
41. Act of March 22, 1972, 86 Stat 96.
42. Executive Order 11920, 41 Federal Register 23665, June 10, 1976.
43. *Ibid.,* Sec. 3 (b).
44. See for example: Callison, "Airline Deregulation—Only Partially a Hoax—The Current Status of the Deregulation Movement," 45 *JALC* 961 (1980). Maloon, "Airline Deregulation in Hindsight, A Good Way to Penalize Shareholders," *New York Times,* Sunday, Dec. 18, 1983, Sec. F, p. 3. Thayer, "More Air Travel Risk?" *New York Times,* Dec. 11, 1973, Sec. E, p. 21. Testimony of George James, Hearings Before the Subcommittee on Administrative Practices and Procedures of the Committee on the Judiciary, U.S. Senate, 94th Congress, First Ses-

sion (1975), p. 99 (Supra Note 12). Thornton, "Deregulation: The CAB and Its Critics," 43 *JALC* 641 (1977). Thayer, "And Now the Deregulators: When Will They Learn?" 43 *JALC* 661 (1977).

45. Hearings Before the Subcommittee on Administrative Practices and Procedures of the Committee on the Judiciary, U.S. Senate, 94th Congress, First Session. Oversight of Civil Aeronautics Board Practices and Prcedures (1975), p. 87–91.

46. See *Oakland Service Case,* CAB Docket No. 30669, CAB Order Nos. 78-4-121 (April 19, 1978) and 78-9-96 (Sept. 21, 1978); *Improved Service to Wichita Case,* CAB Docket No. 28848, CAB Order No. 78-3-78 (March 16, 1978).

47. Published as: Kahn, "The Changing Environment in International Air Commerce," *Air Law,* Vol. IV, No. 3 (1978), p. 163.

48. The paper is worth reading in full as an exercise in sunny confidence and certitude in an environment which one would expect to generate doubt and hesitancy.

49. *Op. cit.,* Note 5, p. 163.

50. At the risk of seeming to argue with Mr. Kahn in the midst of summarizing his paper, it seems only fair to the staff officials concerned to observe that they were evidently only trying to act pursuant to the Bermuda-type agreement between the United States and Belgium. The whole point of the agreement was that routes must be justified by traffic to and from the home country and that the exchange of routes must represent a fair exchange of economic benefits.

51. *Op. cit.,* Note 47, p. 165.

52. Freedom of Entry is generally referred to in international markets as the right of "multiple designation," in recognition of the fact that even under very liberal bilateral agreements, governments insist on the formality of designation of foreign airlines.

53. ICAO Special Air Transport Conference, Montreal, 13-26 April 1977. ICAO Doc. 9199 SATC (1977).

54. According to Callison (Note 44, supra, p. 962) the causes for the domestic airline deregulation movement were: (1) academic support, (2) the experience with unregulated intrastate routes in California and Texas, (3) the influence of pro-deregulation economists who had been taken on by the Ford administration, (4) support by President Ford himself, (5) Congressional support, notably by senators Kennedy and Cannon, (6) President Carter's support, engendered by his observation of how popular the subject had become under President Ford, (7) Chairman Kahn's deregulation efforts, which coincided with an upturn in the economy which made it appear that they were successful.

Thornton (*op. cit.,* Note 44, supra) assigns the following other reasons: (1) the young, well-educated and highly mobile segment of the American population who were active in support of other causes, such as opposition to the Vietnam War and support of racial equality and of environmental movements, also tended to support deregulation of U.S. business as a form of antiestablishment protest, (2) the CAB disapproval of youth fares in 1972 caused dissatisfaction among the young that led to pressure for deregulation (he refers to Ralph Nader's testimony before the Kennedy Committee in 1975), (3) the airline over-capacity that resulted from the introduction of wide-bodied aircraft, and was aggravated by the fuel shortage in the mid 1970s, was blamed in part on over-regulation by government, (4) the creation of the cabinet post of Department of Transportation led to conflict between it and the Civil Aeronautics Board and to the eventual weakening of the CAB.

55. Protocol Relating to Air Transport Services, March 31, 1978, United States-Netherlands, TIAS No. 8998.
56. The Dutch got new route rights to Los Angeles plus a new point to be selected by them. This agreement provides for country-of-origin charter rules and country-of-origin rate control for scheduled service. With respect to capacity, the agreement (Art. 5) provides for a fair opportunity to compete, and that the airlines take one another's interest into consideration. Beyond that it provides that "(c) neither Contracting Pary shall limit the volume, frequency, or aircraft type operated by the designated airlines of the other contracting party, except under uniform conditions consistent with Article 15 of the Convention (i.e. the Chicago Convention, Article 15 of which covers 'airport and similar charges' and requires that every airport that is open to public use by a state's own aircraft shall be open under uniform conditions to the aircraft of all other contracting states); [and] (d) Neither Contracting Party shall impose an uplift ratio with respect to the capacity, frequency or traffic to be carried by the designated airlines of either party." The agreement provides further that the Bermuda capacity provisions contained in the Bilateral Air Transport Agreement of 1957 shall be cancelled, leaving the clause to read as follows in its entirety: "Article 10—The air services made available to the public by the airlines operating under this agreement shall bear a close relationship to the requirements of the public for such services."
57. Protocol Relating to Air Transport Services, Aug. 16, 1978, United States-Israel, TIAS No. 9002.
58. Protocol Relating to Air Transport Services, Nov. 1, 1978, United States-Federal Republic of Germany, TIAS No. 9591.
59. Agreement on Air Transport Services, Dec. 12-14, 1978, United Staes -Belgium, TIAS No. 9207.
60. Understanding on Air Transport Services, Aug. 17, 1979, United States-Costa Rica, superseded by agreement dated Oct. 20 and Nov. 23, 1983, TIAS ____.
61. Agreement on Air Transport Services, Sept. 14, 1979, United States-Singapore, TIAS No. 9654.
62. Agreement on Air Transport Services, Dec. 7, 1979, United States-Thailand, TIAS No. 9704.
63. Understanding on Air Transport Services, Jan. 22, 1980, United States-Netherlands/Antilles, TIAS ____.
64. Protocol Relating to Air Transport Services, April 14, 1979, United States-Jamaica, TIAS No. 9613.
65. United States-Finland Agreement on Air Transport Servics, May 12, 1980, TIAS No. 9845.
66. Agreement on Air Transport Services, March 5, 1980, United States-Jordan, TIAS No. 9777.
67. Bogosian, "Aviation Negotiations and the U.S. Model Agreement," 46 *JALC* 1007 (1981).
68. Agreement Between the United States of America and the United Kingdom of Great Britain and Northern Ireland. Feb. 11, 1946, TIAS 1507. Final Act, Article 4.
69. For example, Peru, Panama, Colombia, Paraguay, Chile and Ecuador.
70. Bermuda 1, TIAS 1507 (1946), and Bermuda 2, TIAS 8641 (1977).
71. TIAS 1679 (1946).
72. Protocol Relating to United States-Israel Agreement of 1950, TIAS 9002, Aug. 16, 1978.
73. Protocol Relating to the United States of America-Federal Republic of Germany Air Transport Agreement of 1958, TIAS 9591, Nov. 1, 1978, Article 3.

74. Protocol Between the Government of the United States of America and the Government of Jamaica, Relating to Air Transport. Protocol amending the agreement of Oct. 2, 1969, TIAS 9613, April 4, 1979, Article 3.
75. Understanding on Air Transport Services Between the Government of the United States of America and the Government of Costa Rica, August 17, 1979, TIAS ____.
76. CAB Order ____.
77. CAB Order ____.
78. CAB Order 79-8-68 (August 1979).
79. CAB Order 80-1-110 (January 1980).
80. CAB Order 80-5-35 (May 1980).
81. CAB Order 80-7-97 (July 1980).
82. CAB Order 80-9-97 (September 1980).
83. CAB Order 81-1-30 (January 1981).
84. That is, with no requirement that the route be operated.
85. Presidential Statement, Aug. 21, 1978. Pamphlet apparently published by the Department of Transportation.
86. PL 96-192; 94 Stat 35 (Feb. 15, 1980).
87. 46 *JALC* 1007 (1981).
88. Viz, Netherlands Antilles TIAS ____, (1980); Finland TIAS 9845 (1980); Jordan TIAS 9777 (1980).
89. Supra, Note 86.
90. PL 95-504; 49 USC 1301, Oct. 24, 1978.
91. U.S. Senate Report to accompany S 1300, 96th Congress, Second Session, Report No. 96–329.
92. *Ibid.,* p. 5.
93. *Ibid.,* p. 7.
94. Airline Deregulation Act of 1978, PL 95-504, 92 Stat 1705, Oct. 24, 1978.
95. In dockets 37730 and 37744, the *Standard Foreign Fare Level Investigation,* CAB Order 80-8-66 (Aug. 12, 1980), the Civil Aeronautics Board reviewed existing international fares in selected markets between the U.S. and Latin America, the Pacific and European countries across the Atlantic to determine whether they were unjust or unreasonable and if so, to determine a new foreign fare level, as required by Section 1002 of the Federal Aviation Act, as amended by the International Competition Act. The administrative law judge recommended a decision approving the existing fares, because he claimed the CAB bureaus had failed to sustain their burden of proof that the existing fares were unreasonable because they had failed to consider the costs of beyond and feeder segments. The Board rejected this approach, but nevertheless refrained from exercising its authority to change the existing foreign fare level, basing its conclusion on the imprecision of airline rate-making as a science, the many unknown elements in the record, and the fact that where excess profits were apparent, they were the result of currency conversions, not of high dollar fares. The Board also referred to its "general policy to exercise restraint intervention in management pricing decisions." This decision seems to have been politically motivated in the light of U.S. aviation relations with other countries. See p. 179–185 infra.
96. 49 USC 11596, Act of Jan. 3, 1975, 88 Stat 2102.
97. In this connection, see *Air Micronesia Inc. and Continental Airlines Inc. against the Japan Civil Air Bureau and Japan Air Lines Co., Ltd.* Civil Aeronautics Board Order 80-9-25 (Sept. 5, 1980), and *United Air Lines, Inc., against the Japan Civil Air Bureau and Japan Air Lines Co., Ltd.,* Civil Aero-

nautics Board Order 81-12-91 (Dec. 14, 1981). The connection these cases have to air transport relations between the U.S. and Japan is described at pages 138–140 supra. The cases have an even greater general importance as an illustration of the willingness of the United States to litigate before a U.S. forum (the Civil Aeronautics Board) the question whether a foreign country was abiding by the terms of a bilateral agreement. One wonders how the U.S. would view the situation if its aviation authorities were made defendants in a similar action in Japan.

98. Federal Aviation Act, Sec. 1102 (b) (11).

9. DEREGULATION: INTERNATIONAL REPERCUSSIONS

1. Taneja. *U.S. International Aviation Policy* (1980), p. 136, Figure 5-6.
2. Federal Aviation Act, Section 403, 72 Stat 758 (1958).
3. CAB Order 72-8-89 (1972).
4. *U.S. v Air France et. al.,* No. 75 C, 1978 (E.D.N.Y., Final Judgment, Sept. 29, 1975); a similar case was held for the Pacific, with similar results, *U.S. v Air New Zealand et al.,* No. C-76-0320 (N.D. Cal. Final Judgment, March 22, 1976).
5. CAB Order 77-6-68 (1977).
6. CAB Order 77-9-55 (1977).
7. *Ibid.*
8. 15 USC § 1 and 2.
9. 15 USC § 15.
10. *Laker Airways Limited v Pan American World Airways, et al.,* Civil Action No. 82-3362, *Laker Airways Limited v Sabena Belgian World Airlines et al.,* Civil Aciton No. 83-0416 U.S. District Court for the District of Columbia. 559 *Federal Supplement* 1124 (1983).
11. *Aviation Daily,* Vol. 270 (Dec. 1, 1983), p. 158.
12. "Justice Closes Investigation of End of Skytrain," *Baltimore Sun,* May 12, 1984.
13. *New York Times,* Nov. 20, 1984, p. 17
14. *Newsday,* Nov. 21, 1984, p. 47. The underlying controversy lived on, however, and figured in a third ICAO Air Transport Conference held in 1985. Dempsey: "The Role of the International Civil Aviation Organization on Deregulation, Discrimination and Dispute Resolution," 52 *JALC* 529 (1987).
15. *Aviation Daily,* Oct. 3, 1985, p. 179.
16. *Order to Show Cause: Agreement Adopted by the International Air Transport Association Relating to Traffic Conferences:* Order 78-6-78 (June 9, 1978).
17. See CAB Order 79-5-113, May 1979.
18. See p. 183 infra.
19. By order 79-5-113 of May 1979, the CAB limited its investigation to the fare-setting functions of IATA.
20. CAB Order 80-4-113, April 1980, and 81-5-27 May 1981. Although the approval was for two years, this was extended. See p. 184, infra.
21. ICAO Doc. 9199 SATC (1977).

22. *Ibid.,* p. 5–8.
23. *Ibid.,* p. 9–12.
24. *Ibid.,* p. 13–17.
25. Dold, "The Competitive Regime in International Air Transportation," 5 *Air Law* (Netherlands), 1980, p. 23–33.
26. ICAO Doc. 9297 At Conf/2. 1980.
27. *Ibid.,* p. 6–12.
28. This definition was: "A scheduled international air service is a series of flights that possesses all of the following characteristics: (a) It passes through the air space over the territory of more than one state; (b) It is performed by aircraft for the transport of passengers, mail or cargo for remuneration, in such manner that each flight is open to the public; (c) It is operated so as to serve traffic between the same two or more points, either (i) According to a published time table, or (ii) With flights so regular or frequent that they constitute a recognizably systematic series"—ICAO Doc. 7278, Adopted by the Council 25 March, 1952.
29. Azzie, "Second Special Air Transport Conference and Bilateral Agreements," 5 *Annals of Air and Space Law* (1980), p. 3.
30. ICAO Doc. 9199 SATC (1977) p. 13–26.
31. *Ibid.,* p. 27–57.
32. That is, the rate would be approved unless both governments concerned wished to disapprove it.
33. That is, the government of the country where the transportation starts can approve or dissapprove the rate.
34. For further evidence of the vehement and virtually total rejection of the U.S. position in the international community, see the transcripts of the meetings held by the United States in Bogotá, Manila and Brussels to explain the CAB's IATA show cause order to other nations. These were available in the docket section of the Civil Aeronautics Board, and are now presumably available in the Department of Transportation. The Bogotá meeting was held on July 24, 1979. The other meetings were held shortly after. For critical press comments, see: Thomka-Gazdik, "Multilateralism in Civil Aviation," 4 *Air Law* (Netherlands), 1979, p. 130; Veil, "25th Anniversary of the European Civil Aviation Conference," 6 *Air Law* (Netherlands), p. 2; Magdelenat, "The Story of the Life and Death of the CAB Show Cause Order," 5 *Air Law* (Netherlands), 1980, p. 83; Dold, "The Competitive Regime in International Air Transportation," 5 *Air Law* (Netherlands), 1980, p. 139.
35. CAB Order 81-5-27 (May 5, 1981).
36. CAB Order Jan. 7, 1982 extending effectiveness of CAB Order 81-5-27 until March 15, 1982.
37. CAB Order 82-3-77 (March 12, 1982).
38. The countries that had signed "pro-competitive" bilateral agreements with the United States would be somewhat hampered by the rate article in their endeavor to impose unilateral fare restrictions, but they contrived to get around the rate articles by claiming that the fares of U.S. airlines were "predatory," which under the rate articles gave them some color of right to act unilaterally.
39. Memorandum of Understanding Between the United States and Members of the European Civil Aviation Conference (ECAC) Concerning Scheduled Transatlantic Passenger Air Fares, With Annexes. Done at Paris, Dec. 17, 1982. Entered into force Feb. 1, 1983.

Protocol to the Memorandum of Understanding with Annexes. Done at Washington, D.C., Oct. 29, 1983. Entered into force Nov. 1, 1983.

40. *Ibid.,* Article (3) (2).
41. *Ibid.,* Article 5.
42. *Ibid.,* Article 6.
43. *Ibid.,* Article 7.
44. This article was the cause of vigorous dispute between the United States and the ECAC parties. The ECAC parties claimed the article was self-executing and directly compelled the U.S. to permit the airlines to set fares in the IATA traffic conferences. The U.S. insisted that in order for the CAB to grant the airlines antitrust immunity for that purpose it must go through quasijudicial procedures that open the possibility that it may not grant the necessary immunity. The U.S. pointed out that since the Understanding was not in the form of a treaty, it could not take precedence over the requirements of U.S. laws. This dispute is still unresolved as this is being written.
45. CAB Order 82-9-108 (Sept. 24, 1982).
46. TIAS.
47. "Reagan Administration Proposes New Strategy of Short Term Deals," *Aviation Daily,* Vol. 261 (May 28, 1982), p. 153.
48. "State Department Official Questions Value of Mini Deals," *Aviation Daily,* Vol. 262 (Aug. 12, 1982), p. 238.
49. It seems likely that the disparaging tone of Scocozza's remarks had less to do with a difference of opinion on policy than with the continuation of the struggle for primacy in dealing with international aviation matters between the Departments of State and Transportation.
50. *Report of the Subcommittee on Investigations and Oversight of the Committee on Public Works and Transportation, U.S. House of Representatives on the Improvement Needed in the Implementation of the United States International Aviation Policy.* 98th Congress, 1st Session, Aug. 1983.
51. "IATCA" is the "International Air Transportation Competition Act" of 1979, 94 Stat 35 (1980).
52. "Transportation Official Sees Change in U.S. Strategy," *Aviation Daily,* Vol. 269 (Sept. 23, 1983), p. 125.
53. "U.S. Changes Emphasis in Bilateral Negotiations," *Aviation Daily,* Vol. 263, (Oct. 21, 1982), p. 278.
54. This statement can be compared with the views of CAB chairman Alfred Kahn implying that anyone who considered the exchange of air traffic rights to be a "zero sum game" was mentally defective.
55. "Thailand Unsuccessful in Bid for Fifth Frequency," *Aviation Daily,* Vol. 270 (Dec. 15, 1983), p. 235.
56. TIAS 9704, Dec. 7, 1979.
57. "U.S. Imposes Moratorium on International Aviation Talks," *Aviation Daily,* Vol. 271 (Jan. 16, 1984), p. 74.
58. This is the same Mr. Scocozza who in 1982 was deputy assistant secretary of state for transportation and telecommunications.
59. TIAS 9704, Dec. 7, 1979.
60. CAB Annual Report, Fiscal Year 1980. CAB Order 80-1-43 (Jan. 7, 1980).
61. *Aviation Daily* (1983).
62. See CAB Order 81-12-171 (Dec. 12, 1981) and CAB Annual Report for the Fiscal Years 1981 and 1982, p. 80: "In the wake of repressive measures in Poland, President Reagan decided in December of 1981 to suspend the U.S.-Poland Air Service Agreements until further notice. The President also requested that the Board suspend the operating authority of the Polish carrier LOT until further notice."

63. See *International Trade Service News Letter,* Vol. 1, Issue 4 (Jan.-June 1981). Published by Office of the U.S. Trade Representative, Executive Office of the President.
64. *Ibid.,* p. 5 (emphasis supplied).
65. According to the ICAO Statistical Yearbooks for 1981 and 1985 (Tables 2 & 3 on page 35, in both cases), U.S. airlines carried 17.2% of the international revenue passenger kilometers performed by the airlines of ICAO members in 1980 and 18.16% of such passenger kilometers in 1985. The figures are as follows:

	All Airlines		U.S. Airlines	U.S.%
1980	466,464		82,639	17.72
1985	590,227	(+26.5%)	107,197	18.16

(During the same period, there was a slight decrease in the percentage of passengers carried by U.S. airlines, but revenue passenger kilometers performed seems the more pertinent figure, since it is the basis for airline revenues.)

On the North Atlantic route between the United States and Europe, the U.S. participation in the total passengers carried increased from 42.5% in 1980 to 43.1% in 1985. (Since these percentages relate to traffic on a single route, so that each unit produces roughly similar revenue, they appear to be a valid measure of the participation of U.S. airlines in the traffic). Source: IATA, North Atlantic Carrier Analysis, Dec. 1980 and Dec. 1986. Page 5, "U.S.A.-Europe Total in Both Directions," in both publications.
66. ICAO Statistical Yearbooks 1981 and 1985, Note 164 supra.
67. Note 66 supra.
68. "ECAC President says Europe Moving to Greater Aviation Flexibility," *Aviation Daily,* April 18, 1985, p. 78; "Air Transport Commission Pushes for Action on (European) Air Transport Liberalization," *Ibid.,* Jan. 15, 1986, p. 79; "Court Decision may Spur Liberalization of European Civil Aviation," *Ibid.,* May 2, 1986, p. 185; "European Airlines Asked to Comply With Competition Rules," *Ibid.,* July 11, 1986, p. 59; "Pressure Increases for European Deregulation," *Ibid.,* Aug. 20, 1986, p. 285.
69. "U.K. Heads Move Toward European Air Transport Deregulation," *Aviation Daily,* May 21, 1984, p. 119; "U.K. Lord's Committee Found An 'Overwhelming Case' for Creating a More Competitve Climate in European Air Transport," *Ibid.,* May 15, 1984, p. 87; "U.K. Aviation Ministers Reviews Liberalizaiton," *Ibid.,* Dec. 23, 1986, p. 446.
70. "B-Cal Chairman Concerned over Dominant U.S. Carriers," *Aviation Daily,* Vol. 279 (June 26, 1985), p. 219; "U.S.-Style Deregulation Impractical for Europe, Air France Says," *Ibid.,* Vol. 277 (Jan. 16, 1985), p. 85; "U.K. Official Says Capacity Controls Necessary," *Ibid.,* Vol. 283 (Feb. 19, 1986), p. 271; "European Ministers Fail to Act on Liberalization Proposals," *Ibid.,* Vol. 285 (July 3, 1986), p. 22.

BIBLIOGRAPHY

BOOKS

Bender, Marian, and Altschul, Selig. *The Chosen Instrument.* New York: Simon and Schuster, 1982.
Billyou, DeForest. *Air Law,* 2nd ed. New York: Ad Press Ltd., 1964.
Bluestone, D.W., and William, E.W. *Rationale of Federal Aviation Policy.* Washington, D.C.: U.S. Department of Commerce, 1930.
Burden, W.A.M. *The Struggle for Airways in Latin America.* New York: Council on Foreign Relations, 1943.
Caves, Richard. E. *Air Transport and Its Regulators.* Cambridge, Mass.: Harvard University Press, 1962.
Cheng, Bin. *The Law of International Air Transport.* London: Stevens and Sons; New York: Oceania Publications, 1962.
Cleveland, Reginald W. *Air Transport at War.* New York: Harper Bros., 1946.
Cooper, J.C. *The Right to Fly.* New York: Henry Holt, 1947.
Corbett, David. *Politics and the Airlines.* Toronto: University of Toronto Press, 1965.
Daley, Robert. *An American Saga.* New York: Random House, 1980.
Davies, R.E.G. *Airlines of the United States Since 1944.* London: Putnam, 1972.
Delascio, Victor José. *Manual de Derecho de la Aviación.* Caracas: Editora Grafos, 1959.
Encyclopaedia Britannica, 11th ed., Chicago, 1957.
Ferreira, Enrique A. *Doctrina Argentina en Derecho Internacional Aéreo.* Córdoba, Argentina: Universidad de Córdoba, 1947.
Folchi, Mario O. *Política Aeronáutica Argentina.* Buenos Aires: Universidad de Buenos Aires, 1966.
Friedman, Jesse J. *A New Air Transport Policy for the North Atlantic—Saving an Endangered System.* New York: Atheneum, 1976.
Gidwitz, Betsy. *The Politics of International Air Transport.* Lexington, Mass./Toronto: D.C. Heath, 1980.
Hamilton, Eduardo. *Manual de Derecho Aeronáutico* (2nda edición). Santiago: Editorial Jurídica, 1960.
Hazeltine, Harold D. *The Law of the Air.* London: London University Press, 1911.
Hooper, Rene. *El Derecho Aeronáutico en el Perú.* Lima: Editorial Universitaria, 1964.
Institute of Air and Space Law, 25th Anniversary Conference, Nov. 17–19, 1976, Proceedings. *International Air Transport: Law, Organization and Policies for the Future.* Toronto: Carswell; Paris: A. Pedone Editions, 1976.

International Air Transport Association. *IATA, The First Three Decades*. Montreal, 1949.
Johnson, D.H.N. *Rights in Air Space*. Manchester: Manchester University Press; New York: Oceania, 1965.
Lowenfeld, Andreas F., and Burger, James M. *Aviation Law*. New York: Matthew Bender, 1981.
Lissitzyn, Oliver J. *World Air Transport and National Policy*. New York: Council on Foreign Relations, 1942.
Marchand, Jacques. *Un Paradoxe Economique, La Renaissance du Mercantilisme à l'Epoque Contemporaine*. Paris: Librairie Technique et Economique, 1937.
Matte, Nicolas Mateesco. *Treatise on Air-Aeronautical Law*. Toronto: Carswell, 1981.
Phillips, Charles F., Jr. *The Economics of Regulation*. Homewood, Ill.: Richard D. Irwin; Georgetown, Ont.: Irwin Dorsey, 1969.
Pillai, K.G.J. *The Air Net, the Case Against the World Aviaton Cartel*. New York: Grossman Publishers, 1960.
Primeras Jornadas Latino Americanas de Derecho Aeronáutico. Buenos Aires: Ediciones Depalma, 1962.
Schleit, Philip. *Shelton's Barefoot Airlines*. Annapolis: Fishergate Publishing Co., 1982.
Semphill, Colonel, the Master of. *The Law of the Air*. London: Eckins Matthews and Marrot, 1931.
Simond, Frank H., and Emeny, Brooks. *The Great Powers in World Politics*. New York: American Book Co., 1939.
Straszheim, Mahlon R. *The International Airline Industry*. Washington, D.C.: Brookings Institute, 1969.
Taneja, N.K. *International Aviation Policy*. Lexington, Mass.: Lexington Books/D.C. Heath & Co., 1980.
Thayer, Frederick C. *Air Transport Policy and National Security*. Chapel Hill: University of North Carolina Press, 1965.
Thornton, R.L. *International Airlines and Politics*. Ann Arbor: University of Michigan Press, 1970.
Tombs, Laurence C. *International Organization in European Air Transport*. New York: Columbia University Press, 1936.
Van Zandt, J. Parker. *Civil Aviation and Peace*. Washington, D.C.: Brookings Institution, 1944.
Wagner, Wenceslas J. *International Air Transportation as Affected by State Sovereignty*. Brussels: Etablissements Emile Bruylant, 1979.
Wassenbergh, H.A. *Postwar Civil Aviation Policy and the Law of the Air*. The Hague: Martinus Nijhoff, 1957.
Wheatcroft, Stephen. *The Economics of European Air Transport*. Cambridge, Mass.: Harvard University Press, 1956.
________. *Air Transport Policy*. London: Michael Joseph, 1964.
World Airline Record. Chicago: Roadcap Associates, 1965.

ARTICLES

Azzie, Ralph. "Second Special Air Transport Conference and Bilateral Agreements." 5 *Annals of Air and Space Law* (1980), p. 3.

Bogolasky, José C. "The Expanding Role of the Latin American Civil Aviation Commission." 44 *Journal of Air Law and Commerce* (1978), p. 75.

Bogosian, Richard W. "Aviation Negotiations and the Model Agreement." 46 *Journal of Air Law and Commerce* (1981), p. 1007.

Callison, J.W. "Airline Deregulation, Only Partially a Hoax-The Current Status of the Deregulation Movement." 45 *Journal of Air Law and Commerce* (1980), p. 961.

Cohen, Ralph S. "Confessions of a Former IATA Man." 34 *Journal of Air Law and Commerce* (1968), p. 610.

Cooper, John C. "The International Aviation Conference, Paris, 1910." 19 *Journal of Air Law* (1952), p. 127.

________. "The Russian Satellite." 24 *Journal of Air Law* (1957), p. 349.

________. "United States Participation in Drafting the Paris Convention." 18 *Journal of Air Law* (1951), p. 266.

Craig, Broward. "National Sovereignty at High Altitudes." 24 *Journal of Air Law* (1957), p. 379.

Dempsey, Paul Stephen. "The Role of the International Civil Aviation Organization on Deregulation, Discrimination and Dispute Resolution." 52 *Journal of Air Law and Commerce* (1987), p. 529.

Diamond, Barry R. "The Bermuda Agreement Revisited: A Look at the Past, Present and Future of Bilateral Agreements." 41 *Journal of Air Law and Commerce* (1975), p. 419.

Dold, Gaylord L. "The Competitive Regime in International Air Transpotation." 5 *Air Law* (1980), p. 139.

Fauchille, Paul. "La Circulation Aérienne et les Droits des Etats en Temps de Paix." 17 *Revue Générale du Droit International Publique* (1910), p. 55.

________. "Le Domain Aerien et le Régime Juridique des Aerostats." 8 *Revue Générale du Droit International Publique* (1901), p. 44.

Gazdik, Julien G. "Nationality of Aircraft and Nationality of Airlines as Means of Control in International Air Transportation." 24 *Journal of Air Law* (1957), p. 1.

________. "Rate Making and the IATA Traffic Conferences." 16 *Journal of Air Law* (1949), p. 298.

Healy, H. Max. "Revisions to the Mexico-United States Air Transport Agreement 1965-1970." 32 *Journal of Air Law and Commerce* (1966), p. 167.

Jordan, William A. "Airline Capacity Agreements, Correcting a Regulatory Imperfection." 39 *Journal of Air Law and Commerce* (1973), p. 179.

Kahn, Alfred E. "The Changing Environment in International Air Commerce," 4 *Air Law* (1978), p. 163.

Kalijarvi, T.J. "The Paradox of Foreign Economic Policy." 36 *Department of State Bulletin* (1957), p. 1009.

Keyes, Lucille Sheppard. "The Charter Policy of the U.S.A.'" 39 *Journal of Air Law and Commerce* (1973), p. 215.

Kieler, Theodore E. "Airline Regulation and Market Performance." 3 *Bell Journal of Economics and Management* (1972), p. 399.

Koffler, Warren K. "IATA, Its Legal Structure, A Critical Review." 32 *Journal of Air Law and Commerce* (1966), p. 222.

Larsen, Paul B. "Arbitration of the United States-France Air Traffic Dispute." 30 *Journal of Air Law and Commerce* (1964), p. 231.

________. "Status Report on the Renegotiation of the U.S.-U.K. Bilateral Air Transport Agreement (Bermuda Agreement)." 2 *Air Law* (1977), p. 82.

________. "The United States-Italy Air Transport Arbitration: Problems of Treaty

Interpretation and Enforcement." 61 *American Journal of International Law* (1967), p. 496.

Lowenfeld, Andreas F. "CAB v KLM, Bermuda at Bay." 1 *Air Law* (1975), p. 2.

________. "A New Takeoff for International Air Transport." 54 *Foreign Affairs* (1975), p. 36.

________, and Mendelsohn, Allen. "Economics, Politics and the Law: Recent Developments in the World of International Air Charters." 44 *Journal of Air Law and Commerce* (1979), p. 479.

Magdelenat, Jean-Louis. "The Story of the Life and Death of the CAB Show-Cause Order." 5 *Air Law* (1980), p. 83.

Maloon, J.H. "Airline Deregulation in Hindsight, A Good Way to Penalize Share Holders." *New York Times,* Sunday, Dec. 18, 1983, Section F, p. 3.

Masefield, Peter G. "Anglo-American Civil Aviation." 1 *Air Affairs* (1947), p. 310.

"Otra Vez el Entreguismo." *Marka* (Lima), Dec. 7, 1978.

Robinson, G.S. "Changing Concepts of Cabotage." 34 *Journal of Air Law and Commerce* (1968), p. 553.

Ryan, Oswald. "Recent Developments in United States Air Transportation Policy." 1 *Air Affairs* (1946), p. 45.

Salacuse, J.W. "The Little Prince and the Business Man—Conflicts and Tensions in Public International Air Law." 45 *Journal of Air Law and Commerce* (1980), p. 807.

Sheehan, W.M. "Air Cabotage and the Chicago Convention." 63 *Harvard Law Review* (1950), p. 1157.

Slotemaker, L.H. "The Internationalization of Civil Aviation." 3 *Journal of Air Law* (1932), p. 648.

Thayer, Frederick E. "And Now the Deregulators—When Will They Learn?" 43 *Journal of Air Law and Commerce* (1977), p. 661.

________. "More Air Travel Risk?" *New York Times,* Dec. 11, 1973, Section E, p. 21.

Thomka-Gazdik, Julien. "Multilateralism in Civil Aviation." 4 *Air Law* (1979), p. 130.

Thornton, Robert L. "Deregulation: The CAB and Its Critics." 43 *Journal of Air Law and Commerce* (1977), p. 641.

Tymms, Frederick. "Let's Clear the Record on Chicago's 'Freedoms'." 3 *Air Transport World,* No. 5 (May 1966), p. 17.

Veil, Simone. "25th Anniversary of the European Civil Aviation Conference." 6 *Air Law* (1981), p. 2.

Von Hesser, E. "Aeroplanes in War." 4 *The Aero,* No. 88 (Wed., Jan. 25, 1911), p. 71.

Westwood, Howard, and Bennett, Alex. "A Footnote to the Legislative History of the Civil Aeronautics Act of 1938 and Afterword." 3 *Notre Dame Lawyer* (1967), p. 310.

MISCELLANEOUS

"Bilateral Air Transport Agreements: Some Problems of Finding a Fair Route Exchange." Remarks by Frank E. Loy at the International Conference on the Freedom of the Air, McGill University, Institute of Air and Space Law, Montreal, Nov. 3 & 4, 1967.

"Remarks by the Honorable Herbert Hoover, Jr., Acting Secretary of State," at Government-Industry Aviation Meeting, Department of State, Wed., Nov. 14, 1956. U.S. Department of State Press Release No. 582, Nov. 14, 1956.

"U.S. International Aviation Policy, Reflections and Objectives." Speech by Alfred Kahn at the International Aviation Club, Washington, D.C., Jan. 16, 1981.

U.S. GOVERNMENT PUBLICATIONS

Executive Branch

"Aspects of United States Participation in Civil Aviation." Department of State Publication 3209. International Organization and Conference Series, IV, International Civil Aviation Organization 21.

"Civil Aeronautics Board." Annual Reports, 1966–.

"Civil Air Policy." A Report of the Air Coordinating Committee, by Direction of the President, May 1954. U.S. Gov. Printing Office, 1954.

Executive Order 11920. Establishing Executive Branch Procedures Solely for the Purpose of Facilitating Presidential Review of Decisions Submitted to the President by the Civil Aeronautics Board. 41 *Federal Register* 23665; 3 CFR 1976 Comp, p. 121.

"Intergovernmental Consultation on the United States Civil Aeronautics Board's 'IATA Show Cause Order'." Transcript, Cámera de Comercio, Bogotá, Colombia, July 23, 1979. (This publication was available in the Docket Section of the Civil Aeronautics Board. Presumably, it is now available in the corresponding section of the Department of Transportation.)

"International Air Transport Policy." Report by the Attorney General. U.S. Gov. Printing Office, 1945.

"International Air Transport Policy." Joint Statement by the U.S. and British Governments. 15 *Department of State Bulletin* (1946), p. 577–578.

"International Air Transport Policy of the United States." White House Press Release of Presidential Approval, Sept. 8, 1976.

"International Civil Aviation 1945–1948." Report of the United States of America to the International Civil Aviation Organization. Department of State Pamphlet, 1948.

"A Statement of National Transportation Policy." Department of Transportation Press Release, Sept. 17, 1975.

"Statement on Air Transport Policy." White House Press Release, April 24, 1963.

"Statement on International Air Transportation Policy." 63 *Department of State Bulletin* (1970), p. 86.

"Survival in the Air Age." A Report by the President's Air Policy Commission. U.S. Gov. Printing Office, 1948. (Reprinted, 15 *Journal of Air Law* (1948), p. 69.)

"United States Policy for the Conduct of Air Transport Negotiations." Presidential Statement, Aug. 21, 1978, apparently published by the Department of Transportation (1978).

United States Treaties in Force. U.S. Gov. Printing Office, 1982–.

Legislative Branch—Senate

Air Laws and Treaties of the World. 3 vols. Prepared at the request of Warren G. Magnuson, chairman of the Committee on Commerce, United States Senate. U.S. Gov. Printing Office, 1965.

"Aviation Study," prepared for the Committee on Interstate and Foreign Commerce, United States Senate on Hearings on S2647 (an omnibus aviation bill). Senate Document No. 163, 83rd Congress, Second Session, 1955.

"Aviation Study, Section VII." Presented by John W. Bricker, Chairman, Interstate and Foreign Commerce, 83rd Congress. Senate Document 163, 83rd Congress, Second Session, released Jan. 11, 1955.

"Hearings on S292 and S689 Before the Subcommittee on Aviation of the Senate Committee on Commerce." 95th Congress, First Session, 1977.

"International Air Agreements." Report of the Committee on Interstate and Foreign Commerce. ("Smathers Report.") Report No. 1875, 84th Congress, Second Session, 1956.

"International Air Transportation Problems." Hearing before the Aviation Subcommittee of the Committee on Commerce, United States Senate, 87th Congress, First Session, Sept. 22, 1961.

"International Air Transportation Rates and S1539 and S1540." Hearings before the Senate Committee on Commerce, 88th Congress, 1st Session, 1963.

"Investigation of Airmail Contracts." Hearings Pursuant to S. Res. 349, before a Special Committee on Investigation of Airmail Contracts. 73rd Congress, 2nd Session, 1934. Pt. 6 2459.

"Joint Explanatory Statement" of the Committee of Conference of the House and Senate on S2493, H.R. Rep. No. 1779, 95th Congress, Second Session, 1978.

"Oversight of Civil Aeronautics Board Practices and Procedures." Hearings Before the Subcommittee on Administrative Practices and Procedures of the Committee on the Judiciary. United States Senate, 94th Congress, First Session, 1975.

"Regulatory Reform in Air Transportation." Hearings Before the Subcommittee on Aviation of the Senate Committee on Commerce, 94th Congress, Second Session, 1976.

Senate Report No. 1811, Federal Aviation Act of 1958, Report of Committee on Interstate and Foreign Commerce to Accompany S3880, July 9, 1958.

Senate Report to Accompany S1300, 96th Congress, Second Session Report No. 96-329, 1979.

Legislative Branch—House of Representatives

"Aviation Regulatory Reform." Hearings on H.R. 9297 and H.R. 11,145. Before the House Committee on Public Works and Transportation, 95th Congress, Second Session, 1978.

"Civil Air Policy." Hearings Before a Subcommittee of the Committee on Interstate and Foreign Commerce, House of Representatives, 84th Congress, on H.R. 4648 and H.R. 4677, Bills to Amend the Civil Aeronautics Act of 1938, and H.R. 8902 and H.R. 8903, Bills to Amend Subsection 406 (b) of the Civil Aeronautics Act of 1938, as amended. House reprint, 1956.

"Hearings." Before a Subcommittee of the Committee on Interstate and Foreign Commerce, House of Representatives, 84th Congress, March 18 and July 22, 1955, and Jan. 17, 18, 19, 20, Feb. 9, 10, 28, 29, March 2, April 18 and 20, 1956 on H.R. 4698, H.R. 4677, H.R. 8902 and H.R. 8903.

"Reform of Economics of Air Carriers." Hearings Before the Subcommittee on Aviation of the House Committee on Public Works and Transportation, 94th Congress, Second Session, 1976.

"Report." Of the Subcommittee on Investigation and Oversight of the Committee on Public Works and Transportation, U.S. House of Representatives, on the

Improvement Needed in the Implementation of the United States International Aviation Policy. 98th Congress, First Session, Aug. 1983.

"United States International Aviation Negotiations." Hearings Before the Subcommittee on Public Works and Transportation, House of Representatives, 95th Congress, First Session, Sept. 29, and Oct. 3, 1977.

Foreign Documents

Argentina: Política Nacional de Transporte Aéreo Commercial. Ley No. 19,030, Modificada por Ley. No. 19,534 (B.O. 22, 392, 29 March 1972).

United Kingdom: House of Lords' Debates, 5th Series, Vol. 129, Col. 214, Oct. 20, 1943. House of Commons Debates, 5th Series, Vol. 387, Col. 995, March 11, 1943.

International Civil Aviation Organization Documents

Commission International Pour la Navegation Aeriene. *Official Bulletin,* 28 Vols., 1919-1939.

"ICAO Special Air Transport Conference, Montreal 13-26 April 1977." International Civil Aviation Organization Document 9199 SATC (1977).

ICAO Statistical Yearbook 1981: Document 9180/7.

ICAO Statistical Yearbook 1985; Document 9180/11.

International Air Transport Association. North Atlantic Carrier Analysis, Dec. 1980.

________. North Atlantic Carrier Analyses, Dec. 1986.

"Proceedings of the First Session of the Assembly, 6 May-27 May, 1947." International Civil Aviation Organization, Montreal, 1947.

Proceedings of the International Civil Aviation Conference, Chicago, Nov. 1-Dec. 7, 1944. 2 vols. U.S. Gov. Printing Office, 1948.

"Records of the Commission on Multilateral Agreement on Commercial Rights in International Civil Air Transport." Session Held at Geneva, Nov. 4-27, 1947. International Civil Aviation Organization, Montreal, 1948.

"Report of the First Interim Assembly of PICAO, May 21-June 8, 1946." *PICAO Journal* Vol. 1, No. 6 (Montreal), (Aug.-June, 1946).

Cases Cited

United States Courts

American Airlines v CAB 348 Fed. 2d. (USCA DC) 1965.

Chicago and Southern Airlines v Waterman Steamship Co. 333 U.S. 103 (1948).

Laker Airways Ltd. v Pan American World Airways et al., Civil Action No. 82-3362.

Laker Airways Ltd. v Sabena Belgian World Airlines et al., Civil Action No. 83-0416, United States District Court for the District of Columbia. 559 Fed. Supp. 1124 (1983).

Pacific Air Transport v The United States 98 Court of Claims 649 (1942).

Pan American Airways Corp. v CAB et al. 121 Fed 2d 810 (1941).
U.S. v Air France et al. No. 75 C, 1978 (ED NY, Final Judgment Sept. 29, 1975).
U.S. v Air New Zealand et al. No. C-76-0320 (ND Cal. Final Judgment March 22, 1976).

Civil Aeronautics Board

Aeroflot, Foreign Air Carrier Permit. CAB Order 79-10-210 (Oct. 31, 1979).
Aeroflot Schedules. CAB Order 80-1-43 (Jan. 1980).
Aeroflot Schedules. CAB Order 81-12-171 (Dec. 1981).
Aerolíneas Argentinas Schedules. 60 CAB 931 (1972).
Aerolíneas Argentinas Schedules. CAB orders 77-3-59 and 77-3-60 (March 11, 1977).
Aeronaves de Mexico, Foreign Air Carrier Permit Amendment. 44 CAB 289 (1966).
Air France Schedules. CAB Order 78-5-45. 76 CAB 1122 (1978).
Air France Schedules. CAB Order 78-7-33 (July, 11, 1978).
Air Jamaica Ltd. Foreign Air Carrier Permit. 44 CAB 169 (1966).
Air Jamaica (1968) Ltd., Foreign Air Carrier Permit. 50 CAB 392 (1968).
Bermuda Show Cause Proceeding. CAB Order 89-9-97 (Sept. 1980).
British Overseas Airways Corp. Foreign Permit. 31 CAB 583 (1959).
Central America Show Cause Proceeding. CAB Order 80-5-35 (May 1980).
Discussions Re Flight Schedule Adjustments. 53 CAB 890 (1970).
Foreign Air Carrier Permit Terms Investigation. 54 CAB 175 (1970).
IATA Agreements Related to Transatlantic Fares. 53 CAB 266 (1970).
IATA Fares Agreement. CAB Order 77-9-55 (Sept. 1977).
Improved Service to Wichita Case. CAB Order 78-3-78 (March 16, 1978).
Investigation of North Atlantic Passenger Market. CAB Order 72-8-89 (Aug. 1972).
Joint Application of National Airlines and British Overseas Airways Corporation. CAB Order 74-2-93 (Feb. 22, 1974) and CAB Order 74-11-34 (Nov. 7, 1974).
KLM Schedules. CAB Order 74-11-83 (Nov. 19, 1974).
Laker Foreign Air Carrier Permit. CAB Order 77-6-68 (June 1977).
Laker Foreign Permit. CAB Order 72-8-89 (Aug. 1972).
Líneas Aéreas Costarricenses SA, Foreign Permit. 26 CAB 429 (1958).
LOT Schedules. CAB Order 81-12-171 (Dec. 12, 1981).
Lufthansa, Foreign Permit. 43 CAB 301 (1965).
Midway Airport, Expanded Services. 54 CAB 841 (1970), 60 CAB 920 (1972).
Oakland Service Case. CAB Order 78-4-121 (April 19, 1978) and CAB Order 78-9-96 (Sept. 21, 1978).
Order to Show Cause: Agreements Adopted by the International Air Transport Association Relating to the Traffic Conferences. CAB Orders 78-6-78 (June 9, 1978), 79-5-113 (May 1979), 80-4-113 (April 15, 1980), 81-5-27 (May 1981) and 82-3-77 (May 1982).
PAA eg al., Joint Discussions. 56 CAB 615 (1971).
Pan American-Venezuelan Traffic Arrangements. Agreement CAB No. 15385. 34 CAB 800 (1961).
Pan American World Airways, Inc.-Trans World Airways, Inc., Route Agreement. CAB Order 77-11-7 (Nov. 16, 1976).
Qantas Airways Schedules Docket 23347. 56 CAB 728 (1971) and 57 CAB 599 (1971).
San Juan Capacity Restricitons. 60 CAB 923 (1972).
Schedule Adjustments Within Hawaii. 55 CAB 983 (1970).

Scheduling Committee Agreements. 49 CAB 893 (1968).
Sociedad Aeronáutica Medellín, Foreign Permit. 26 CAB 53 (1957).
Transatlantic Charter Investigation. 40 CAB 233 (1963).
Transmediterranean Airways SAC, Foreign Permit. 57 CAB 18 (1971).
Transpacific Low Fare Route Investigation. CAB Order 81-1-30 (Jan. 1981).
Transpacific Route Case. 32 CAB 928 (1961).
Transportes Aéreos Nacionales, Foreign Air Carrier Permit. 31 CAB 246 (1960).
U.S.-Bahamas Proceedings. CAB Order 79-8-68 (Aug. 1979).
U.S.-Benelux Low Fares Proceeding.
U.S.-Costa Rica Show Cause Proceeding. CAB Order 80-1-110 (Jan. 1980).
U.S.-Germany Show Cause Proceeding. CAB Order 80-7-97 (July 1980).
U.S.-Zurich/Tel Aviv Show Cause Proceeding.
Varig Foreign Permit. 40 CAB 351 (1964).

INDEX